We Have
Root

We Have Root

Even More Advice from Schneier on Security

Bruce Schneier

WILEY

We Have Root: Even More Advice from Schneier on Security

Published by
John Wiley & Sons, Inc.
10475 Crosspoint Boulevard
Indianapolis, IN 46256
www.wiley.com

Copyright © 2019 Bruce Schneier

Published by John Wiley & Sons, Inc., Indianapolis, Indiana

Published simultaneously in Canada

ISBN: 978-1-119-64301-2
ISBN: 978-1-119-64346-3 (ebk)
ISBN: 978-1-119-64312-8 (ebk)

Manufactured in the United States of America

For general information on our other products and services please contact our Customer Care Department within the United States at (877) 762-2974, outside the United States at (317) 572-3993 or fax (317) 572-4002.

Wiley publishes in a variety of print and electronic formats and by print-on-demand. Some material included with standard print versions of this book may not be included in e-books or in print-on-demand. If this book refers to media such as a CD or DVD that is not included in the version you purchased, you may download this material at http://booksupport.wiley.com. For more information about Wiley products, visit www.wiley.com.

Library of Congress Control Number: 2019945771

About the Author

Bruce Schneier is an internationally renowned security technologist, called a security guru by the *Economist*. He is the author of 14 books—including the best-seller *Click Here to Kill Everybody*—as well as hundreds of articles, essays, and academic papers. His influential newsletter Crypto-Gram and blog Schneier on Security are read by over 250,000 people. Schneier is a fellow at the Berkman Klein Center for Internet and Society at Harvard University; a Lecturer in Public Policy at the Harvard Kennedy School; a board member of the Electronic Frontier Foundation, AccessNow, and the Tor Project; and an advisory board member of EPIC and VerifiedVoting.org. He can be found online at www.schneier.com and @schneierblog.

Contents

Introduction

Why I Write about Tech for Popular Audiences

I write essays because I enjoy it. It's fun, and I'm good at it. I like the exposure. Having an essay published in a popular and influential newspaper or magazine is a good way to get new readers. And having to explain something to a general audience in 1,200 words is a good way for me to crystallize my own thinking.

That's not all: I also write because it's important.

I consider myself a technologist. Technology is complicated. It requires expertise to understand. Technological systems are full of nonlinear effects, emergent properties, and wicked problems. In the broader context of how we use technology, they are complex socio-technical systems. These socio-technical systems are also full of even-more-complex nonlinear effects, emergent properties, and wicked problems. Understanding all this is hard: it requires understanding both the underlying technology and the broader social context. Explaining any of this to a popular audience is even harder. But it's something that technologists need to do.

We need to do it because understanding it matters.

What really matters is not the technology part, but the socio-technical whole. Addressing Congress in a 2011 essay, journalist Joshua Kopstein wrote: "It's no longer OK not to understand how the Internet works." He's right, but he's also wrong. The Internet is pervasive and powerful precisely because you do not need to understand how it works. You can just use it, just as you use any other specialized hard-to-understand technology. Similarly, Congress doesn't need to understand how the Internet works in order to effectively legislate it. It had better not be true that only those who know how something works can effectively legislate. We know that governments that can legislate aviation without understanding aerodynamics, health without understanding medicine, and climate change without understanding the science of climate change.

Where Kopstein is right is that policy makers need to understand enough about how the Internet works to understand its broader socio-technical implications, and enough about how the Internet works to defer to technologists when they reach the end of their understanding—just as they need to do with aviation, health, and the enormous ongoing catastrophe that is climate change. When policy makers ignore the science and tech in favor of their own agendas, or when they defer to lobbyists, tech policy starts to go off the rails. It is our job as technologists to explain what we do to a broader audience. Not just now technology works, but how it fits in to society. We have a unique perspective.

It's also a vital perspective. Kopstein is also right when he said that "it's no longer okay." It once was okay, but now it's not. The Internet, and information technologies in general, are fundamental to society. In some ways, this is a surprise. The people who designed and built the Internet created a system that—at its start—didn't matter. Email, file transfer, remote access, webpages—even commerce—were nice-to-have add-ons. They might have been important to us, but they weren't important to society. This has completely changed. The Internet is vital to society. Social media is vital to public discourse. The web is vital for commerce. Even more critically, the Internet now affects the world in a direct physical manner. And in the future, as the Internet of Things permeates more of our society, the Internet will directly affect life and property. And, of course, enable a level of pervasive surveillance the world has never seen.

This is what policy makers, and everyone else, needs, to understand. This is what we need to help explain.

One of the ways we can help bridge this gap is by writing about technology for popular audiences. Whether it's security and privacy—my areas of expertise—artificial intelligence and robotics, algorithms, synthetic biology, food security, climate change, or any of the other major science and technology issues facing society, we technologists need to share what we know.

This is one aspect of what is coming to be known as public-interest technology. It's a broad umbrella of a term, encompassing technologists who work on public policy—either inside government or from without—people who work on technological projects for the public good, academics who teach courses at the intersection of technology and policy, and a lot more. It's what we need more of in a world where society's critical problems have a strong technological basis—and whose solutions will be similarly technological.

This is my third volume of essays, covering July 2013 through December 2017. It includes essays on topics I have written about for decades, like privacy and surveillance. It includes essays on topics that are pretty new to me, like the Internet of Things. It includes essays written during the period that Edward Snowden's NSA documents were made public. Every word in this book has been published elsewhere (including these), and all are available for free on my website. What this book does is make them available in a curated-by-topic, easy-to-carry, ink-on-paper format that I hope looks good on your shelf. Or an e-book version, if you prefer to read that way.

Over the course of my career, I've written over 600 essays and op-eds. I wouldn't do it—I couldn't do it—if you weren't reading them. Thank you for that.

1 Crime, Terrorism, Spying, and War

Cyberconflicts and National Security ──

Originally published in UN Chronicle, *July 18, 2013*

Whenever national cybersecurity policy is discussed, the same stories come up again and again. Whether the examples are called acts of cyberwar, cyberespionage, hacktivism, or cyberterrorism, they all affect national interest, and there is a corresponding call for some sort of national cyberdefense.

Unfortunately, it is very difficult to identify attackers and their motivations in cyberspace. As a result, nations are classifying all serious cyberattacks as cyberwar. This perturbs national policy and fuels a cyberwar arms race, resulting in more instability and less security for everyone. We need to dampen our cyberwar rhetoric, even as we adopt stronger law enforcement policies towards cybersecurity, and work to demilitarize cyberspace.

Let us consider three specific cases:

In Estonia, in 2007, during a period of political tensions between the Russian Federation and Estonia, there were a series of denial-of-service cyberattacks against many Estonian websites, including those run by the Estonian Parliament, government ministries, banks, newspapers and television stations. Though Russia was blamed for these attacks based on circumstantial evidence, the Russian Government never admitted its involvement. An ethnic Russian living in Tallinn, who was upset by Estonia's actions and who had been acting alone, was convicted in an Estonian court for his part in these attacks.

In Dharamsala, India, in 2009, security researchers uncovered a sophisticated surveillance system in the Dalai Lama's computer network. Called GhostNet, further research found the same network had infiltrated political, economic and media targets in 103 countries. China was the presumed origin of this surveillance network, although the evidence was circumstantial. It was also unclear whether this network was run by an organization of the Chinese Government, or by Chinese nationals for either profit or nationalist reasons.

In Iran, in 2010, the Stuxnet computer worm severely damaged, and possibly destroyed, centrifuge machines in the Natanz uranium enrichment facility, in an effort to set back the Iranian nuclear program. Subsequent analysis of the worm indicated that it was a well-designed and well-executed cyberweapon, requiring an engineering effort that implied a nation-state sponsor. Further investigative reporting pointed to the United States and Israel as designers and deployers of the worm, although neither country has officially taken credit for it.

Ordinarily, you could determine who the attacker was by the weaponry. When you saw a tank driving down your street, you knew the military was involved because only the military could afford tanks. Cyberspace is different. In cyberspace, technology is broadly spreading its capability, and everyone is using the same weaponry: hackers, criminals, politically motivated hacktivists, national spies, militaries, even the potential cyberterrorist. They are all exploiting the same vulnerabilities, using the same sort of hacking tools, engaging in the same attack tactics, and leaving the same traces behind. They all eavesdrop or steal data. They all engage in denial-of-service attacks. They all probe cyberdefenses and do their best to cover their tracks.

Despite this, knowing the attacker is vitally important. As members of society, we have several different types of organizations that can defend us from an attack. We can call the police or the military. We can call on our national anti-terrorist agency and our corporate lawyers. Or we can defend ourselves with a variety of commercial products and services. Depending on the situation, all of these are reasonable choices.

The legal regime in which any defense operates depends on two things: who is attacking you and why. Unfortunately, when you are being attacked in cyberspace, the two things you often do not know are who is attacking you and why. It is not that everything can be defined as cyberwar; it is that we are increasingly seeing warlike tactics used in broader cyberconflicts. This makes defense and national cyberdefense policy difficult.

The obvious tendency is to assume the worst. If every attack is potentially an act of war perpetrated by a foreign military, then the logical assumption is that the military needs to be in charge of all cyberdefense, and military problems beg for military solutions. This is the rhetoric we hear from many of the world's leaders: the problem is cyberwar and we are all fighting one right now. This is just not true; there is no war in cyberspace. There is an enormous amount of criminal activity, some of it organized and much of it international. There is politically motivated hacking—hacktivism—against countries, companies, organizations and individuals. There is espionage, sometimes by lone actors and sometimes by national espionage organizations. There are also offensive actions by national organizations, ranging from probing each other's cyberdefenses to actual damage-causing cyberweapons like Stuxnet.

The word "war" really has two definitions: the literal definition of war which evokes guns and tanks and advancing armies, and the rhetorical definition of war as in war on crime, war on poverty, war on drugs, and war on terror. The term "cyberwar" has aspects of both literal and rhetorical war, making it a very loaded term to use when discussing cybersecurity and cyberattacks.

Words matter. To the police, we are citizens to protect. To the military, we are a population to be managed. Framing cybersecurity in terms of war reinforces the notion that we are helpless in the face of the threat, and we need a government—indeed, a military—to protect us.

The framing of the issue as a war affects policy debates around the world. From the notion of government control over the Internet, to wholesale surveillance and eavesdropping facilitation, to an Internet kill switch, to calls to eliminate anonymity—many measures proposed by different countries might make sense in wartime but not in peacetime. (Except that like the war on drugs or terror, there is no winning condition, which means placing a population in a permanent state of emergency). We are seeing a power grab in cyberspace by the world's militaries. We are in the early years of a cyberwar arms race.

Arms races stem from ignorance and fear: ignorance of the other side's capabilities and fear that its capabilities are greater than one's own. Once cyberweapons exist, there will be an impetus to use them.

Stuxnet damaged networks other than its intended targets. Any military-inserted back doors in Internet systems will make us more vulnerable to criminals and hackers.

The cyberwar arms race is destabilizing. It is only a matter of time before something big happens, perhaps by the rash actions of a low-level military officer, an enthusiastic hacker who thinks he is working in his country's best interest, or by accident. If the target nation retaliates, we could find ourselves in a real cyberwar.

I am not proposing that cyberwar is complete fiction. War expands to fill all available theatres, and any future war will have a cyberspace component. It makes sense for countries to establish cyberspace commands within their militaries, and to prepare for cyberwar. Similarly, cyberespionage is not going away anytime soon. Espionage is as old as civilization, and there is simply too much good information in cyberspace for countries not to avail themselves of hacking tools to get at it.

We need to dampen the war rhetoric and increase international cybersecurity cooperation. We need to continue talking about cyberwar treaties. We need to establish rules of engagement in cyberspace, including ways to identify where attacks are coming from and clear definitions of what does or does not constitute an offensive action. We need to understand the role of cybermercenaries, and the role of non-state actors. Cyberterrorism is still a media and political myth, but there will come a time when it will not be. Lastly, we need to build resilience into our infrastructure. Many cyberattacks, regardless of origin, exploit fragilities in the Internet. The more we can reduce those, the safer we will be.

Cyberspace threats are real, but militarizing cyberspace will do more harm than good. The value of a free and open Internet is too important to sacrifice to our fears.

Counterterrorism Mission Creep

Originally published in TheAtlantic.com, *July 16, 2013*

One of the assurances I keep hearing about the US government's spying on American citizens is that it's only used in cases of terrorism. Terrorism is, of course, an extraordinary crime, and its horrific nature is supposed to justify permitting all sorts of excesses to prevent it. But there's a problem with this line of reasoning: mission creep. The definitions of "terrorism" and "weapon of mass destruction" are broadening, and these extraordinary powers are being used, and will continue to be used, for crimes other than terrorism.

Back in 2002, the Patriot Act greatly broadened the definition of terrorism to include all sorts of "normal" violent acts as well as non-violent protests. The term "terrorist" is surprisingly broad; since the terrorist attacks of 9/11, it has been applied to people you wouldn't normally consider terrorists.

The most egregious example of this are the three anti-nuclear pacifists, including an 82-year-old nun, who cut through a chain-link fence at the Oak Ridge nuclear-weapons-production facility in 2012. While they were originally arrested on a misdemeanor trespassing charge, the government kept increasing their charges as the facility's security lapses became more embarrassing. Now the protestors have been convicted of violent crimes of terrorism—and remain in jail.

Meanwhile, a Tennessee government official claimed that complaining about water quality could be considered an act of terrorism. To the government's credit, he was subsequently demoted for those remarks.

The notion of making a terrorist threat is older than the current spate of anti-terrorism craziness. It basically means threatening people in order to terrorize them, and can include things like pointing a fake gun at someone, threatening to set off a bomb, and so on. A Texas high-school student recently spent five months in jail for writing the following on Facebook: "I think I'ma shoot up a kindergarten. And watch the blood of the innocent rain down. And eat the beating heart of one of them." Last year, two Irish tourists were denied entry at the Los Angeles Airport because of some misunderstood tweets.

Another term that's expanded in meaning is "weapon of mass destruction." The law is surprisingly broad, and includes anything that explodes, leading political scientist and terrorism-fear skeptic John Mueller to comment:

As I understand it, not only is a grenade a weapon of mass destruction, but so is a maliciously-designed child's rocket even if it doesn't have a warhead. On the other hand, although a missile-propelled firecracker would be considered a weapon of mass destruction if its designers had wanted to think of it as a weapon, it would not be so considered if it had previously been designed for use as a weapon and then redesigned for pyrotechnic use or if it was surplus and had been sold, loaned, or given to you (under certain circumstances) by the secretary of the army...

All artillery, and virtually every muzzle-loading military long arm for that matter, legally qualifies as a WMD. It does make the bombardment of Ft. Sumter all the more sinister. To say nothing of the revelation that The Star Spangled Banner is in fact an account of a WMD attack on American shores.

After the Boston Marathon bombings, one commentator described our use of the term this way: "What the United States means by terrorist violence is, in large part, 'public violence some weirdo had the gall to carry out using a weapon other than a gun.' ... Mass murderers who strike with guns (and who don't happen to be Muslim) are typically read as psychopaths disconnected from the larger political sphere." Sadly, there's a lot of truth to that.

Even as the definition of terrorism broadens, we have to ask how far we will extend that arbitrary line. Already, we're using these surveillance systems in other areas. A raft of secret court rulings has recently expanded the NSA's eavesdropping powers to include "people possibly involved in nuclear proliferation, espionage and cyberattacks." A "little-noticed provision" in a 2008 law expanded the definition of "foreign intelligence" to include "weapons of mass destruction," which, as we've just seen, is surprisingly broad.

A recent *Atlantic* essay asks, somewhat facetiously, "If PRISM is so good, why stop with terrorism?" The author's point was to discuss the value of the Fourth Amendment, even if it makes the police less efficient. But it's actually a very good question. Once the NSA's ubiquitous surveillance of all Americans is complete—once it has the ability to collect and process all of our emails, phone calls, text messages, Facebook posts, location data, physical mail, financial transactions, and who knows what else—why limit its use to cases of terrorism? I can easily imagine a public groundswell of support to use to help solve some other heinous crime, like a kidnapping.

Or maybe a child-pornography case. From there, it's an easy step to enlist NSA surveillance in the continuing war on drugs; that's certainly important enough to warrant regular access to the NSA's databases. Or maybe to identify illegal immigrants. After all, we've already invested in this system, we might as well get as much out of it as we possibly can. Then it's a short jump to the trivial examples suggested in the *Atlantic* essay: speeding and illegal downloading. This "slippery slope" argument is largely speculative, but we've already started down that incline.

Criminal defendants are starting to demand access to the NSA data that they believe will exonerate themselves. How can a moral government refuse this request?

More humorously, the NSA might have created the best backup system ever.

Technology changes slowly, but political intentions can change very quickly. In 2000, I wrote in my book *Secrets and Lies* about police surveillance technologies: "Once the technology is in place, there will always be the temptation to use it. And it is poor civic hygiene to install technologies that could someday facilitate a police state." Today we're installing technologies of ubiquitous surveillance, and the temptation to use them will be overwhelming.

Syrian Electronic Army Cyberattacks

Originally published in the Wall Street Journal *website,*
August 29, 2013

The Syrian Electronic Army attacked again this week, compromising the websites of the *New York Times*, Twitter, the Huffington Post, and others.

Political hacking isn't new. Hackers were breaking into systems for political reasons long before commerce and criminals discovered the Internet. Over the years, we've seen U.K. vs. Ireland, Israel vs. Arab states, Russia vs. its former Soviet republics, India vs. Pakistan, and US vs. China.

There was a big one in 2007, when the government of Estonia was attacked in cyberspace following a diplomatic incident with Russia. It was hyped as the first cyberwar, but the Kremlin denied any Russian government involvement. The only individuals positively identified were young ethnic Russians living in Estonia.

Poke at any of these international incidents, and what you find are kids playing politics. The Syrian Electronic Army doesn't seem to be an actual army. We don't even know if they're Syrian. And—to be fair—I don't know their ages. Looking at the details of their attacks, it's pretty clear they didn't target the *New York Times* and others directly. They reportedly hacked into an Australian domain name registrar called Melbourne IT, and used that access to disrupt service at a bunch of big-name sites.

We saw this same tactic last year from Anonymous: hack around at random, then retcon a political reason why the sites they successfully broke into deserved it. It makes them look a lot more skilled than they actually are.

This isn't to say that cyberattacks by governments aren't an issue, or that cyberwar is something to be ignored. Attacks from China reportedly are a mix of government-executed military attacks, government-sponsored independent attackers, and random hacking groups that work with tacit government approval. The US also engages in active cyberattacks around the world. Together with Israel, the US employed a sophisticated computer virus (Stuxnet) to attack Iran in 2010.

For the typical company, defending against these attacks doesn't require anything different than what you've been traditionally been doing to secure yourself in cyberspace. If your network is secure, you're secure against amateur geopoliticians who just want to help their side.

The Limitations of Intelligence

Originally published in CNN.com, *September 11, 2013*

We recently learned that US intelligence agencies had at least three days' warning that Syrian President Bashar al-Assad was preparing to launch a chemical attack on his own people, but wasn't able to stop it. At least that's what an intelligence briefing from the White House reveals. With the combined abilities of our national intelligence apparatus—the CIA, NSA, National Reconnaissance Office and all the rest—it's not surprising that we had advance notice. It's not known whether the US shared what it knew.

More interestingly, the US government did not choose to act on that knowledge (for example, launch a preemptive strike), which left some wondering why.

There are several possible explanations, all of which point to a fundamental problem with intelligence information and our national intelligence apparatuses.

The first possibility is that we may have had the data, but didn't fully understand what it meant. This is the proverbial connect-the-dots problem. As we've learned again and again, connecting the dots is hard. Our intelligence services collect billions of individual pieces of data every day. After the fact, it's easy to walk backward through the data and notice all the individual pieces that point to what actually happened. Before the fact, though, it's much more difficult. The overwhelming majority of those bits of data point in random directions, or nowhere at all. Almost all the dots don't connect to anything.

Rather than thinking of intelligence as a connect-the-dots picture, think of it as a million unnumbered pictures superimposed on top of each other. Which picture is the relevant one? We have no idea. Turning that data into actual information is an extraordinarily difficult problem, and one that the vast scope of our data-gathering programs makes even more difficult.

The second possible explanation is that while we had some information about al-Assad's plans, we didn't have enough confirmation to act on that information. This is probably the most likely explanation. We can't act on inklings, hunches, or possibilities. We probably can't even act on probabilities; we have to be sure. But when it comes to intelligence, it's hard to be sure. There could always be something else going on—something we're not able to eavesdrop on, spy on, or see from our satellites. Again, our knowledge is most obvious after the fact.

The third is that while we were sure of our information, we couldn't act because that would reveal "sources and methods." This is probably the most frustrating explanation. Imagine we are able to eavesdrop on al-Assad's most private conversations with his generals and aides, and are absolutely sure of his plans. If we act on them, we reveal that we are eavesdropping. As a result, he's likely to change how he communicates, costing us our ability to eavesdrop. It might sound perverse, but often the fact that we are able to successfully spy on someone is a bigger secret than the information we learn from that spying.

This dynamic was vitally important during World War II. During the war, the British were able to break the German Enigma encryption machine and eavesdrop on German military communications. But while the Allies knew a lot, they would only act on information they learned when there was another plausible way they could have learned it. They even occasionally manufactured plausible explanations. It was just too risky to tip the Germans off that their encryption machines' code had been broken.

The fourth possibility is that there was nothing useful we could have done. And it is hard to imagine how we could have prevented the use of chemical weapons in Syria. We couldn't have launched a preemptive strike, and it's probable that it wouldn't have been effective. The only feasible action would be to alert the opposition—and that, too, might not have accomplished anything. Or perhaps there wasn't sufficient agreement for any one course of action—so, by default, nothing was done.

All of these explanations point out the limitations of intelligence. The NSA serves as an example. The agency measures its success by amount of data collected, not by information synthesized or knowledge gained. But it's knowledge that matters.

The NSA's belief that more data is always good, and that it's worth doing anything in order to collect it, is wrong. There are diminishing returns, and the NSA almost certainly passed that point long ago. But the idea of trade-offs does not seem to be part of its thinking.

The NSA missed the Boston Marathon bombers, even though the suspects left a really sloppy Internet trail and the older brother was on the terrorist watch list. With all the NSA is doing eavesdropping on the world, you would think the least it could manage would be keeping track of people on the terrorist watch list. Apparently not.

I don't know how the CIA measures its success, but it failed to predict the end of the Cold War.

More data does not necessarily mean better information. It's much easier to look backward than to predict. Information does not necessarily enable the government to act. Even when we know something, protecting the methods of collection can be more valuable than the possibility of taking action based on gathered information. But there's not a lot of value to intelligence that can't be used for action. These are the paradoxes of intelligence, and it's time we started remembering them.

Of course, we need organizations like the CIA, the NSA, the NRO and all the rest. Intelligence is a vital component of national security, and can be invaluable in both wartime and peacetime. But it is just one security tool among many, and there are significant costs and limitations.

We've just learned from the recently leaked "black budget" that we're spending $52 billion annually on national intelligence. We need to take a serious look at what kind of value we're getting for our money, and whether it's worth it.

Computer Network Exploitation vs. Computer Network Attack

Originally published in TheAtlantic.com, *March 6, 2014*

Back when we first started getting reports of the Chinese breaking into US computer networks for espionage purposes, we described it in some very strong language. We called the Chinese actions cyber-attacks. We sometimes even invoked the word cyberwar, and declared that a cyber-attack was an act of war.

When Edward Snowden revealed that the NSA has been doing exactly the same thing as the Chinese to computer networks around the world, we used much more moderate language to describe US actions: words like espionage, or intelligence gathering, or spying. We stressed that it's a peacetime activity, and that everyone does it.

The reality is somewhere in the middle, and the problem is that our intuitions are based on history.

Electronic espionage is different today than it was in the pre-Internet days of the Cold War. Eavesdropping isn't passive anymore. It's not the electronic equivalent of sitting close to someone and overhearing a conversation. It's not passively monitoring a communications circuit. It's more likely to involve actively breaking into an adversary's computer network—be it Chinese, Brazilian, or Belgian—and installing malicious software designed to take over that network.

In other words, it's hacking. Cyber-espionage is a form of cyber-attack. It's an offensive action. It violates the sovereignty of another country, and we're doing it with far too little consideration of its diplomatic and geopolitical costs.

The abbreviation-happy US military has two related terms for what it does in cyberspace. CNE stands for "computer network exploitation."

That's spying. CNA stands for "computer network attack." That includes actions designed to destroy or otherwise incapacitate enemy networks. That's—among other things—sabotage.

CNE and CNA are not solely in the purview of the US; everyone does it. We know that other countries are building their offensive cyberwar capabilities. We have discovered sophisticated surveillance networks from other countries with names like GhostNet, Red October, The Mask. We don't know who was behind them—these networks are very difficult to trace back to their source—but we suspect China, Russia, and Spain, respectively. We recently learned of a hacking tool called RCS that's used by 21 governments: Azerbaijan, Colombia, Egypt, Ethiopia, Hungary, Italy, Kazakhstan, Korea, Malaysia, Mexico, Morocco, Nigeria, Oman, Panama, Poland, Saudi Arabia, Sudan, Thailand, Turkey, UAE, and Uzbekistan.

When the Chinese company Huawei tried to sell networking equipment to the US, the government considered that equipment a "national security threat," rightly fearing that those switches were backdoored to allow the Chinese government both to eavesdrop and attack US networks. Now we know that the NSA is doing the exact same thing to American-made equipment sold in China, as well as to those very same Huawei switches.

The problem is that, from the point of view of the object of an attack, CNE and CNA look the same as each other, except for the end result. Today's surveillance systems involve breaking into the computers and installing malware, just as cybercriminals do when they want your money. And just like Stuxnet: the US/Israeli cyberweapon that disabled the Natanz nuclear facility in Iran in 2010.

This is what Microsoft's General Counsel Brad Smith meant when he said: "Indeed, government snooping potentially now constitutes an 'advanced persistent threat,' alongside sophisticated malware and cyber attacks."

When the Chinese penetrate US computer networks, which they do with alarming regularity, we don't really know what they're doing. Are they modifying our hardware and software to just eavesdrop, or are they leaving "logic bombs" that could be triggered to do real damage at some future time? It can be impossible to tell. As a 2011 EU cybersecurity policy document stated (page 7):

> ...technically speaking, CNA requires CNE to be effective. In other words, what may be preparations for cyberwarfare can well be cyberespionage initially or simply be disguised as such.

We can't tell the intentions of the Chinese, and they can't tell ours, either.

Much of the current debate in the US is over what the NSA should be allowed to do, and whether limiting the NSA somehow empowers other governments. That's the wrong debate. We don't get to choose between a world where the NSA spies and one where the Chinese spy. Our choice is between a world where our information infrastructure is vulnerable to all attackers or secure for all users.

As long as cyber-espionage equals cyber-attack, we would be much safer if we focused the NSA's efforts on securing the Internet from these attacks. True, we wouldn't get the same level of access to information flows around the world. But we would be protecting the world's information flows—including our own—from both eavesdropping and more damaging attacks. We would be protecting our information flows from governments, nonstate actors, and criminals. We would be making the world safer.

Offensive military operations in cyberspace, be they CNE or CNA, should be the purview of the military. In the US, that's CyberCommand. Such operations should be recognized as offensive military actions, and should be approved at the highest levels of the executive branch, and be subject to the same international law standards that govern acts of war in the offline world.

If we're going to attack another country's electronic infrastructure, we should treat it like any other attack on a foreign country. It's no longer just espionage, it's a cyber-attack.

iPhone Encryption and the Return of the Crypto Wars

Originally published in CNN.com, *October 3, 2014*

Last week, Apple announced that it is closing a serious security vulnerability in the iPhone. It used to be that the phone's encryption only protected a small amount of the data, and Apple had the ability to bypass security on the rest of it.

From now on, all the phone's data is protected. It can no longer be accessed by criminals, governments, or rogue employees. Access to it can no longer be demanded by totalitarian governments. A user's iPhone data is now more secure.

To hear US law enforcement respond, you'd think Apple's move heralded an unstoppable crime wave. See, the FBI had been using that vulnerability to get into people's iPhones. In the words of cyberlaw professor Orin Kerr, "How is the public interest served by a policy that only thwarts lawful search warrants?"

Ah, but that's the thing: You can't build a backdoor that only the good guys can walk through. Encryption protects against cybercriminals, industrial competitors, the Chinese secret police and the FBI. You're either vulnerable to eavesdropping by any of them, or you're secure from eavesdropping from all of them.

Backdoor access built for the good guys is routinely used by the bad guys. In 2005, some unknown group surreptitiously used the lawful-intercept capabilities built into the Greek cell phone system. The same thing happened in Italy in 2006.

In 2010, Chinese hackers subverted an intercept system Google had put into Gmail to comply with US government surveillance requests. Back doors in our cell phone system are currently being exploited by the FBI and unknown others.

This doesn't stop the FBI and Justice Department from pumping up the fear. Attorney General Eric Holder threatened us with kidnappers and sexual predators.

The former head of the FBI's criminal investigative division went even further, conjuring up kidnappers who are also sexual predators. And, of course, terrorists.

FBI Director James Comey claimed that Apple's move allows people to "place themselves beyond the law" and also invoked that now overworked "child kidnapper." John J. Escalante, chief of detectives for the Chicago police department now holds the title of most hysterical: "Apple will become the phone of choice for the pedophile."

It's all bluster. Of the 3,576 major offenses for which warrants were granted for communications interception in 2013, exactly one involved kidnapping. And, more importantly, there's no evidence that encryption hampers criminal investigations in any serious way. In 2013, encryption foiled the police nine times, up from four in 2012—and the investigations proceeded in some other way.

This is why the FBI's scare stories tend to wither after public scrutiny. A former FBI assistant director wrote about a kidnapped man who would never have been found without the ability of the FBI to decrypt an iPhone, only to retract the point hours later because it wasn't true.

We've seen this game before. During the crypto wars of the 1990s, FBI Director Louis Freeh and others would repeatedly use the example of mobster John Gotti to illustrate why the ability to tap telephones was so vital. But the Gotti evidence was collected using a room bug, not a telephone tap. And those same scary criminal tropes were trotted out then, too. Back then we called them the Four Horsemen of the Infocalypse: pedophiles, kidnappers, drug dealers, and terrorists. Nothing has changed.

Strong encryption has been around for years. Both Apple's File-Vault and Microsoft's BitLocker encrypt the data on computer hard drives. PGP encrypts email. Off-the-Record encrypts chat sessions. HTTPS Everywhere encrypts your browsing. Android phones already come with encryption built-in. There are literally thousands of encryption products without back doors for sale, and some have been around for decades. Even if the US bans the stuff, foreign companies will corner the market because many of us have legitimate needs for security.

Law enforcement has been complaining about "going dark" for decades now. In the 1990s, they convinced Congress to pass a law requiring phone companies to ensure that phone calls would remain tappable even as they became digital. They tried and failed to ban strong encryption and mandate back doors for their use. The FBI tried and failed again to ban strong encryption in 2010. Now, in the post-Snowden era, they're about to try again.

We need to fight this. Strong encryption protects us from a panoply of threats. It protects us from hackers and criminals. It protects our businesses from competitors and foreign spies. It protects people in totalitarian governments from arrest and detention. This isn't just me talking: The FBI also recommends you encrypt your data for security.

As for law enforcement? The recent decades have given them an unprecedented ability to put us under surveillance and access our data. Our cell phones provide them with a detailed history of our movements. Our call records, email history, buddy lists, and Facebook pages tell them who we associate with. The hundreds of companies that track us on the Internet tell them what we're thinking about.

Ubiquitous cameras capture our faces everywhere. And most of us back up our iPhone data on iCloud, which the FBI can still get a warrant for. It truly is the golden age of surveillance.

After considering the issue, Orin Kerr rethought his position, looking at this in terms of a technological-legal trade-off. I think he's right.

Given everything that has made it easier for governments and others to intrude on our private lives, we need both technological security and legal restrictions to restore the traditional balance between government access and our security/privacy. More companies should follow Apple's lead and make encryption the easy-to-use default. And let's wait for some actual evidence of harm before we acquiesce to police demands for reduced security.

Attack Attribution and Cyber Conflict

Originally published in the Christian Science Monitor,
March 4, 2015

The vigorous debate after the Sony Pictures breach pitted the Obama administration against many of us in the cybersecurity community who didn't buy Washington's claim that North Korea was the culprit.

What's both amazing—and perhaps a bit frightening—about that dispute over who hacked Sony is that it happened in the first place.

But what it highlights is the fact that we're living in a world where we can't easily tell the difference between a couple of guys in a basement apartment and the North Korean government with an estimated $10 billion military budget. And that ambiguity has profound implications for how countries will conduct foreign policy in the Internet age.

Clandestine military operations aren't new. Terrorism can be hard to attribute, especially the murky edges of state-sponsored terrorism. What's different in cyberspace is how easy it is for an attacker to mask his identity—and the wide variety of people and institutions that can attack anonymously.

In the real world, you can often identify the attacker by the weaponry. In 2006, Israel attacked a Syrian nuclear facility. It was a conventional attack—military airplanes flew over Syria and bombed the plant—and there was never any doubt who did it. That shorthand doesn't work in cyberspace.

When the US and Israel attacked an Iranian nuclear facility in 2010, they used a cyberweapon and their involvement was a secret for years. On the Internet, technology broadly disseminates capability. Everyone from lone hackers to criminals to hypothetical cyberterrorists to nations' spies and soldiers are using the same tools and the same tactics. Internet traffic doesn't come with a return address, and it's easy for an attacker to obscure his tracks by routing his attacks through some innocent third party.

And while it now seems that North Korea did indeed attack Sony, the attack it most resembles was conducted by members of the hacker group Anonymous against a company called HBGary Federal in 2011. In the same year, other members of Anonymous threatened NATO, and in 2014, still others announced that they were going to attack ISIS. Regardless of what you think of the group's capabilities, it's a new world when a bunch of hackers can threaten an international military alliance.

Even when a victim does manage to attribute a cyberattack, the process can take a long time. It took the US weeks to publicly blame North Korea for the Sony attacks. That was relatively fast; most of that time was probably spent trying to figure out how to respond. Attacks by China against US companies have taken much longer to attribute.

This delay makes defense policy difficult. Microsoft's Scott Charney makes this point: When you're being physically attacked, you can call on a variety of organizations to defend you—the police, the military, whoever does antiterrorism security in your country, your lawyers. The legal structure justifying that defense depends on knowing two things: who's attacking you, and why. Unfortunately, when you're being attacked in cyberspace, the two things you often don't know are who's attacking you, and why.

Whose job was it to defend Sony? Was it the US military's, because it believed the attack to have come from North Korea? Was it the FBI, because this wasn't an act of war? Was it Sony's own problem, because it's a private company? What about during those first weeks, when no one knew who the attacker was? These are just a few of the policy questions that we don't have good answers for.

Certainly Sony needs enough security to protect itself regardless of who the attacker was, as do all of us. For the victim of a cyberattack, who the attacker is can be academic. The damage is the same, whether it's a couple of hackers or a nation-state.

In the geopolitical realm, though, attribution is vital. And not only is attribution hard, providing evidence of any attribution is even harder. Because so much of the FBI's evidence was classified—and probably provided by the National Security Agency—it was not able to explain why it was so sure North Korea did it. As I recently wrote: "The agency might have intelligence on the planning process for the hack. It might, say, have phone calls discussing the project, weekly PowerPoint status reports, or even Kim Jong-un's sign-off on the plan." Making any of this public would reveal the NSA's "sources and methods," something it regards as a very important secret.

Different types of attribution require different levels of evidence. In the Sony case, we saw the US government was able to generate enough evidence to convince itself. Perhaps it had the additional evidence required to convince North Korea it was sure, and provided that over diplomatic channels. But if the public is expected to support any government retaliatory action, they are going to need sufficient evidence made public to convince them. Today, trust in US intelligence agencies is low, especially after the 2003 Iraqi weapons-of-mass-destruction debacle.

What all of this means is that we are in the middle of an arms race between attackers and those that want to identify them: deception and deception detection. It's an arms race in which the US—and, by extension, its allies—has a singular advantage. We spend more money on electronic eavesdropping than the rest of the world combined, we have more technology companies than any other country, and the architecture of the Internet ensures that most of the world's traffic passes through networks the NSA can eavesdrop on.

In 2012, then US Secretary of Defense Leon Panetta said publicly that the US—presumably the NSA—has "made significant advances in ... identifying the origins" of cyberattacks. We don't know if this means they have made some fundamental technological advance, or that their espionage is so good that they're monitoring the planning processes. Other US government officials have privately said that they've solved the attribution problem.

We don't know how much of that is real and how much is bluster. It's actually in America's best interest to confidently accuse North Korea, even if it isn't sure, because it sends a strong message to the rest of the world: "Don't think you can hide in cyberspace. If you try anything, we'll know it's you."

Strong attribution leads to deterrence. The detailed NSA capabilities leaked by Edward Snowden help with this, because they bolster an image of an almost-omniscient NSA.

It's not, though—which brings us back to the arms race. A world where hackers and governments have the same capabilities, where governments can masquerade as hackers or as other governments, and where much of the attribution evidence intelligence agencies collect remains secret, is a dangerous place.

So is a world where countries have secret capabilities for deception and detection deception, and are constantly trying to get the best of each other. This is the world of today, though, and we need to be prepared for it.

Metal Detectors at Sports Stadiums ━━━

Originally published in the Washington Post, *April 14, 2015*

Fans attending Major League Baseball games are being greeted in a new way this year: with metal detectors at the ballparks. Touted as a counterterrorism measure, they're nothing of the sort. They're pure security theater: They look good without doing anything to make us safer. We're stuck with them because of a combination of buck passing, CYA thinking, and fear.

As a security measure, the new devices are laughable. The ballpark metal detectors are much more lax than the ones at an airport checkpoint. They aren't very sensitive—people with phones and keys in their pockets are sailing through—and there are no X-ray machines. Bags get the same cursory search they've gotten for years. And fans wanting to avoid the detectors can opt for a "light pat-down search" instead.

There's no evidence that this new measure makes anyone safer. A halfway competent ticketholder would have no trouble sneaking a gun into the stadium. For that matter, a bomb exploded at a crowded checkpoint would be no less deadly than one exploded in the stands. These measures will, at best, be effective at stopping the random baseball fan who's carrying a gun or knife into the stadium. That may be a good idea, but unless there's been a recent spate of fan shootings and stabbings at baseball games—and there hasn't—this is a whole lot of time and money being spent to combat an imaginary threat.

But imaginary threats are the only ones baseball executives have to stop this season; there's been no specific terrorist threat or actual intelligence to be concerned about. MLB executives forced this change on ballparks based on unspecified discussions with the Department of Homeland Security after the Boston Marathon bombing in 2013. Because, you know, that was also a sporting event.

This system of vague consultations and equally vague threats ensure that no one organization can be seen as responsible for the change. MLB can claim that the league and teams "work closely" with DHS. DHS can claim that it was MLB's initiative. And both can safely relax because if something happens, at least they did something.

It's an attitude I've seen before: "Something must be done. This is something. Therefore, we must do it." Never mind if the something makes any sense or not.

In reality, this is CYA security, and it's pervasive in post-9/11 America. It no longer matters if a security measure makes sense, if it's cost-effective or if it mitigates any actual threats. All that matters is that you took the threat seriously, so if something happens you won't be blamed for inaction. It's security, all right—security for the careers of those in charge.

I'm not saying that these officials care only about their jobs and not at all about preventing terrorism, only that their priorities are skewed. They imagine vague threats, and come up with correspondingly vague security measures intended to address them. They experience none of the costs. They're not the ones who have to deal with the long lines and confusion at the gates. They're not the ones who have to arrive early to avoid the messes the new policies have caused around the league. And if fans spend more money at the concession stands because they've arrived an hour early and have had the food and drinks they tried to bring along confiscated, so much the better, from the team owners' point of view.

I can hear the objections to this as I write. You don't know these measures won't be effective! What if something happens? Don't we have to do everything possible to protect ourselves against terrorism?

That's worst-case thinking, and it's dangerous. It leads to bad decisions, bad design and bad security. A better approach is to realistically assess the threats, judge security measures on their effectiveness and take their costs into account. And the result of that calm, rational look will be the realization that there will always be places where we pack ourselves densely together, and that we should spend less time trying to secure those places and more time finding terrorist plots before they can be carried out.

So far, fans have been exasperated but mostly accepting of these new security measures. And this is precisely the problem—most of us don't care all that much. Our options are to put up with these measures, or stay home. Going to a baseball game is not a political act, and metal detectors aren't worth a boycott. But there's an undercurrent of fear as well. If it's in the name of security, we'll accept it. As long as our leaders are scared of the terrorists, they're going to continue the security theater. And we're similarly going to accept whatever measures are forced upon us in the name of security. We're going to accept the National Security Agency's surveillance of every American, airport security procedures that make no sense and metal detectors at baseball and football stadiums. We're going to continue to waste money overreacting to irrational fears.

We no longer need the terrorists. We're now so good at terrorizing ourselves.

This essay previously appeared in the *Washington Post*.

The Future of Ransomware

Originally published in the Washington Post, *May 16, 2017*

Ransomware isn't new, but it's increasingly popular and profitable.

The concept is simple: Your computer gets infected with a virus that encrypts your files until you pay a ransom. It's extortion taken to its networked extreme. The criminals provide step-by-step instructions on how to pay, sometimes even offering a help line for victims unsure how to buy bitcoin. The price is designed to be cheap enough for people to pay instead of giving up: a few hundred dollars in many cases. Those who design these systems know their market, and it's a profitable one.

The ransomware that has affected systems in more than 150 countries recently, WannaCry, made press headlines last week, but it doesn't seem to be more virulent or more expensive than other ransomware. This one has a particularly interesting pedigree: It's based on a vulnerability developed by the National Security Agency that can be used against many versions of the Windows operating system. The NSA's code was, in turn, stolen by an unknown hacker group called Shadow Brokers—widely believed by the security community to be the Russians—in 2014 and released to the public in April.

Microsoft patched the vulnerability a month earlier, presumably after being alerted by the NSA that the leak was imminent. But the vulnerability affected older versions of Windows that Microsoft no longer supports, and there are still many people and organizations that don't regularly patch their systems. This allowed whoever wrote WannaCry—it could be anyone from a lone individual to an organized crime syndicate—to use it to infect computers and extort users.

The lessons for users are obvious: Keep your system patches up to date and regularly backup your data. This isn't just good advice to defend against ransomware, but good advice in general. But it's becoming obsolete.

Everything is becoming a computer. Your microwave is a computer that makes things hot. Your refrigerator is a computer that keeps things cold. Your car and television, the traffic lights and signals in your city and our national power grid are all computers. This is the much-hyped Internet of Things (IoT). It's coming, and it's coming faster than you might think. And as these devices connect to the Internet, they become vulnerable to ransomware and other computer threats.

It's only a matter of time before people get messages on their car screens saying that the engine has been disabled and it will cost $200 in bitcoin to turn it back on. Or a similar message on their phones about their Internet-enabled door lock: Pay $100 if you want to get into your house tonight. Or pay far more if they want their embedded heart defibrillator to keep working.

This isn't just theoretical. Researchers have already demonstrated a ransomware attack against smart thermostats, which may sound like a nuisance at first but can cause serious property damage if it's cold enough outside. If the device under attack has no screen, you'll get the message on the smartphone app you control it from.

Hackers don't even have to come up with these ideas on their own; the government agencies whose code was stolen were already doing it. One of the leaked CIA attack tools targets Internet-enabled Samsung smart televisions.

Even worse, the usual solutions won't work with these embedded systems. You have no way to back up your refrigerator's software, and it's unclear whether that solution would even work if an attack targets the functionality of the device rather than its stored data.

These devices will be around for a long time. Unlike our phones and computers, which we replace every few years, cars are expected to last at least a decade. We want our appliances to run for 20 years or more, our thermostats even longer.

What happens when the company that made our smart washing machine—or just the computer part—goes out of business, or otherwise decides that they can no longer support older models? WannaCry affected Windows versions as far back as XP, a version that Microsoft no longer supports. The company broke with policy and released a patch for those older systems, but it has both the engineering talent and the money to do so.

That won't happen with low-cost IoT devices.

Those devices are built on the cheap, and the companies that make them don't have the dedicated teams of security engineers ready to craft and distribute security patches. The economics of the IoT doesn't allow for it. Even worse, many of these devices aren't patchable. Remember last fall when the Mirai botnet infected hundreds of thousands of Internet-enabled digital video recorders, webcams and other devices and launched a massive denial-of-service attack that resulted in a host of popular websites dropping off the Internet? Most of those devices couldn't be fixed with new software once they were attacked. The way you update your DVR is to throw it away and buy a new one.

Solutions aren't easy and they're not pretty. The market is not going to fix this unaided. Security is a hard-to-evaluate feature against a possible future threat, and consumers have long rewarded companies that provide easy-to-compare features and a quick time-to-market at its expense. We need to assign liabilities to companies that write insecure software that harms people, and possibly even issue and enforce regulations that require companies to maintain software systems throughout their life cycle. We may need minimum security standards for critical IoT devices. And it would help if the NSA got more involved in securing our information infrastructure and less in keeping it vulnerable so the government can eavesdrop.

I know this all sounds politically impossible right now, but we simply cannot live in a future where everything—from the things we own to our nation's infrastructure—can be held for ransom by criminals again and again.

2 Travel and Security

Hacking Airplanes

Originally published in CNN.com, *April 16, 2015*

Imagine this: A terrorist hacks into a commercial airplane from the ground, takes over the controls from the pilots and flies the plane into the ground. It sounds like the plot of some "Die Hard" reboot, but it's actually one of the possible scenarios outlined in a new Government Accountability Office report on security vulnerabilities in modern airplanes.

It's certainly possible, but in the scheme of Internet risks I worry about, it's not very high. I'm more worried about the more pedestrian attacks against more common Internet-connected devices. I'm more worried, for example, about a multination cyber arms race that stockpiles capabilities such as this, and prioritizes attack over defense in an effort to gain relative advantage. I worry about the democratization of cyberattack techniques, and who might have the capabilities currently reserved for nation-states. And I worry about a future a decade from now if these problems aren't addressed.

First, the airplanes. The problem the GAO identifies is one computer security experts have talked about for years. Newer planes such as the Boeing 787 Dreamliner and the Airbus A350 and A380 have a single network that is used both by pilots to fly the plane and passengers for their Wi-Fi connections. The risk is that a hacker sitting in the back of the plane, or even one on the ground, could use the Wi-Fi connection to hack into the avionics and then remotely fly the plane.

The report doesn't explain how someone could do this, and there are currently no known vulnerabilities that a hacker could exploit. But all systems are vulnerable—we simply don't have the engineering expertise to design and build perfectly secure computers and networks—so of course we believe this kind of attack is theoretically possible.

Previous planes had separate networks, which is much more secure.

As terrifying as this movie-plot threat is—and it has been the plot of several recent works of fiction—this is just one example of an increasingly critical problem: As the computers already critical to running our infrastructure become connected, our vulnerability to cyberattack grows. We've already seen vulnerabilities in baby monitors, cars, medical equipment and all sorts of other Internet-connected devices. In February, Toyota recalled 1.9 million Prius cars because of a software vulnerability. Expect similar vulnerabilities in our smart thermostats, smart light bulbs and everything else connected to the smart power grid. The Internet of Things will bring computers into every aspect of our life and society. Those computers will be on the network and will be vulnerable to attack.

And because they'll all be networked together, a vulnerability in one device will affect the security of everything else. Right now, a vulnerability in your home router can compromise the security of your entire home network. A vulnerability in your Internet-enabled refrigerator can reportedly be used as a launching pad for further attacks.

Future attacks will be exactly like what's happening on the Internet today with your computer and smartphones, only they will be with everything. It's all one network, and it's all critical infrastructure.

Some of these attacks will require sufficient budget and organization to limit them to nation-state aggressors. But that's hardly comforting. North Korea is last year believed to have launched a massive cyberattack against Sony Pictures. Last month, China used a cyberweapon called the "Great Cannon" against the website GitHub. In 2010, the US and Israeli governments launched a sophisticated cyberweapon called Stuxnet against the Iranian Natanz nuclear power plant; it used a series of vulnerabilities to cripple centrifuges critical for separating nuclear material. In fact, the United States has done more to weaponize the Internet than any other country.

Governments only have a fleeting advantage over everyone else, though. Today's top-secret National Security Agency programs become tomorrow's Ph.D. theses and the next day's hacker's tools. So while remotely hacking the 787 Dreamliner's avionics might be well beyond the capabilities of anyone except Boeing engineers today, that's not going to be true forever.

What this all means is that we have to start thinking about the security of the Internet of Things—whether the issue in question is today's airplanes or tomorrow's smart clothing. We can't repeat the mistakes of the early days of the PC and then the Internet, where we initially ignored security and then spent years playing catch-up. We have to build security into everything that is going to be connected to the Internet.

This is going to require both significant research and major commitments by companies. It's also going to require legislation mandating certain levels of security on devices connecting to the Internet, and at network providers that make the Internet work. This isn't something the market can solve on its own, because there are just too many incentives to ignore security and hope that someone else will solve it.

As a nation, we need to prioritize defense over offense. Right now, the NSA and US Cyber Command have a strong interest in keeping the Internet insecure so they can better eavesdrop on and attack our enemies. But this prioritization cuts both ways: We can't leave others' networks vulnerable without also leaving our own vulnerable. And as one of the most networked countries on the planet, we are highly vulnerable to attack. It would be better to focus the NSA's mission on defense and harden our infrastructure against attack.

Remember the GAO's nightmare scenario: A hacker on the ground exploits a vulnerability in the airplane's Wi-Fi system to gain access to the airplane's network. Then he exploits a vulnerability in the firewall that separates the passengers' network from the avionics to gain access to the flight controls. Then he uses other vulnerabilities both to lock the pilots out of the cockpit controls and take control of the plane himself.

It's a scenario made possible by insecure computers and insecure networks. And while it might take a government-led secret project on the order of Stuxnet to pull it off today, that won't always be true.

Of course, this particular movie-plot threat might never become a real one. But it is almost certain that some equally unlikely scenario will. I just hope we have enough security expertise to deal with whatever it ends up being.

Reassessing Airport Security

Originally published in CNN.com, *June 5, 2015*

News that the Transportation Security Administration missed a whopping 95% of guns and bombs in recent airport security "red team" tests was justifiably shocking. It's clear that we're not getting value for the $7 billion we're paying the TSA annually.

But there's another conclusion, inescapable and disturbing to many, but good news all around: we don't need $7 billion worth of airport security. These results demonstrate that there isn't much risk of airplane terrorism, and we should ratchet security down to pre-9/11 levels.

We don't need perfect airport security. We just need security that's good enough to dissuade someone from building a plot around evading it. If you're caught with a gun or a bomb, the TSA will detain you and call the FBI. Under those circumstances, even a medium chance of getting caught is enough to dissuade a sane terrorist. A 95% failure rate is too high, but a 20% one isn't.

For those of us who have been watching the TSA, the 95% number wasn't that much of a surprise. The TSA has been failing these sorts of tests since its inception: failures in 2003, a 91% failure rate at Newark Liberty International in 2006, a 75% failure rate at Los Angeles International in 2007, more failures in 2008. And those are just the public test results; I'm sure there are many more similarly damning reports the TSA has kept secret out of embarrassment.

Previous TSA excuses were that the results were isolated to a single airport, or not realistic simulations of terrorist behavior. That almost certainly wasn't true then, but the TSA can't even argue that now. The current test was conducted at many airports, and the testers didn't use super-stealthy ninja-like weapon-hiding skills.

This is consistent with what we know anecdotally: the TSA misses a lot of weapons. Pretty much everyone I know has inadvertently carried a knife through airport security, and some people have told me about guns they mistakenly carried on airplanes. The TSA publishes statistics about how many guns it detects; last year, it was 2,212. This doesn't mean the TSA missed 44,000 guns last year; a weapon that is mistakenly left in a carry-on bag is going to be easier to detect than a weapon deliberately hidden in the same bag. But we now know that it's not hard to deliberately sneak a weapon through.

So why is the failure rate so high? The report doesn't say, and I hope the TSA is going to conduct a thorough investigation as to the causes. My guess is that it's a combination of things. Security screening is an incredibly boring job, and almost all alerts are false alarms. It's very hard for people to remain vigilant in this sort of situation, and sloppiness is inevitable.

There are also technology failures. We know that current screening technologies are terrible at detecting the plastic explosive PETN—that's what the underwear bomber had—and that a disassembled weapon has an excellent chance of getting through airport security. We know that some items allowed through airport security make excellent weapons.

The TSA is failing to defend us against the threat of terrorism. The only reason they've been able to get away with the scam for so long is that there isn't much of a threat of terrorism to defend against.

Even with all these actual and potential failures, there have been no successful terrorist attacks against airplanes since 9/11. If there were lots of terrorists just waiting for us to let our guard down to destroy American planes, we would have seen attacks—attempted or successful—after all these years of screening failures. No one has hijacked a plane with a knife or a gun since 9/11. Not a single plane has blown up due to terrorism.

Terrorists are much rarer than we think, and launching a terrorist plot is much more difficult than we think. I understand this conclusion is counterintuitive, and contrary to the fearmongering we hear every day from our political leaders. But it's what the data shows.

This isn't to say that we can do away with airport security altogether. We need some security to dissuade the stupid or impulsive, but any more is a waste of money. The very rare smart terrorists are going to be able to bypass whatever we implement or choose an easier target. The more common stupid terrorists are going to be stopped by whatever measures we implement.

Smart terrorists are very rare, and we're going to have to deal with them in two ways. One, we need vigilant passengers—that's what protected us from both the shoe and the underwear bombers. And two, we're going to need good intelligence and investigation—that's how we caught the liquid bombers in their London apartments.

The real problem with airport security is that it's only effective if the terrorists target airplanes. I generally am opposed to security measures that require us to correctly guess the terrorists' tactics and targets. If we detect solids, the terrorists will use liquids. If we defend airports, they bomb movie theaters. It's a lousy game to play, because we can't win.

We should demand better results out of the TSA, but we should also recognize that the actual risk doesn't justify their $7 billion budget. I'd rather see that money spent on intelligence and investigation—security that doesn't require us to guess the next terrorist tactic and target, and works regardless of what the terrorists are planning next.

3 Internet of Things

Hacking Consumer Devices

Originally published in CNN.com, *August 15, 2013*

Last weekend, a Texas couple apparently discovered that the electronic baby monitor in their children's bedroom had been hacked. According to a local TV station, the couple said they heard an unfamiliar voice coming from the room, went to investigate and found that someone had taken control of the camera monitor remotely and was shouting profanity-laden abuse. The child's father unplugged the monitor.

What does this mean for the rest of us? How secure are consumer electronic systems, now that they're all attached to the Internet?

The answer is not very, and it's been this bad for many years. Security vulnerabilities have been found in all types of webcams, cameras of all sorts, implanted medical devices, cars, and even smart toilets—not to mention yachts, ATM machines, industrial control systems and military drones.

All of these things have long been hackable. Those of us who work in security are often amazed that most people don't know about it.

Why are they hackable? Because security is very hard to get right. It takes expertise, and it takes time. Most companies don't care because most customers buying security systems and smart appliances don't know enough to care. Why should a baby monitor manufacturer spend all sorts of money making sure its security is good when the average customer won't even notice?

Even worse, that consumer will look at two competing baby monitors—a more expensive one with better security, and a cheaper one with minimal security—and buy the cheaper. Without the expertise to make an informed buying decision, cheaper wins.

A lot of hacks happen because the users don't configure or install their devices properly, but that's really the fault of the manufacturer. These are supposed to be consumer devices, not specialized equipment for security experts only.

This sort of thing is true in other aspects of society, and we have a variety of mechanisms to deal with it. Government regulation is one of them. For example, few of us can differentiate real pharmaceuticals from snake oil, so the FDA regulates what can be sold and what sorts of claims vendors can make. Independent product testing is another. You and I might not be able to tell a well-made car from a poorly-made one at a glance, but we can both read the reports from a variety of testing agencies.

Computer security has resisted these mechanisms, both because the industry changes so quickly and because this sort of testing is hard and expensive. But the effect is that we're all being sold a lot of insecure consumer products with embedded computers. And as these computers get connected to the Internet, the problems will get worse.

The moral here isn't that your baby monitor could be hacked. The moral is that pretty much every "smart" everything can be hacked, and because consumers don't care, the market won't fix the problem.

****

This essay previously appeared on CNN.com. I wrote it in about half an hour, on request, and I'm not really happy with it. I should have talked more about the economics of good security, as well as the economics of hacking. The point is that we don't have to worry about hackers smart enough to figure out these vulnerabilities, but those dumb hackers who just use software tools written and distributed by the smart hackers. Ah well, next time.

Security Risks of Embedded Systems

Originally published in Wired.com, *January 6, 2014*

We're at a crisis point now with regard to the security of embedded systems, where computing is embedded into the hardware itself—

as with the Internet of Things. These embedded computers are riddled with vulnerabilities, and there's no good way to patch them.

It's not unlike what happened in the mid-1990s, when the insecurity of personal computers was reaching crisis levels. Software and operating systems were riddled with security vulnerabilities, and there was no good way to patch them. Companies were trying to keep vulnerabilities secret, and not releasing security updates quickly. And when updates were released, it was hard—if not impossible—to get users to install them. This has changed over the past twenty years, due to a combination of full disclosure—publishing vulnerabilities to force companies to issue patches quicker—and automatic updates: automating the process of installing updates on users' computers. The results aren't perfect, but they're much better than ever before.

But this time the problem is much worse, because the world is different: All of these devices are connected to the Internet. The computers in our routers and modems are much more powerful than the PCs of the mid-1990s, and the Internet of Things will put computers into all sorts of consumer devices. The industries producing these devices are even less capable of fixing the problem than the PC and software industries were.

If we don't solve this soon, we're in for a security disaster as hackers figure out that it's easier to hack routers than computers. At a recent Def Con, a researcher looked at thirty home routers and broke into half of them—including some of the most popular and common brands.

To understand the problem, you need to understand the embedded systems market.

Typically, these systems are powered by specialized computer chips made by companies such as Broadcom, Qualcomm, and Marvell. These chips are cheap, and the profit margins slim. Aside from price, the way the manufacturers differentiate themselves from each other is by features and bandwidth. They typically put a version of the Linux operating system onto the chips, as well as a bunch of other open-source and proprietary components and drivers. They do as little engineering as possible before shipping, and there's little incentive to update their "board support package" until absolutely necessary.

The system manufacturers—usually original device manufacturers (ODMs) who often don't get their brand name on the finished product—choose a chip based on price and features, and then build a router, server, or whatever. They don't do a lot of engineering, either. The brand-name company on the box may add a user interface and maybe some new features, make sure everything works, and they're done, too.

The problem with this process is that no one entity has any incentive, expertise, or even ability to patch the software once it's shipped. The chip manufacturer is busy shipping the next version of the chip, and the ODM is busy upgrading its product to work with this next chip. Maintaining the older chips and products just isn't a priority.

And the software is old, even when the device is new. For example, one survey of common home routers found that the software components were four to five years older than the device. The minimum age of the Linux operating system was four years. The minimum age of the Samba file system software: six years. They may have had all the security patches applied, but most likely not. No one has that job. Some of the components are so old that they're no longer being patched. This patching is especially important because security vulnerabilities are found "more easily" as systems age.

To make matters worse, it's often impossible to patch the software or upgrade the components to the latest version. Often, the complete source code isn't available. Yes, they'll have the source code to Linux and any other open-source components. But many of the device drivers and other components are just "binary blobs"—no source code at all. That's the most pernicious part of the problem: No one can possibly patch code that's just binary.

Even when a patch is possible, it's rarely applied. Users usually have to manually download and install relevant patches. But since users never get alerted about security updates, and don't have the expertise to manually administer these devices, it doesn't happen. Sometimes the ISPs have the ability to remotely patch routers and modems, but this is also rare.

The result is hundreds of millions of devices that have been sitting on the Internet, unpatched and insecure, for the last five to ten years.

Hackers are starting to notice. Malware DNS Changer attacks home routers as well as computers. In Brazil, 4.5 million DSL routers were compromised for purposes of financial fraud. Last month, Symantec reported on a Linux worm that targets routers, cameras, and other embedded devices.

This is only the beginning. All it will take is some easy-to-use hacker tools for the script kiddies to get into the game.

And the Internet of Things will only make this problem worse, as the Internet—as well as our homes and bodies—becomes flooded with new embedded devices that will be equally poorly maintained and unpatchable. But routers and modems pose a particular problem, because they're: (1) between users and the Internet, so turning them off is increasingly not an option; (2) more powerful and more general in function than other embedded devices; (3) the one 24/7 computing device in the house, and are a natural place for lots of new features.

We were here before with personal computers, and we fixed the problem. But disclosing vulnerabilities in an effort to force vendors to fix the problem won't work the same way as with embedded systems. The last time, the problem was computers, ones mostly not connected to the Internet, and slow-spreading viruses. The scale is different today: more devices, more vulnerability, viruses spreading faster on the Internet, and less technical expertise on both the vendor and the user sides. Plus vulnerabilities that are impossible to patch.

Combine full function with lack of updates, add in a pernicious market dynamic that has inhibited updates and prevented anyone else from updating, and we have an incipient disaster in front of us. It's just a matter of when.

We simply have to fix this. We have to put pressure on embedded system vendors to design their systems better. We need open-source driver software—no more binary blobs!—so third-party vendors and ISPs can provide security tools and software updates for as long as the device is in use. We need automatic update mechanisms to ensure they get installed.

The economic incentives point to large ISPs as the driver for change. Whether they're to blame or not, the ISPs are the ones who get the service calls for crashes. They often have to send users new hardware because it's the only way to update a router or modem, and that can easily cost a year's worth of profit from that customer. This problem is only going to get worse, and more expensive. Paying the cost up front for better embedded systems is much cheaper than paying the costs of the resultant security disasters.

Samsung Television Spies on Viewers

Originally published in CNN.com, *February 11, 2015*

Earlier this week, we learned that Samsung televisions are eavesdropping on their owners. If you have one of their Internet-connected smart TVs, you can turn on a voice command feature that saves you the trouble of finding the remote, pushing buttons and scrolling through menus. But making that feature work requires the television to listen to everything you say. And what you say isn't just processed by the television; it may be forwarded over the Internet for remote processing. It's literally Orwellian.

This discovery surprised people, but it shouldn't have. The things around us are increasingly computerized, and increasingly connected to the Internet. And most of them are listening.

Our smartphones and computers, of course, listen to us when we're making audio and video calls. But the microphones are always there, and there are ways a hacker, government, or clever company can turn those microphones on without our knowledge. Sometimes we turn them on ourselves. If we have an iPhone, the voice-processing system Siri listens to us, but only when we push the iPhone's button. Like Samsung, iPhones with the "Hey Siri" feature enabled listen all the time. So do Android devices with the "OK Google" feature enabled, and so does an Amazon voice-activated system called Echo. Facebook has the ability to turn your smartphone's microphone on when you're using the app.

Even if you don't speak, our computers are paying attention. Gmail "listens" to everything you write, and shows you advertising based on it. It might feel as if you're never alone. Facebook does the same with everything you write on that platform, and even listens to the things you type but don't post. Skype doesn't listen—we think—but as *Der Spiegel* notes, data from the service "has been accessible to the NSA's snoops" since 2011.

So the NSA certainly listens. It listens directly, and it listens to all these companies listening to you. So do other countries like Russia and China, which we really don't want listening so closely to their citizens.

It's not just the devices that listen; most of this data is transmitted over the Internet. Samsung sends it to what was referred to as a "third party" in its policy statement. It later revealed that third party to be a company you've never heard of—Nuance—that turns the voice into text for it. Samsung promises that the data is erased immediately. Most of the other companies that are listening promise no such thing and, in fact, save your data for a long time. Governments, of course, save it, too.

This data is a treasure trove for criminals, as we are learning again and again as tens and hundreds of millions of customer records are repeatedly stolen. Last week, it was reported that hackers had accessed the personal records of some 80 million Anthem Health customers and others. Last year, it was Home Depot, JP Morgan, Sony and many others. Do we think Nuance's security is better than any of these companies? I sure don't.

At some level, we're consenting to all this listening. A single sentence in Samsung's 1,500-word privacy policy, the one most of us don't read, stated: "Please be aware that if your spoken words include personal or other sensitive information, that information will be among the data captured and transmitted to a third party through your use of Voice Recognition." Other services could easily come with a similar warning: Be aware that your email provider knows what you're saying to your colleagues and friends and be aware that your cell phone knows where you sleep and whom you're sleeping with—assuming that you both have smartphones, that is.

The Internet of Things is full of listeners. Newer cars contain computers that record speed, steering wheel position, pedal pressure, even tire pressure—and insurance companies want to listen. And, of course, your cell phone records your precise location at all times you have it on—and possibly even when you turn it off. If you have a smart thermostat, it records your house's temperature, humidity, ambient light and any nearby movement. Any fitness tracker you're wearing records your movements and some vital signs; so do many computerized medical devices. Add security cameras and recorders, drones and other surveillance airplanes, and we're being watched, tracked, measured and listened to almost all the time.

It's the age of ubiquitous surveillance, fueled by both Internet companies and governments. And because it's largely happening in the background, we're not really aware of it.

This has to change. We need to regulate the listening: both what is being collected and how it's being used. But that won't happen until we know the full extent of surveillance: who's listening and what they're doing with it. Samsung buried its listening details in its privacy policy—they have since amended it to be clearer—and we're only having this discussion because a Daily Beast reporter stumbled upon it. We need more explicit conversation about the value of being able to speak freely in our living rooms without our televisions listening, or having email conversations without Google or the government listening. Privacy is a prerequisite for free expression, and losing that would be an enormous blow to our society.

Volkswagen and Cheating Software

Originally published in CNN.com, *September 28, 2015*

For the past six years, Volkswagen has been cheating on the emissions testing for its diesel cars. The cars' computers were able to detect when they were being tested, and temporarily alter how their engines worked so they looked much cleaner than they actually were. When they weren't being tested, they belched out 40 times the pollutants. Their CEO has resigned, and the company will face an expensive recall, enormous fines and worse.

Cheating on regulatory testing has a long history in corporate America. It happens regularly in automobile emissions control and elsewhere. What's important in the VW case is that the cheating was preprogrammed into the algorithm that controlled cars' emissions.

Computers allow people to cheat in ways that are new. Because the cheating is encapsulated in software, the malicious actions can happen at a far remove from the testing itself. Because the software is "smart" in ways that normal objects are not, the cheating can be subtler and harder to detect.

We've already had examples of smartphone manufacturers cheating on processor benchmark testing: detecting when they're being tested and artificially increasing their performance. We're going to see this in other industries.

The Internet of Things is coming. Many industries are moving to add computers to their devices, and that will bring with it new opportunities for manufacturers to cheat. Light bulbs could fool regulators into appearing more energy efficient than they are. Temperature sensors could fool buyers into believing that food has been stored at safer temperatures than it has been. Voting machines could appear to work perfectly—except during the first Tuesday of November, when they undetectably switch a few percent of votes from one party's candidates to another's.

My worry is that some corporate executives won't interpret the VW story as a cautionary tale involving just punishments for a bad mistake but will see it instead as a demonstration that you can get away with something like that for six years.

And they'll cheat smarter. For all of VW's brazenness, its cheating was obvious once people knew to look for it. Far cleverer would be to make the cheating look like an accident. Overall software quality is so bad that products ship with thousands of programming mistakes.

Most of them don't affect normal operations, which is why your software generally works just fine. Some of them do, which is why your software occasionally fails, and needs constant updates. By making cheating software appear to be a programming mistake, the cheating looks like an accident. And, unfortunately, this type of deniable cheating is easier than people think.

Computer-security experts believe that intelligence agencies have been doing this sort of thing for years, both with the consent of the software developers and surreptitiously.

This problem won't be solved through computer security as we normally think of it. Conventional computer security is designed to prevent outside hackers from breaking into your computers and networks. The car analogue would be security software that prevented an owner from tweaking his own engine to run faster but in the process emit more pollutants. What we need to contend with is a very different threat: malfeasance programmed in at the design stage.

We already know how to protect ourselves against corporate misbehavior. Ronald Reagan once said "trust, but verify" when speaking about the Soviet Union cheating on nuclear treaties. We need to be able to verify the software that controls our lives.

Software verification has two parts: transparency and oversight. Transparency means making the source code available for analysis. The need for this is obvious; it's much easier to hide cheating software if a manufacturer can hide the code.

But transparency doesn't magically reduce cheating or improve software quality, as anyone who uses open-source software knows. It's only the first step. The code must be analyzed. And because software is so complicated, that analysis can't be limited to a once-every-few-years government test. We need private analysis as well.

It was researchers at private labs in the United States and Germany that eventually outed Volkswagen. So transparency can't just mean making the code available to government regulators and their representatives; it needs to mean making the code available to everyone.

Both transparency and oversight are being threatened in the software world. Companies routinely fight making their code public and attempt to muzzle security researchers who find problems, citing the proprietary nature of the software. It's a fair complaint, but the public interests of accuracy and safety need to trump business interests.

Proprietary software is increasingly being used in critical applications: voting machines, medical devices, breathalyzers, electric power distribution, systems that decide whether or not someone can board an airplane. We're ceding more control of our lives to software and algorithms. Transparency is the only way verify that they're not cheating us.

There's no shortage of corporate executives willing to lie and cheat their way to profits. We saw another example of this last week: Stewart Parnell, the former CEO of the now-defunct Peanut Corporation of America, was sentenced to 28 years in prison for knowingly shipping out salmonella-tainted products. That may seem excessive, but nine people died and many more fell ill as a result of his cheating.

Software will only make malfeasance like this easier to commit and harder to prove. Fewer people need to know about the conspiracy. It can be done in advance, nowhere near the testing time or site. And, if the software remains undetected for long enough, it could easily be the case that no one in the company remembers that it's there.

We need better verification of the software that controls our lives, and that means more—and more public—transparency.

DMCA and the Internet of Things

Originally published in TheAtlantic.com, *December 24, 2015*

In theory, the Internet of Things—the connected network of tiny computers inside home appliances, household objects, even clothing—promises to make your life easier and your work more efficient. These computers will communicate with each other and the Internet in homes and public spaces, collecting data about their environment and making changes based on the information they receive. In theory, connected sensors will anticipate your needs, saving you time, money, and energy.

Except when the companies that make these connected objects act in a way that runs counter to the consumer's best interests—as the technology company Philips did recently with its smart ambient-lighting system, Hue, which consists of a central controller that can remotely communicate with light bulbs. In mid-December, the company pushed out a software update that made the system incompatible with some other manufacturers' light bulbs, including bulbs that had previously been supported.

The complaints began rolling in almost immediately. The Hue system was supposed to be compatible with an industry standard called ZigBee, but the bulbs that Philips cut off were ZigBee-compliant. Philips backed down and restored compatibility a few days later.

But the story of the Hue debacle—the story of a company using copy protection technology to lock out competitors—isn't a new one. Plenty of companies set up proprietary standards to ensure that their customers don't use someone else's products with theirs. Keurig, for example, puts codes on its single-cup coffee pods, and engineers its coffeemakers to work only with those codes. HP has done the same thing with its printers and ink cartridges.

To stop competitors just reverse-engineering the proprietary standard and making compatible peripherals (for example, another coffee manufacturer putting Keurig's codes on its own pods), these companies rely on a 1998 law called the Digital Millennium Copyright Act (DCMA). The law was originally passed to prevent people from pirating music and movies; while it hasn't done a lot of good in that regard (as anyone who uses BitTorrent can attest), it has done a lot to inhibit security and compatibility research.

Specifically, the DMCA includes an anti-circumvention provision, which prohibits companies from circumventing "technological protection measures" that "effectively control access" to copyrighted works. That means it's illegal for someone to create a Hue-compatible light bulb without Philips' permission, a K-cup-compatible coffee pod without Keurigs', or an HP-printer compatible cartridge without HP's.

By now, we're used to this in the computer world. In the 1990s, Microsoft used a strategy it called "embrace, extend, extinguish," in which it gradually added proprietary capabilities to products that already adhered to widely used standards. Some more recent examples: Amazon's e-book format doesn't work on other companies' readers, music purchased from Apple's iTunes store doesn't work with other music players, and every game console has its own proprietary game cartridge format.

Because companies can enforce anti-competitive behavior this way, there's a litany of things that just don't exist, even though they would make life easier for consumers in significant ways. You can't have custom software for your cochlear implant, or your programmable thermostat, or your computer-enabled Barbie doll. An auto repair shop can't design a better diagnostic system that interfaces with a car's computers. And John Deere has claimed that it owns the software on all of its tractors, meaning the farmers that purchase them are prohibited from repairing or modifying their property.

As the Internet of Things becomes more prevalent, so too will this kind of anti-competitive behavior—which undercuts the purpose of having smart objects in the first place. We'll want our light bulbs to communicate with a central controller, regardless of manufacturer. We'll want our clothes to communicate with our washing machines and our cars to communicate with traffic signs.

We can't have this when companies can cut off compatible products, or use the law to prevent competitors from reverse-engineering their products to ensure compatibility across brands. For the Internet of Things to provide any value, what we need is a world that looks like the automotive industry, where you can go to a store and buy replacement parts made by a wide variety of different manufacturers. Instead, the Internet of Things is on track to become a battleground of competing standards, as companies try to build monopolies by locking each other out.

Real-World Security and the Internet of Things

Originally published in Vice Motherboard, *July 25, 2016*

Disaster stories involving the Internet of Things are all the rage. They feature cars (both driven and driverless), the power grid, dams, and tunnel ventilation systems. A particularly vivid and realistic one, near-future fiction published last month in *New York Magazine*, described a cyberattack on New York that involved hacking of cars, the water system, hospitals, elevators, and the power grid. In these stories, thousands of people die. Chaos ensues. While some of these scenarios overhype the mass destruction, the individual risks are all real. And traditional computer and network security isn't prepared to deal with them.

Classic information security is a triad: confidentiality, integrity, and availability. You'll see it called "CIA," which admittedly is confusing in the context of national security. But basically, the three things I can do with your data are steal it (confidentiality), modify it (integrity), or prevent you from getting it (availability).

So far, Internet threats have largely been about confidentiality. These can be expensive; one survey estimated that data breaches cost an average of $3.8 million each. They can be embarrassing, as in the theft of celebrity photos from Apple's iCloud in 2014 or the Ashley Madison breach in 2015. They can be damaging, as when the government of North Korea stole tens of thousands of internal documents from Sony or when hackers stole data about 83 million customer accounts from JPMorgan Chase, both in 2014. They can even affect national security, as in the case of the Office of Personnel Management data breach by—presumptively—China in 2015.

On the Internet of Things, integrity and availability threats are much worse than confidentiality threats. It's one thing if your smart door lock can be eavesdropped upon to know who is home. It's another thing entirely if it can be hacked to allow a burglar to open the door— or prevent you from opening your door. A hacker who can deny you control of your car, or take over control, is much more dangerous than one who can eavesdrop on your conversations or track your car's location.

With the advent of the Internet of Things and cyber-physical systems in general, we've given the Internet hands and feet: the ability to directly affect the physical world. What used to be attacks against data and information have become attacks against flesh, steel, and concrete.

Today's threats include hackers crashing airplanes by hacking into computer networks, and remotely disabling cars, either when they're turned off and parked or while they're speeding down the highway. We're worried about manipulated counts from electronic voting machines, frozen water pipes through hacked thermostats, and remote murder through hacked medical devices. The possibilities are pretty literally endless. The Internet of Things will allow for attacks we can't even imagine.

The increased risks come from three things: software control of systems, interconnections between systems, and automatic or autonomous systems. Let's look at them in turn:

> **Software Control**. The Internet of Things is a result of everything turning into a computer. This gives us enormous power and flexibility, but it brings insecurities with it as well. As more things come under software control, they become vulnerable to all the attacks we've seen against computers. But because many of these things are both inexpensive and long-lasting, many of the patch and update systems that work with computers and smartphones won't work. Right now, the only way to patch most home routers is to throw them away and buy new ones. And the security that comes from replacing your computer and phone every few years won't work with your refrigerator and thermostat: on the average, you replace the former every 15 years, and the latter approximately never. A recent Princeton survey found 500,000 insecure devices on the Internet. That number is about to explode.

> **Interconnections**. As these systems become interconnected, vulnerabilities in one lead to attacks against others. Already we've seen Gmail accounts compromised through vulnerabilities in Samsung smart refrigerators, hospital IT networks compromised through vulnerabilities in medical devices, and Target Corporation hacked

through a vulnerability in its HVAC system. Systems are filled with externalities that affect other systems in unforeseen and potentially harmful ways. What might seem benign to the designers of a particular system becomes harmful when it's combined with some other system. Vulnerabilities on one system cascade into other systems, and the result is a vulnerability that no one saw coming and no one bears responsibility for fixing. The Internet of Things will make exploitable vulnerabilities much more common. It's simple mathematics. If 100 systems are all interacting with each other, that's about 5,000 interactions and 5,000 potential vulnerabilities resulting from those interactions. If 300 systems are all interacting with each other, that's 45,000 interactions. 1,000 systems: 12.5 million interactions. Most of them will be benign or uninteresting, but some of them will be very damaging.

Autonomy. Increasingly, our computer systems are autonomous. They buy and sell stocks, turn the furnace on and off, regulate electricity flow through the grid, and—in the case of driverless cars—automatically pilot multi-ton vehicles to their destinations. Autonomy is great for all sorts of reasons, but from a security perspective it means that the effects of attacks can take effect immediately, automatically, and ubiquitously. The more we remove humans from the loop, faster attacks can do their damage and the more we lose our ability to rely on actual smarts to notice something is wrong before it's too late.

We're building systems that are increasingly powerful, and increasingly useful. The necessary side effect is that they are increasingly dangerous. A single vulnerability forced Chrysler to recall 1.4 million vehicles in 2015. We're used to computers being attacked at scale—think of the large-scale virus infections from the last decade—but we're not prepared for this happening to everything else in our world.

Governments are taking notice. Last year, both Director of National Intelligence James Clapper and NSA Director Mike Rogers testified before Congress, warning of these threats. They both believe we're vulnerable.

This is how it was phrased in the DNI's 2015 Worldwide Threat Assessment: "Most of the public discussion regarding cyber threats has focused on the confidentiality and availability of information;

cyber espionage undermines confidentiality, whereas denial-of-service operations and data-deletion attacks undermine availability. In the future, however, we might also see more cyber operations that will change or manipulate electronic information in order to compromise its integrity (i.e. accuracy and reliability) instead of deleting it or disrupting access to it. Decision-making by senior government officials (civilian and military), corporate executives, investors, or others will be impaired if they cannot trust the information they are receiving."

The DNI 2016 threat assessment included something similar: "Future cyber operations will almost certainly include an increased emphasis on changing or manipulating data to compromise its integrity (i.e., accuracy and reliability) to affect decision making, reduce trust in systems, or cause adverse physical effects. Broader adoption of IoT devices and AI—in settings such as public utilities and healthcare—will only exacerbate these potential effects."

Security engineers are working on technologies that can mitigate much of this risk, but many solutions won't be deployed without government involvement. This is not something that the market can solve. Like data privacy, the risks and solutions are too technical for most people and organizations to understand; companies are motivated to hide the insecurity of their own systems from their customers, their users, and the public; the interconnections can make it impossible to connect data breaches with resultant harms; and the interests of the companies often don't match the interests of the people.

Governments need to play a larger role: setting standards, policing compliance, and implementing solutions across companies and networks. And while the White House Cybersecurity National Action Plan says some of the right things, it doesn't nearly go far enough, because so many of us are phobic of any government-led solution to anything.

The next president will probably be forced to deal with a large-scale Internet disaster that kills multiple people. I hope he or she responds with both the recognition of what government can do that industry can't, and the political will to make it happen.

Lessons from the Dyn DDoS Attack

Originally published in the SecurityIntelligence website, *November 1, 2016*

A week ago Friday, someone took down numerous popular websites in a massive distributed denial-of-service (DDoS) attack against the domain name provider Dyn. DDoS attacks are neither new nor sophisticated. The attacker sends a massive amount of traffic, causing the victim's system to slow to a crawl and eventually crash. There are more or less clever variants, but basically, it's a datapipe-size battle between attacker and victim. If the defender has a larger capacity to receive and process data, he or she will win. If the attacker can throw more data than the victim can process, he or she will win.

The attacker can build a giant data cannon, but that's expensive. It is much smarter to recruit millions of innocent computers on the Internet. This is the "distributed" part of the DDoS attack, and pretty much how it's worked for decades. Cybercriminals infect innocent computers around the Internet and recruit them into a botnet. They then target that botnet against a single victim.

You can imagine how it might work in the real world. If I can trick tens of thousands of others to order pizzas to be delivered to your house at the same time, I can clog up your street and prevent any legitimate traffic from getting through. If I can trick many millions, I might be able to crush your house from the weight. That's a DDoS attack—it's simple brute force.

As you'd expect, DDoSers have various motives. The attacks started out as a way to show off, then quickly transitioned to a method of intimidation—or a way of just getting back at someone you didn't like. More recently, they've become vehicles of protest. In 2013, the hacker group Anonymous petitioned the White House to recognize DDoS attacks as a legitimate form of protest. Criminals have used these attacks as a means of extortion, although one group found that just the fear of attack was enough. Military agencies are also thinking about DDoS as a tool in their cyberwar arsenals. A 2007 DDoS attack against Estonia was blamed on Russia and widely called an act of cyberwar.

The DDoS attack against Dyn two weeks ago was nothing new, but it illustrated several important trends in computer security.

These attack techniques are broadly available. Fully capable DDoS attack tools are available for free download. Criminal groups offer DDoS services for hire. The particular attack technique used against Dyn was first used a month earlier. It's called Mirai, and since the source code was released four weeks ago, over a dozen botnets have incorporated the code.

The Dyn attacks were probably not originated by a government. The perpetrators were most likely hackers mad at Dyn for helping Brian Krebs identify—and the FBI arrest—two Israeli hackers who were running a DDoS-for-hire ring. Recently I have written about probing DDoS attacks against Internet infrastructure companies that appear to be perpetrated by a nation-state. But, honestly, we don't know for sure.

This is important. Software spreads capabilities. The smartest attacker needs to figure out the attack and write the software. After that, anyone can use it. There's not even much of a difference between government and criminal attacks. In December 2014, there was a legitimate debate in the security community as to whether the massive attack against Sony had been perpetrated by a nation-state with a $20 billion military budget or a couple of guys in a basement somewhere. The Internet is the only place where we can't tell the difference. Everyone uses the same tools, the same techniques and the same tactics.

These attacks are getting larger. The Dyn DDoS attack set a record at 1.2 Tbps. The previous record holder was the attack against cybersecurity journalist Brian Krebs a month prior at 620 Gbps. This is much larger than required to knock the typical website offline. A year ago, it was unheard of. Now it occurs regularly.

The botnets attacking Dyn and Brian Krebs consisted largely of unsecure Internet of Things (IoT) devices—webcams, digital video recorders, routers and so on. This isn't new, either. We've already seen Internet-enabled refrigerators and TVs used in DDoS botnets. But again, the scale is bigger now. In 2014, the news was hundreds of thousands of IoT devices—the Dyn attack used millions. Analysts expect the IoT to increase the number of things on the Internet by a factor of 10 or more. Expect these attacks to similarly increase.

The problem is that these IoT devices are unsecure and likely to remain that way. The economics of Internet security don't trickle down to the IoT. Commenting on the Krebs attack last month, I wrote:

> *The market can't fix this because neither the buyer nor the seller cares. Think of all the CCTV cameras and DVRs used in the attack against Brian Krebs. The owners of those devices don't care. Their devices were cheap to buy, they still work, and they don't even know Brian. The sellers of those devices don't care: They're now selling newer and better models, and the original buyers only cared about price and features. There is no market solution because the insecurity is what economists call an externality: It's an effect of the purchasing decision that affects other people. Think of it kind of like invisible pollution.*

To be fair, one company that made some of the unsecure things used in these attacks recalled its unsecure webcams. But this is more of a publicity stunt than anything else. I would be surprised if the company got many devices back. We already know that the reputational damage from having your unsecure software made public isn't large and doesn't last. At this point, the market still largely rewards sacrificing security in favor of price and time-to-market.

DDoS prevention works best deep in the network, where the pipes are the largest and the capability to identify and block the attacks is the most evident. But the backbone providers have no incentive to do this. They don't feel the pain when the attacks occur and they have no way of billing for the service when they provide it. So they let the attacks through and force the victims to defend themselves. In many ways, this is similar to the spam problem. It, too, is best dealt with in the backbone, but similar economics dump the problem onto the endpoints.

We're unlikely to get any regulation forcing backbone companies to clean up either DDoS attacks or spam, just as we are unlikely to get any regulations forcing IoT manufacturers to make their systems secure. This is me again:

What this all means is that the IoT will remain insecure unless government steps in and fixes the problem. When we have market failures, government is the only solution. The government could impose security regulations on IoT manufacturers, forcing them to make their devices secure even though their customers don't care. They could impose liabilities on manufacturers, allowing people like Brian Krebs to sue them. Any of these would raise the cost of insecurity and give companies incentives to spend money making their devices secure.

That leaves the victims to pay. This is where we are in much of computer security. Because the hardware, software and networks we use are so unsecure, we have to pay an entire industry to provide after-the-fact security.

There are solutions you can buy. Many companies offer DDoS protection, although they're generally calibrated to the older, smaller attacks. We can safely assume that they'll up their offerings, although the cost might be prohibitive for many users. Understand your risks. Buy mitigation if you need it, but understand its limitations. Know the attacks are possible and will succeed if large enough. And the attacks are getting larger all the time. Prepare for that.

Regulation of the Internet of Things

Originally published in the Washington Post, *November 3, 2016*

Late last month, popular websites like Twitter, Pinterest, Reddit and PayPal went down for most of a day. The distributed denial-of-service attack that caused the outages, and the vulnerabilities that made the attack possible, was as much a failure of market and policy as it was of technology. If we want to secure our increasingly computerized and connected world, we need more government involvement in the security of the "Internet of Things" and increased regulation of what are now critical and life-threatening technologies. It's no longer a question of if, it's a question of when.

First, the facts. Those websites went down because their domain name provider—a company named Dyn—was forced offline. We don't know who perpetrated that attack, but it could have easily been a lone hacker. Whoever it was launched a distributed denial-of-service attack against Dyn by exploiting a vulnerability in large numbers—possibly millions—of Internet-of-Things devices like webcams and digital video recorders, then recruiting them all into a single botnet. The botnet bombarded Dyn with traffic, so much that it went down. And when it went down, so did dozens of websites.

Your security on the Internet depends on the security of millions of Internet-enabled devices, designed and sold by companies you've never heard of to consumers who don't care about your security.

The technical reason these devices are insecure is complicated, but there is a market failure at work. The Internet of Things is bringing computerization and connectivity to many tens of millions of devices worldwide. These devices will affect every aspect of our lives, because they're things like cars, home appliances, thermostats, light bulbs, fitness trackers, medical devices, smart streetlights and sidewalk squares. Many of these devices are low-cost, designed and built offshore, then rebranded and resold. The teams building these devices don't have the security expertise we've come to expect from the major computer and smartphone manufacturers, simply because the market won't stand for the additional costs that would require. These devices don't get security updates like our more expensive computers, and many don't even have a way to be patched. And, unlike our computers and phones, they stay around for years and decades.

An additional market failure illustrated by the Dyn attack is that neither the seller nor the buyer of those devices cares about fixing the vulnerability. The owners of those devices don't care. They wanted a webcam—or thermostat, or refrigerator—with nice features at a good price. Even after they were recruited into this botnet, they still work fine—you can't even tell they were used in the attack. The sellers of those devices don't care: They've already moved on to selling newer and better models. There is no market solution because the insecurity primarily affects other people. It's a form of invisible pollution.

And, like pollution, the only solution is to regulate. The government could impose minimum security standards on IoT manufacturers, forcing them to make their devices secure even though their customers don't care. They could impose liabilities on manufacturers, allowing companies like Dyn to sue them if their devices are used in DDoS attacks. The details would need to be carefully scoped, but either of these options would raise the cost of insecurity and give companies incentives to spend money making their devices secure.

It's true that this is a domestic solution to an international problem and that there's no US regulation that will affect, say, an Asian-made product sold in South America, even though that product could still be used to take down US websites. But the main costs in making software come from development. If the United States and perhaps a few other major markets implement strong Internet-security regulations on IoT devices, manufacturers will be forced to upgrade their security if they want to sell to those markets. And any improvements they make in their software will be available in their products wherever they are sold, simply because it makes no sense to maintain two different versions of the software. This is truly an area where the actions of a few countries can drive worldwide change.

Regardless of what you think about regulation vs. market solutions, I believe there is no choice. Governments will get involved in the IoT, because the risks are too great and the stakes are too high. Computers are now able to affect our world in a direct and physical manner.

Security researchers have demonstrated the ability to remotely take control of Internet-enabled cars. They've demonstrated ransomware against home thermostats and exposed vulnerabilities in implanted medical devices. They've hacked voting machines and power plants. In one recent paper, researchers showed how a vulnerability in smart light bulbs could be used to start a chain reaction, resulting in them *all* being controlled by the attackers—that's everyone in a city. Security flaws in these things could mean people dying and property being destroyed.

Nothing motivates the US government like fear. Remember 2001? A small-government Republican president created the Department of Homeland Security in the wake of the 9/11 terrorist attacks: a rushed and ill-thought-out decision that we've been trying to fix for more than a decade. A fatal IoT disaster will similarly spur our government into action, and it's unlikely to be well-considered and thoughtful action. Our choice isn't between government involvement and no government involvement. Our choice is between smarter government involvement and stupider government involvement. We have to start thinking about this now. Regulations are necessary, important and complex—and they're coming. We can't afford to ignore these issues until it's too late.

In general, the software market demands that products be fast and cheap and that security be a secondary consideration. That was okay when software didn't matter—it was okay that your spreadsheet crashed once in a while. But a software bug that literally crashes your car is another thing altogether. The security vulnerabilities in the Internet of Things are deep and pervasive, and they won't get fixed if the market is left to sort it out for itself. We need to proactively discuss good regulatory solutions; otherwise, a disaster will impose bad ones on us.

Security and the Internet of Things

Originally published in New York Magazine, *January 27, 2017*

Last year, on October 21, your digital video recorder—or at least a DVR like yours—knocked Twitter off the Internet. Someone used your DVR, along with millions of insecure webcams, routers, and other connected devices, to launch an attack that started a chain reaction, resulting in Twitter, Reddit, Netflix, and many sites going off the Internet. You probably didn't realize that your DVR had that kind of power. But it does.

All computers are hackable. This has as much to do with the computer market as it does with the technologies. We prefer our software full of features and inexpensive, at the expense of security and reliability. That your computer can affect the security of Twitter is a market failure. The industry is filled with market failures that, until now, have been largely ignorable. As computers continue to permeate our homes, cars, businesses, these market failures will no longer be tolerable. Our only solution will be regulation, and that regulation will be foisted on us by a government desperate to "do something" in the face of disaster.

In this article I want to outline the problems, both technical and political, and point to some regulatory solutions. *Regulation* might be a dirty word in today's political climate, but security is the exception to our small-government bias. And as the threats posed by computers become greater and more catastrophic, regulation will be inevitable. So now's the time to start thinking about it.

We also need to reverse the trend to connect everything to the Internet. And if we risk harm and even death, we need to think twice about what we connect and what we deliberately leave uncomputerized.

If we get this wrong, the computer industry will look like the pharmaceutical industry, or the aircraft industry. But if we get this right, we can maintain the innovative environment of the Internet that has given us so much.

****

We no longer have things with computers embedded in them. We have computers with things attached to them.

Your modern refrigerator is a computer that keeps things cold. Your oven, similarly, is a computer that makes things hot. An ATM is a computer with money inside. Your car is no longer a mechanical device with some computers inside; it's a computer with four wheels and an engine. Actually, it's a distributed system of over 100 computers with four wheels and an engine. And, of course, your phones became full-power general-purpose computers in 2007, when the iPhone was introduced.

We wear computers: fitness trackers and computer-enabled medical devices—and, of course, we carry our smartphones everywhere. Our homes have smart thermostats, smart appliances, smart door locks, even smart light bulbs. At work, many of those same smart devices are networked together with CCTV cameras, sensors that detect customer movements, and everything else. Cities are starting to embed smart sensors in roads, streetlights, and sidewalk squares, also smart energy grids and smart transportation networks. A nuclear power plant is really just a computer that produces electricity, and—like everything else we've just listed—it's on the Internet.

The Internet is no longer a web that we connect to. Instead, it's a computerized, networked, and interconnected world that we live in. This is the future, and what we're calling the Internet of Things.

Broadly speaking, the Internet of Things has three parts. There are the sensors that collect data about us and our environment: smart thermostats, street and highway sensors, and those ubiquitous smartphones with their motion sensors and GPS location receivers. Then there are the "smarts" that figure out what the data means and what to do about it. This includes all the computer processors on these devices and—increasingly—in the cloud, as well as the memory that stores all of this information. And finally, there are the actuators that affect our environment. The point of a smart thermostat isn't to record the temperature; it's to control the furnace and the air conditioner. Driverless cars collect data about the road and the environment to steer themselves safely to their destinations.

You can think of the sensors as the eyes and ears of the Internet. You can think of the actuators as the hands and feet of the Internet. And you can think of the stuff in the middle as the brain. We are building an Internet that senses, thinks, and acts.

This is the classic definition of a robot. We're building a world-size robot, and we don't even realize it.

To be sure, it's not a robot in the classical sense. We think of robots as discrete autonomous entities, with sensors, brain, and actuators all together in a metal shell. The world-size robot is distributed. It doesn't have a singular body, and parts of it are controlled in different ways by different people. It doesn't have a central brain, and it has nothing even remotely resembling a consciousness. It doesn't have a single goal or focus. It's not even something we deliberately designed. It's something we have inadvertently built out of the everyday objects we live with and take for granted. It is the extension of our computers and networks into the real world.

This world-size robot is actually more than the Internet of Things. It's a combination of several decades-old computing trends: mobile computing, cloud computing, always-on computing, huge databases of personal information, the Internet of Things—or, more precisely, cyber-physical systems—autonomy, and artificial intelligence. And while it's still not very smart, it'll get smarter. It'll get more powerful and more capable through all the interconnections we're building.

It'll also get much more dangerous.

****

Computer security has been around for almost as long as computers have been. And while it's true that security wasn't part of the design of the original Internet, it's something we have been trying to achieve since its beginning.

I have been working in computer security for over 30 years: first in cryptography, then more generally in computer and network security, and now in general security technology. I have watched computers become ubiquitous, and have seen firsthand the problems—and solutions—of securing these complex machines and systems. I'm telling you all this because what used to be a specialized area of expertise now affects everything. Computer security is now everything security. There's one critical difference, though: The threats have become greater.

Traditionally, computer security is divided into three categories: confidentiality, integrity, and availability. For the most part, our security concerns have largely centered around confidentiality. We're concerned about our data and who has access to it—the world of privacy and surveillance, of data theft and misuse.

But threats come in many forms. Availability threats: computer viruses that delete our data, or ransomware that encrypts our data and demands payment for the unlock key. Integrity threats: hackers who can manipulate data entries can do things ranging from changing grades in a class to changing the amount of money in bank accounts. Some of these threats are pretty bad. Hospitals have paid tens of thousands of dollars to criminals whose ransomware encrypted critical medical files. JPMorgan Chase spends half a billion on cybersecurity a year.

Today, the integrity and availability threats are much worse than the confidentiality threats. Once computers start affecting the world in a direct and physical manner, there are real risks to life and property. There is a fundamental difference between crashing your computer and losing your spreadsheet data, and crashing your pacemaker and losing your life. This isn't hyperbole; recently researchers found serious security vulnerabilities in St. Jude Medical's implantable heart devices. Give the Internet hands and feet, and it will have the ability to punch and kick.

Take a concrete example: modern cars, those computers on wheels. The steering wheel no longer turns the axles, nor does the accelerator pedal change the speed. Every move you make in a car is processed by a computer, which does the actual controlling. A central computer controls the dashboard. There's another in the radio. The engine has 20 or so computers. These are all networked, and increasingly autonomous.

Now, let's start listing the security threats. We don't want car navigation systems to be used for mass surveillance, or the microphone for mass eavesdropping. We might want it to be used to determine a car's location in the event of a 911 call, and possibly to collect information about highway congestion. We don't want people to hack their own cars to bypass emissions-control limitations. We don't want manufacturers or dealers to be able to do that, either, as Volkswagen did for years. We can imagine wanting to give police the ability to remotely and safely disable a moving car; that would make high-speed chases a thing of the past. But we definitely don't want hackers to be able to do that. We definitely don't want them disabling the brakes in every car without warning, at speed. As we make the transition from driver-controlled cars to cars with various driver-assist capabilities to fully driverless cars, we don't want any of those critical components subverted. We don't want someone to be able to accidentally crash your car, let alone do it on purpose. And equally, we don't want them to be able to manipulate the navigation software to change your route, or the door-lock controls to prevent you from opening the door. I could go on.

That's a lot of different security requirements, and the effects of getting them wrong range from illegal surveillance to extortion by ransomware to mass death.

****

Our computers and smartphones are as secure as they are because companies like Microsoft, Apple, and Google spend a lot of time testing their code before it's released, and quickly patch vulnerabilities when they're discovered. Those companies can support large, dedicated teams because those companies make a huge amount of money, either directly or indirectly, from their software—and, in part, compete on its security. Unfortunately, this isn't true of embedded systems like digital video recorders or home routers. Those systems are sold at a much lower margin, and are often built by offshore third parties. The companies involved simply don't have the expertise to make them secure.

At a recent hacker conference, a security researcher analyzed 30 home routers and was able to break into half of them, including some of the most popular and common brands. The denial-of-service attacks that forced popular websites like Reddit and Twitter off the Internet last October were enabled by vulnerabilities in devices like webcams and digital video recorders. In August, two security researchers demonstrated a ransomware attack on a smart thermostat.

Even worse, most of these devices don't have any way to be patched. Companies like Microsoft and Apple continuously deliver security patches to your computers. Some home routers are technically patchable, but in a complicated way that only an expert would attempt. And the only way for you to update the firmware in your hackable DVR is to throw it away and buy a new one.

The market can't fix this because neither the buyer nor the seller cares. The owners of the webcams and DVRs used in the denial-of-service attacks don't care. Their devices were cheap to buy, they still work, and they don't know any of the victims of the attacks. The sellers of those devices don't care: They're now selling newer and better models, and the original buyers only cared about price and features. There is no market solution, because the insecurity is what economists call an externality: It's an effect of the purchasing decision that affects other people. Think of it kind of like invisible pollution.

****

Security is an arms race between attacker and defender. Technology perturbs that arms race by changing the balance between attacker and defender. Understanding how this arms race has unfolded on the Internet is essential to understanding why the world-size robot we're building is so insecure, and how we might secure it. To that end, I have five truisms, born from what we've already learned about computer and Internet security. They will soon affect the security arms race everywhere.

Truism No. 1: On the Internet, attack is easier than defense.

There are many reasons for this, but the most important is the complexity of these systems. More complexity means more people involved, more parts, more interactions, more mistakes in the design and development process, more of everything where hidden insecurities can be found. Computer-security experts like to speak about the attack surface of a system: all the possible points an attacker might target and that must be secured. A complex system means a large attack surface. The defender has to secure the entire attack surface. The attacker just has to find one vulnerability—one unsecured avenue for attack—and gets to choose how and when to attack. It's simply not a fair battle.

There are other, more general, reasons why attack is easier than defense. Attackers have a natural agility that defenders often lack. They don't have to worry about laws, and often not about morals or ethics. They don't have a bureaucracy to contend with, and can more quickly make use of technical innovations. Attackers also have a first-mover advantage. As a society, we're generally terrible at proactive security; we rarely take preventive security measures until an attack actually happens. So more advantages go to the attacker.

Truism No. 2: Most software is poorly written and insecure.

If complexity isn't enough, we compound the problem by producing lousy software. Well-written software, like the kind found in airplane avionics, is both expensive and time-consuming to produce. We don't want that. For the most part, poorly written software has been good enough. We'd all rather live with buggy software than pay the prices good software would require. We don't mind if our games crash regularly, or our business applications act weird once in a while. Because software has been largely benign, it hasn't mattered. This has permeated the industry at all levels. At universities, we don't teach how to code well. Companies don't reward quality code in the same way they reward fast and cheap. And we consumers don't demand it.

But poorly written software is riddled with bugs, sometimes as many as one per 1,000 lines of code. Some of them are inherent in the complexity of the software, but most are programming mistakes. Not all bugs are vulnerabilities, but some are.

Truism No. 3: Connecting everything to each other via the Internet will expose new vulnerabilities.

The more we network things together, the more vulnerabilities on one thing will affect other things. On October 21, vulnerabilities in a wide variety of embedded devices were all harnessed together to create what hackers call a botnet. This botnet was used to launch a distributed denial-of-service attack against a company called Dyn. Dyn provided a critical Internet function for many major Internet sites. So when Dyn went down, so did all those popular websites.

These chains of vulnerabilities are everywhere. In 2012, journalist Mat Honan suffered a massive personal hack because of one of them. A vulnerability in his Amazon account allowed hackers to get into his Apple account, which allowed them to get into his Gmail account. And in 2013, the Target Corporation was hacked by someone stealing credentials from its HVAC contractor.

Vulnerabilities like these are particularly hard to fix, because no one system might actually be at fault. It might be the insecure interaction of two individually secure systems.

Truism No. 4: Everybody has to stop the best attackers in the world.

One of the most powerful properties of the Internet is that it allows things to scale. This is true for our ability to access data or control systems or do any of the cool things we use the Internet for, but it's also true for attacks. In general, fewer attackers can do more damage because of better technology. It's not just that these modern attackers are more efficient, it's that the Internet allows attacks to scale to a degree impossible without computers and networks.

This is fundamentally different from what we're used to. When securing my home against burglars, I am only worried about the burglars who live close enough to my home to consider robbing me. The Internet is different. When I think about the security of my network, I have to be concerned about the best attacker possible, because he's the one who's going to create the attack tool that everyone else will use. The attacker that discovered the vulnerability used to attack Dyn released the code to the world, and within a week there were a dozen attack tools using it.

Truism No. 5: Laws inhibit security research.

The Digital Millennium Copyright Act is a terrible law that fails at its purpose of preventing widespread piracy of movies and music. To make matters worse, it contains a provision that has critical side effects. According to the law, it is a crime to bypass security mechanisms that protect copyrighted work, even if that bypassing would otherwise be legal. Since all software can be copyrighted, it is arguably illegal to do security research on these devices and to publish the result.

Although the exact contours of the law are arguable, many companies are using this provision of the DMCA to threaten researchers who expose vulnerabilities in their embedded systems. This instills fear in researchers, and has a chilling effect on research, which means two things: (1) Vendors of these devices are more likely to leave them insecure, because no one will notice and they won't be penalized in the market, and (2) security engineers don't learn how to do security better. Unfortunately, companies generally like the DMCA. The provisions against reverse-engineering spare them the embarrassment of having their shoddy security exposed. It also allows them to build proprietary systems that lock out competition. (This is an important one. Right now, your toaster cannot force you to only buy a particular brand of bread. But because of this law and an embedded computer, your Keurig coffee maker can force you to buy a particular brand of coffee.)

****

In general, there are two basic paradigms of security. We can either try to secure something well the first time, or we can make our security agile. The first paradigm comes from the world of dangerous things: from planes, medical devices, buildings. It's the paradigm that gives us secure design and secure engineering, security testing and certifications, professional licensing, detailed preplanning and complex government approvals, and long times-to-market. It's security for a world where getting it right is paramount because getting it wrong means people dying.

The second paradigm comes from the fast-moving and heretofore largely benign world of software. In this paradigm, we have rapid prototyping, on-the-fly updates, and continual improvement. In this paradigm, new vulnerabilities are discovered all the time and security disasters regularly happen. Here, we stress survivability, recoverability, mitigation, adaptability, and muddling through. This is security for a world where getting it wrong is okay, as long as you can respond fast enough.

These two worlds are colliding. They're colliding in our cars—literally—in our medical devices, our building control systems, our traffic control systems, and our voting machines. And although these paradigms are wildly different and largely incompatible, we need to figure out how to make them work together.

So far, we haven't done very well. We still largely rely on the first paradigm for the dangerous computers in cars, airplanes, and medical devices. As a result, there are medical systems that can't have security patches installed because that would invalidate their government approval. In 2015, Chrysler recalled 1.4 million cars to fix a software vulnerability. In September 2016, Tesla remotely sent a security patch to all of its Model S cars overnight. Tesla sure sounds like it's doing things right, but what vulnerabilities does this remote patch feature open up?

****

Until now we've largely left computer security to the market. Because the computer and network products we buy and use are so lousy, an enormous after-market industry in computer security has emerged. Governments, companies, and people buy the security they think they need to secure themselves. We've muddled through well enough, but the market failures inherent in trying to secure this world-size robot will soon become too big to ignore.

Markets alone can't solve our security problems. Markets are motivated by profit and short-term goals at the expense of society. They can't solve collective-action problems. They won't be able to deal with economic externalities, like the vulnerabilities in DVRs that resulted in Twitter going offline. And we need a counterbalancing force to corporate power.

This all points to policy. While the details of any computer-security system are technical, getting the technologies broadly deployed is a problem that spans law, economics, psychology, and sociology. And getting the policy right is just as important as getting the technology right because, for Internet security to work, law and technology have to work together. This is probably the most important lesson of Edward Snowden's NSA disclosures. We already knew that technology can subvert law. Snowden demonstrated that law can also subvert technology. Both fail unless each work. It's not enough to just let technology do its thing.

Any policy changes to secure this world-size robot will mean significant government regulation. I know it's a sullied concept in today's world, but I don't see any other possible solution. It's going to be especially difficult on the Internet, where its permissionless nature is one of the best things about it and the underpinning of its most world-changing innovations. But I don't see how that can continue when the Internet can affect the world in a direct and physical manner.

****

I have a proposal: a new government regulatory agency. Before dismissing it out of hand, please hear me out.

We have a practical problem when it comes to Internet regulation. There's no government structure to tackle this at a systemic level. Instead, there's a fundamental mismatch between the way government works and the way this technology works that makes dealing with this problem impossible at the moment.

Government operates in silos. In the US, the FAA regulates aircraft. The NHTSA regulates cars. The FDA regulates medical devices. The FCC regulates communications devices. The FTC protects consumers in the face of "unfair" or "deceptive" trade practices. Even worse, who regulates data can depend on how it is used. If data is used to influence a voter, it's the Federal Election Commission's jurisdiction. If that same data is used to influence a consumer, it's the FTC's. Use those same technologies in a school, and the Department of Education is now in charge. Robotics will have its own set of problems, and no one is sure how that is going to be regulated. Each agency has a different approach and different rules. They have no expertise in these new issues, and they are not quick to expand their authority for all sorts of reasons.

Compare that with the Internet. The Internet is a freewheeling system of integrated objects and networks. It grows horizontally, demolishing old technological barriers so that people and systems that never previously communicated now can. Already, apps on a smartphone can log health information, control your energy use, and communicate with your car. That's a set of functions that crosses jurisdictions of at least four different government agencies, and it's only going to get worse.

Our world-size robot needs to be viewed as a single entity with millions of components interacting with each other. Any solutions here need to be holistic. They need to work everywhere, for everything. Whether we're talking about cars, drones, or phones, they're all computers.

This has lots of precedent. Many new technologies have led to the formation of new government regulatory agencies. Trains did, cars did, airplanes did. Radio led to the formation of the Federal Radio Commission, which became the FCC. Nuclear power led to the formation of the Atomic Energy Commission, which eventually became the Department of Energy. The reasons were the same in every case.

New technologies need new expertise because they bring with them new challenges. Governments need a single agency to house that new expertise, because its applications cut across several preexisting agencies. It's less that the new agency needs to regulate—although that's often a big part of it—and more that governments recognize the importance of the new technologies.

The Internet has famously eschewed formal regulation, instead adopting a multi-stakeholder model of academics, businesses, governments, and other interested parties. My hope is that we can keep the best of this approach in any regulatory agency, looking more at the new US Digital Service or the 18F office inside the General Services Administration. Both of those organizations are dedicated to providing digital government services, and both have collected significant expertise by bringing people in from outside of government, and both have learned how to work closely with existing agencies. Any Internet regulatory agency will similarly need to engage in a high level of collaborate regulation—both a challenge and an opportunity.

I don't think any of us can predict the totality of the regulations we need to ensure the safety of this world, but here's a few. We need government to ensure companies follow good security practices: testing, patching, secure defaults—and we need to be able to hold companies liable when they fail to do these things. We need government to mandate strong personal data protections, and limitations on data collection and use. We need to ensure that responsible security research is legal and well-funded. We need to enforce transparency in design, some sort of code escrow in case a company goes out of business, and interoperability between devices of different manufacturers, to counterbalance the monopolistic effects of interconnected technologies. Individuals need the right to take their data with them. And Internet-enabled devices should retain some minimal functionality if disconnected from the Internet.

I'm not the only one talking about this. I've seen proposals for a National Institutes of Health analogue for cybersecurity. University of Washington law professor Ryan Calo has proposed a Federal Robotics Commission. I think it needs to be broader: maybe a Department of Technology Policy.

Of course there will be problems. There's a lack of expertise in these issues inside government. There's a lack of willingness in government to do the hard regulatory work. Industry is worried about any new bureaucracy: both that it will stifle innovation by regulating too much and that it will be captured by industry and regulate too little. A domestic regulatory agency will have to deal with the fundamentally international nature of the problem.

But government is the entity we use to solve problems like this. Governments have the scope, scale, and balance of interests to address the problems. It's the institution we've built to adjudicate competing social interests and internalize market externalities. Left to their own devices, the market simply can't. That we're currently in the middle of an era of low government trust, where many of us can't imagine government doing anything positive in an area like this, is to our detriment.

Here's the thing: Governments will get involved, regardless. The risks are too great, and the stakes are too high. Government already regulates dangerous physical systems like cars and medical devices. And nothing motivates the US government like fear. Remember 2001? A nominally small-government Republican president created the Office of Homeland Security 11 days after the terrorist attacks: a rushed and ill-thought-out decision that we've been trying to fix for over a decade. A fatal disaster will similarly spur our government into action, and it's unlikely to be well-considered and thoughtful action. Our choice isn't between government involvement and no government involvement. Our choice is between smarter government involvement and stupider government involvement. We have to start thinking about this now. Regulations are necessary, important, and complex; and they're coming. We can't afford to ignore these issues until it's too late.

We also need to start disconnecting systems. If we cannot secure complex systems to the level required by their real-world capabilities, then we must not build a world where everything is computerized and interconnected.

There are other models. We can enable local communications only. We can set limits on collected and stored data. We can deliberately design systems that don't interoperate with each other. We can deliberately fetter devices, reversing the current trend of turning everything into a general-purpose computer. And, most important, we can move toward less centralization and more distributed systems, which is how the Internet was first envisioned.

This might be a heresy in today's race to network everything, but large, centralized systems are not inevitable. The technical elites are pushing us in that direction, but they really don't have any good supporting arguments other than the profits of their ever-growing multinational corporations.

But this will change. It will change not only because of security concerns, it will also change because of political concerns. We're starting to chafe under the worldview of everything producing data about us and what we do, and that data being available to both governments and corporations. Surveillance capitalism won't be the business model of the Internet forever. We need to change the fabric of the Internet so that evil governments don't have the tools to create a horrific totalitarian state. And while good laws and regulations in Western democracies are a great second line of defense, they can't be our only line of defense.

My guess is that we will soon reach a high-water mark of computerization and connectivity, and that afterward we will make conscious decisions about what and how we decide to interconnect. But we're still in the honeymoon phase of connectivity. Governments and corporations are punch-drunk on our data, and the rush to connect everything is driven by an even greater desire for power and market share. One of the presentations released by Edward Snowden contained the NSA mantra: "Collect it all." A similar mantra for the Internet today might be: "Connect it all."

The inevitable backlash will not be driven by the market. It will be deliberate policy decisions that put the safety and welfare of society above individual corporations and industries. It will be deliberate policy decisions that prioritize the security of our systems over the demands of the FBI to weaken them in order to make their law-enforcement jobs easier. It'll be hard policy for many to swallow, but our safety will depend on it.

****

The scenarios I've outlined, both the technological and economic trends that are causing them and the political changes we need to make to start to fix them, come from my years of working in Internet-security technology and policy. All of this is informed by an understanding of both technology and policy. That turns out to be critical, and there aren't enough people who understand both.

This brings me to my final plea: We need more public-interest technologists.

Over the past couple of decades, we've seen examples of getting Internet-security policy badly wrong. I'm thinking of the FBI's "going dark" debate about its insistence that computer devices be designed to facilitate government access, the "vulnerability equities process" about when the government should disclose and fix a vulnerability versus when it should use it to attack other systems, the debacle over paperless touch-screen voting machines, and the DMCA that I discussed above. If you watched any of these policy debates unfold, you saw policy-makers and technologists talking past each other.

Our world-size robot will exacerbate these problems. The historical divide between Washington and Silicon Valley—the mistrust of governments by tech companies and the mistrust of tech companies by governments—is dangerous.

We have to fix this. Getting IoT security right depends on the two sides working together and, even more important, having people who are experts in each working on both. We need technologists to get involved in policy, and we need policy-makers to get involved in technology. We need people who are experts in making both technology and technological policy. We need technologists on congressional staffs, inside federal agencies, working for NGOs, and as part of the press. We need to create a viable career path for public-interest technologists, much as there already is one for public-interest attorneys. We need courses, and degree programs in colleges, for people interested in careers in public-interest technology. We need fellowships in organizations that need these people. We need technology companies to offer sabbaticals for technologists wanting to go down this path. We need an entire ecosystem that supports people bridging the gap between technology and law. We need a viable career path that ensures that even though people in this field won't make as much as they would in a high-tech start-up, they will have viable careers. The security of our computerized and networked future—meaning the security of ourselves, families, homes, businesses, and communities—depends on it.

This plea is bigger than security, actually. Pretty much all of the major policy debates of this century will have a major technological component. Whether it's weapons of mass destruction, robots drastically affecting employment, climate change, food safety, or the increasing ubiquity of ever-shrinking drones, understanding the policy means understanding the technology. Our society desperately needs technologists working on the policy. The alternative is bad policy.

****

The world-size robot is less designed than created. It's coming without any forethought or architecting or planning; most of us are completely unaware of what we're building. In fact, I am not convinced we can actually design any of this. When we try to design complex sociotechnical systems like this, we are regularly surprised by their emergent properties. The best we can do is observe and channel these properties as best we can.

Market thinking sometimes makes us lose sight of the human choices and autonomy at stake. Before we get controlled—or killed—by the world-size robot, we need to rebuild confidence in our collective governance institutions. Law and policy may not seem as cool as digital tech, but they're also places of critical innovation. They're where we collectively bring about the world we want to live in.

While I might sound like a Cassandra, I'm actually optimistic about our future. Our society has tackled bigger problems than this one. It takes work and it's not easy, but we eventually find our way clear to make the hard choices necessary to solve our real problems.

The world-size robot we're building can only be managed responsibly if we start making real choices about the interconnected world we live in. Yes, we need security systems as robust as the threat landscape. But we also need laws that effectively regulate these dangerous technologies. And, more generally, we need to make moral, ethical, and political decisions on how those systems should work. Until now, we've largely left the Internet alone. We gave programmers a special right to code cyberspace as they saw fit. This was okay because cyberspace was separate and relatively unimportant: That is, it didn't matter. Now that that's changed, we can no longer give programmers and the companies they work for this power. Those moral, ethical, and political decisions need, somehow, to be made by everybody. We need to link people with the same zeal that we are currently linking machines. "Connect it all" must be countered with "connect us all."

Botnets

Originally published in the MIT Technology Review, *March/April 2017*

Botnets have existed for at least a decade. As early as 2000, hackers were breaking into computers over the Internet and controlling them en masse from centralized systems. Among other things, the hackers used the combined computing power of these botnets to launch distributed denial-of-service attacks, which flood websites with traffic to take them down.

But now the problem is getting worse, thanks to a flood of cheap webcams, digital video recorders, and other gadgets in the "Internet of things." Because these devices typically have little or no security, hackers can take them over with little effort. And that makes it easier than ever to build huge botnets that take down much more than one site at a time.

In October, a botnet made up of 100,000 compromised gadgets knocked an Internet infrastructure provider partially offline. Taking down that provider, Dyn, resulted in a cascade of effects that ultimately caused a long list of high-profile websites, including Twitter and Netflix, to temporarily disappear from the Internet. More attacks are sure to follow: the botnet that attacked Dyn was created with publicly available malware called Mirai that largely automates the process of co-opting computers.

The best defense would be for everything online to run only secure software, so botnets couldn't be created in the first place. This isn't going to happen anytime soon. Internet of things devices are not designed with security in mind and often have no way of being patched. The things that have become part of Mirai botnets, for example, will be vulnerable until their owners throw them away. Botnets will get larger and more powerful simply because the number of vulnerable devices will go up by orders of magnitude over the next few years.

What do hackers do with them? Many things.

Botnets are used to commit click fraud. Click fraud is a scheme to fool advertisers into thinking that people are clicking on, or viewing, their ads. There are lots of ways to commit click fraud, but the easiest is probably for the attacker to embed a Google ad in a Web page he owns. Google ads pay a site owner according to the number of people who click on them. The attacker instructs all the computers on his botnet to repeatedly visit the Web page and click on the ad. Dot, dot, dot, PROFIT! If the botnet makers figure out more effective ways to siphon revenue from big companies online, we could see the whole advertising model of the Internet crumble.

Similarly, botnets can be used to evade spam filters, which work partly by knowing which computers are sending millions of emails. They can speed up password guessing to break into online accounts, mine bitcoins, and do anything else that requires a large network of computers. This is why botnets are big businesses. Criminal organizations rent time on them.

But the botnet activities that most often make headlines are denial-of-service attacks. Dyn seems to have been the victim of some angry hackers, but more financially motivated groups use these attacks as a form of extortion. Political groups use them to silence websites they don't like. Such attacks will certainly be a tactic in any future cyberwar.

Once you know a botnet exists, you can attack its command-and-control system. When botnets were rare, this tactic was effective. As they get more common, this piecemeal defense will become less so. You can also secure yourself against the effects of botnets. For example, several companies sell defenses against denial-of-service attacks. Their effectiveness varies, depending on the severity of the attack and the type of service.

But overall, the trends favor the attacker. Expect more attacks like the one against Dyn in the coming year.

IoT Cybersecurity: What's Plan B?

Originally published in the Sept/Oct 2017 issue of
IEEE Security & Privacy

In August, four US Senators introduced a bill designed to improve Internet of Things (IoT) security. The IoT Cybersecurity Improvement

Act of 2017 is a modest piece of legislation. It doesn't regulate the IoT market. It doesn't single out any industries for particular attention, or force any companies to do anything. It doesn't even modify the liability laws for embedded software. Companies can continue to sell IoT devices with whatever lousy security they want.

What the bill does do is leverage the government's buying power to nudge the market: any IoT product that the government buys must meet minimum security standards. It requires vendors to ensure that devices can not only be patched, but are patched in an authenticated and timely manner; don't have unchangeable default passwords; and are free from known vulnerabilities. It's about as low a security bar as you can set, and that it will considerably improve security speaks volumes about the current state of IoT security. (Full disclosure: I helped draft some of the bill's security requirements.)

The bill would also modify the Computer Fraud and Abuse and the Digital Millennium Copyright Acts to allow security researchers to study the security of IoT devices purchased by the government. It's a far narrower exemption than our industry needs. But it's a good first step, which is probably the best thing you can say about this legislation.

However, it's unlikely this first step will even be taken. I am writing this column in August, and have no doubt that the bill will have gone nowhere by the time you read it in October or later. If hearings are held, they won't matter. The bill won't have been voted on by any committee, and it won't be on any legislative calendar. The odds of this bill becoming law are zero. And that's not just because of current politics—I'd be equally pessimistic under the Obama administration.

But the situation is critical. The Internet is dangerous—and the IoT gives it not just eyes and ears, but also hands and feet. Security vulnerabilities, exploits, and attacks that once affected only bits and bytes now affect flesh and blood.

Markets, as we've repeatedly learned over the past century, are terrible mechanisms for improving the safety of products and services. It was true for automobile, food, restaurant, airplane, fire, and financial-instrument safety. The reasons are complicated, but basically, sellers don't compete on safety features because buyers can't efficiently differentiate products based on safety considerations. The race-to-the-bottom mechanism that markets use to minimize prices also minimizes quality. Without government intervention, the IoT remains dangerously insecure.

The US government has no appetite for intervention, so we won't see serious safety and security regulations, a new federal agency, or better liability laws. We might have a better chance in the EU. Depending on how the General Data Protection Regulation on data privacy pans out, the EU might pass a similar security law in 5 years. No other country has a large enough market share to make a difference.

Sometimes we can opt out of the IoT, but that option is becoming increasingly rare. Last year, I tried and failed to purchase a new car without an Internet connection. In a few years, it's going to be nearly impossible to not be multiply connected to the IoT. And our biggest IoT security risks will stem not from devices we have a market relationship with, but from everyone else's cars, cameras, routers, drones, and so on.

We can try to shop our ideals and demand more security, but companies don't compete on IoT safety—and we security experts aren't a large enough market force to make a difference.

We need a Plan B, although I'm not sure what that is. Comment if you have any ideas.

4 Security and Technology

The NSA's Cryptographic Capabilities

Originally published in Wired.com, *September 4, 2013*

The latest Snowden document is the US intelligence "black budget." There's a lot of information in the few pages the *Washington Post* decided to publish, including an introduction by Director of National Intelligence James Clapper. In it, he drops a tantalizing hint: "Also, we are investing in groundbreaking cryptanalytic capabilities to defeat adversarial cryptography and exploit Internet traffic."

Honestly, I'm skeptical. Whatever the NSA has up its top-secret sleeves, the mathematics of cryptography will still be the most secure part of any encryption system. I worry a lot more about poorly designed cryptographic products, software bugs, bad passwords, companies that collaborate with the NSA to leak all or part of the keys, and insecure computers and networks. Those are where the real vulnerabilities are, and where the NSA spends the bulk of its efforts.

This isn't the first time we've heard this rumor. In a WIRED article last year, longtime NSA-watcher James Bamford wrote:

> According to another top official also involved with the program, the NSA made an enormous breakthrough several years ago in its ability to cryptanalyze, or break, unfathomably complex encryption systems employed by not only governments around the world but also many average computer users in the US.

We have no further information from Clapper, Snowden, or this other source of Bamford's. But we can speculate.

Perhaps the NSA has some new mathematics that breaks one or more of the popular encryption algorithms: AES, Twofish, Serpent, triple-DES, Serpent. It wouldn't be the first time this happened. Back in the 1970s, the NSA knew of a cryptanalytic technique called "differential cryptanalysis" that was unknown in the academic world. That technique broke a variety of other academic and commercial algorithms that we all thought secure. We learned better in the early 1990s, and now design algorithms to be resistant to that technique.

It's very probable that the NSA has newer techniques that remain undiscovered in academia. Even so, such techniques are unlikely to result in a practical attack that can break actual encrypted plaintext.

The naive way to break an encryption algorithm is to brute-force the key. The complexity of that attack is 2^n, where n is the key length. All cryptanalytic attacks can be viewed as shortcuts to that method. And since the efficacy of a brute-force attack is a direct function of key length, these attacks effectively shorten the key. So if, for example, the best attack against DES has a complexity of 2^{39}, that effectively shortens DES's 56-bit key by 17 bits.

That's a really good attack, by the way.

Right now the upper practical limit on brute force is somewhere under 80 bits. However, using that as a guide gives us some indication as to how good an attack has to be to break any of the modern algorithms. These days, encryption algorithms have, at a minimum, 128-bit keys. That means any NSA cryptanalytic breakthrough has to reduce the effective key length by at least 48 bits in order to be practical.

There's more, though. That DES attack requires an impractical 70 terabytes of known plaintext encrypted with the key we're trying to break. Other mathematical attacks require similar amounts of data. In order to be effective in decrypting actual operational traffic, the NSA needs an attack that can be executed with the known plaintext in a common MS-Word header: much, much less.

So while the NSA certainly has symmetric cryptanalysis capabilities that we in the academic world do not, converting that into practical attacks on the sorts of data it is likely to encounter seems so impossible as to be fanciful.

More likely is that the NSA has some mathematical breakthrough that affects one or more public-key algorithms. There are a lot of mathematical tricks involved in public-key cryptanalysis, and absolutely no theory that provides any limits on how powerful those tricks can be.

Breakthroughs in factoring have occurred regularly over the past several decades, allowing us to break ever-larger public keys. Much of the public-key cryptography we use today involves elliptic curves, something that is even more ripe for mathematical breakthroughs. It is not unreasonable to assume that the NSA has some techniques in this area that we in the academic world do not. Certainly the fact that the NSA is pushing elliptic-curve cryptography is some indication that it can break them more easily.

If we think that's the case, the fix is easy: increase the key lengths.

Assuming the hypothetical NSA breakthroughs don't totally break public-cryptography—and that's a very reasonable assumption—it's pretty easy to stay a few steps ahead of the NSA by using ever-longer keys. We're already trying to phase out 1024-bit RSA keys in favor of 2048-bit keys. Perhaps we need to jump even further ahead and consider 3072-bit keys. And maybe we should be even more paranoid about elliptic curves and use key lengths above 500 bits.

One last blue-sky possibility: a quantum computer. Quantum computers are still toys in the academic world, but have the theoretical ability to quickly break common public-key algorithms—regardless of key length—and to effectively halve the key length of any symmetric algorithm. I think it extraordinarily unlikely that the NSA has built a quantum computer capable of performing the magnitude of calculation necessary to do this, but it's possible. The defense is easy, if annoying: stick with symmetric cryptography based on shared secrets, and use 256-bit keys.

There's a saying inside the NSA: "Cryptanalysis always gets better. It never gets worse." It's naive to assume that, in 2013, we have discovered all the mathematical breakthroughs in cryptography that can ever be discovered. There's a lot more out there, and there will be for centuries.

And the NSA is in a privileged position: It can make use of everything discovered and openly published by the academic world, as well as everything discovered by it in secret.

The NSA has a lot of people thinking about this problem full-time. According to the black budget summary, 35,000 people and

$11 billion annually are part of the Department of Defense-wide Consolidated Cryptologic Program. Of that, 4 percent—or $440 million—goes to "Research and Technology."

That's an enormous amount of money; probably more than everyone else on the planet spends on cryptography research put together. I'm sure that results in a lot of interesting—and occasionally groundbreaking—cryptanalytic research results, maybe some of it even practical.

Still, I trust the mathematics.

iPhone Fingerprint Authentication

Originally published in Wired.com, *September 9, 2013*

When Apple bought AuthenTec for its biometrics technology—reported as one of its most expensive purchases—there was a lot of speculation about how the company would incorporate biometrics in its product line. Many speculate that the new Apple iPhone to be announced tomorrow will come with a fingerprint authentication system, and there are several ways it could work, such as swiping your finger over a slit-sized reader to have the phone recognize you.

Apple would be smart to add biometric technology to the iPhone. Fingerprint authentication is a good balance between convenience and security for a mobile device.

Biometric systems are seductive, but the reality isn't that simple. They have complicated security properties. For example, they are not keys. Your fingerprint isn't a secret; you leave it everywhere you touch.

And fingerprint readers have a long history of vulnerabilities as well. Some are better than others. The simplest ones just check the ridges of a finger; some of those can be fooled with a good photocopy. Others check for pores as well. The better ones verify pulse, or finger temperature. Fooling them with rubber fingers is harder, but often possible. A Japanese researcher had good luck doing this over a decade ago with the gelatin mixture that's used to make Gummi bears.

The best system I've ever seen was at the entry gates of a secure government facility. Maybe you could have fooled it with a fake finger, but a Marine guard with a big gun was making sure you didn't get the opportunity to try. Disney World uses a similar system at its park gates—but without the Marine guards.

A biometric system that authenticates you and you alone is easier to design than a biometric system that is supposed to identify unknown people. That is, the question "Is this the finger belonging to the owner of this iPhone?" is a much easier question for the system to answer than "Whose finger is this?"

There are two ways an authentication system can fail. It can mistakenly allow an unauthorized person access, or it can mistakenly deny access to an authorized person. In any consumer system, the second failure is far worse than the first. Yes, it can be problematic if an iPhone fingerprint system occasionally allows someone else access to your phone. But it's much worse if you can't reliably access your own phone—you'd junk the system after a week.

If it's true that Apple's new iPhone will have biometric security, the designers have presumably erred on the side of ensuring that the user can always get in. Failures will be more common in cold weather, when your shriveled fingers just got out of the shower, and so on. But there will certainly still be the traditional PIN system to fall back on.

So...can biometric authentication be hacked?

Almost certainly. I'm sure that someone with a good enough copy of your fingerprint and some rudimentary materials engineering capability—or maybe just a good enough printer—can authenticate his way into your iPhone. But, honestly, if some bad guy has your iPhone and your fingerprint, you've probably got bigger problems to worry about.

The final problem with biometric systems is the database. If the system is centralized, there will be a large database of biometric information that's vulnerable to hacking. A system by Apple will almost certainly be local—you authenticate yourself to the phone, not to any network—so there's no requirement for a centralized fingerprint database.

Apple's move is likely to bring fingerprint readers into the mainstream. But all applications are not equal. It's fine if your fingers unlock your phone. It's a different matter entirely if your fingerprint is used to authenticate your iCloud account. The centralized database required for that application would create an enormous security risk.

The Future of Incident Response

Originally published in the Sept/Oct 2014 issue of
IEEE Security & Privacy

Security is a combination of protection, detection, and response. It's taken the industry a long time to get to this point, though. The 1990s was the era of protection. Our industry was full of products that would protect your computers and network. By 2000, we realized that detection needed to be formalized as well, and the industry was full of detection products and services.

This decade is one of response. Over the past few years, we've started seeing incident response (IR) products and services. Security teams are incorporating them into their arsenal because of three trends in computing. One, we've lost control of our computing environment. More of our data is held in the cloud by other companies, and more of our actual networks are outsourced. This makes response more complicated, because we might not have visibility into parts of our critical network infrastructures.

Two, attacks are getting more sophisticated. The rise of APT (advanced persistent threat)—attacks that specifically target for reasons other than simple financial theft—brings with it a new sort of attacker, which requires a new threat model. Also, as hacking becomes a more integral part of geopolitics, unrelated networks are increasingly collateral damage in nation-state fights.

And three, companies continue to under-invest in protection and detection, both of which are imperfect even under the best of circumstances, obliging response to pick up the slack.

Way back in the 1990s, I used to say that "security is a process, not a product." That was a strategic statement about the fallacy of thinking you could ever be done with security; you need to continually reassess your security posture in the face of an ever-changing threat landscape.

At a tactical level, security is both a product and a process. Really, it's a combination of people, process, and technology. What changes are the ratios. Protection systems are almost technology, with some assistance from people and process. Detection requires more-or-less equal proportions of people, process, and technology. Response is mostly done by people, with critical assistance from process and technology.

Usability guru Lorrie Faith Cranor once wrote, "Whenever possible, secure system designers should find ways of keeping humans out of the loop." That's sage advice, but you can't automate IR. Everyone's network is different. All attacks are different. Everyone's security environments are different. The regulatory environments are different. All organizations are different, and political and economic considerations are often more important than technical considerations. IR needs people, because successful IR requires thinking.

This is new for the security industry, and it means that response products and services will look different. For most of its life, the security industry has been plagued with the problems of a lemons market. That's a term from economics that refers to a market where buyers can't tell the difference between good products and bad. In these markets, mediocre products drive good ones out of the market; price is the driver, because there's no good way to test for quality. It's been true in anti-virus, it's been true in firewalls, it's been true in IDSs, and it's been true elsewhere. But because IR is people-focused in ways protection and detection are not, it won't be true here. Better products will do better because buyers will quickly be able to determine that they're better.

The key to successful IR is found in Cranor's next sentence: "However, there are some tasks for which feasible, or cost effective, alternatives to humans are not available. In these cases, system designers should engineer their systems to support the humans in the loop, and maximize their chances of performing their security-critical functions successfully." What we need is technology that aids people, not technology that supplants them.

The best way I've found to think about this is OODA loops. OODA stands for "observe, orient, decide, act," and it's a way of thinking about real-time adversarial situations developed by US Air Force military strategist John Boyd. He was thinking about fighter jets, but the general idea has been applied to everything from contract negotiations to boxing—and computer and network IR.

Speed is essential. People in these situations are constantly going through OODA loops in their head. And if you can do yours faster than the other guy—if you can "get inside his OODA loop"—then you have an enormous advantage.

We need tools to facilitate all of these steps:

- Observe, which means knowing what's happening on our networks in real time. This includes real-time threat detection information from IDSs, log monitoring and analysis data, network and system performance data, standard network management data, and even physical security information—and then tools knowing which tools to use to synthesize and present it in useful formats. Incidents aren't standardized; they're all different. The more an IR team can observe what's happening on the network, the more they can understand the attack. This means that an IR team needs to be able to operate across the entire organization.

- Orient, which means understanding what it means in context, both in the context of the organization and the context of the greater Internet community. It's not enough to know about the attack; IR teams need to know what it means. Is there a new malware being used by cybercriminals? Is the organization rolling out a new software package or planning layoffs? Has the organization seen attacks from this particular IP address before? Has the network been opened to a new strategic partner? Answering these questions means tying data from the network to information from the news, network intelligence feeds, and other information from the organization. What's going on in an organization often matters more in IR than the attack's technical details.

- Decide, which means figuring out what to do at that moment. This is actually difficult because it involves knowing who has the authority to decide and giving them the information to decide quickly. IR decisions often involve executive input, so it's important to be able to get those people the information they need quickly and efficiently. All decisions need to be defensible after the fact and documented. Both the regulatory and litigation environments have gotten very complex, and decisions need to be made with defensibility in mind.

- Act, which means being able to make changes quickly and effectively on our networks. IR teams need access to the organization's network—all of the organization's network. Again, incidents differ, and it's impossible to know in advance what sort of access an IR team will need. But ultimately, they need broad access; security will come from audit rather than access control. And they need to train repeatedly, because nothing improves someone's ability to act more than practice.

Pulling all of these tools together under a unified framework will make IR work. And making IR work is the ultimate key to making security work. The goal here is to bring people, process and technology together in a way we haven't seen before in network security. It's something we need to do to continue to defend against the threats.

Drone Self-Defense and the Law

Originally published in CNN.com, *September 9, 2015*

Last month, a Kentucky man shot down a drone that was hovering near his backyard.

WDRB News reported that the camera drone's owners soon showed up at the home of the shooter, William H. Merideth: "Four guys came over to confront me about it, and I happened to be armed, so that changed their minds," Merideth said. "They asked me, 'Are you the S-O-B that shot my drone?' and I said, 'Yes I am,'" he said. "I had my 40 mm Glock on me and they started toward me and I told them, 'If you cross my sidewalk, there's gonna be another shooting.'" Police charged Meredith with criminal mischief and wanton endangerment.

This is a trend. People have shot down drones in southern New Jersey and rural California as well. It's illegal, and they get arrested for it.

Technology changes everything. Specifically, it upends long-standing societal balances around issues like security and privacy. When a capability becomes possible, or cheaper, or more common, the changes can be far-reaching. Rebalancing security and privacy after technology changes capabilities can be very difficult, and take years. And we're not very good at it.

The security threats from drones are real, and the government is taking them seriously. In January, a man lost control of his drone, which crashed on the White House lawn. In May, another man was arrested for trying to fly his drone over the White House fence, and another last week for flying a drone into the stadium where the US Open was taking place.

Drones have attempted to deliver drugs to prisons in Maryland, Ohio and South Carolina—so far.

There have been many near-misses between drones and airplanes. Many people have written about the possible terrorist uses of drones.

Defenses are being developed. Both Lockheed Martin and Boeing sell anti-drone laser weapons. One company sells shotgun shells specifically designed to shoot down drones.

Other companies are working on technologies to detect and disable them safely. Some of those technologies were used to provide security at this year's Boston Marathon. ·

Law enforcement can deploy these technologies, but under current law it's illegal to shoot down a drone, even if it's hovering above your own property. In our society, you're generally not allowed to take the law into your own hands. You're expected to call the police and let them deal with it.

There's an alternate theory, though, from law professor Michael Froomkin. He argues that self-defense should be permissible against drones simply because you don't know their capabilities. We know, for example, that people have mounted guns on drones, which means they could pose a threat to life. Note that this legal theory has not been tested in court.

Increasingly, government is regulating drones and drone flights both at the state level and by the FAA. There are proposals to require that drones have an identifiable transponder, or no-fly zones programmed into the drone software.

Still, a large number of security issues remain unresolved. How do we feel about drones with long-range listening devices, for example? Or drones hovering outside our property and photographing us through our windows?

What's going on is that drones have changed how we think about security and privacy within our homes, by removing the protections we used to get from fences and walls. Of course, being spied on and shot at from above is nothing new, but access to those technologies was expensive and largely the purview of governments and some corporations. Drones put these capabilities into the hands of hobby-ists, and we don't know what to do about it.

The issues around drones will get worse as we move from remotely piloted aircraft to true drones: aircraft that operate autonomously from a computer program. For the first time, autonomous robots—with ever-increasing intelligence and capabilities at an ever-decreasing cost—will have access to public spaces. This will create serious prob-lems for society, because our legal system is largely based on deterring human miscreants rather than their proxies.

Our desire to shoot down a drone hovering nearby is understand-able, given its potential threat. Society's need for people not to take the law into their own hands—and especially not to fire guns into the air—is also understandable. These two positions are increasingly com-ing into conflict, and will require increasing government regulation to sort out. But more importantly, we need to rethink our assumptions of security and privacy in a world of autonomous drones, long-range cameras, face recognition, and the myriad other technologies that are increasingly in the hands of everyone.

Replacing Judgment with Algorithms

Originally published in CNN.com, *January 6, 2016*

China is considering a new "social credit" system, designed to rate everyone's trustworthiness. Many fear that it will become a tool of social control—but in reality it has a lot in common with the algo-rithms and systems that score and classify us all every day.

Human judgment is being replaced by automatic algorithms, and that brings with it both enormous benefits and risks. The technology is enabling a new form of social control, sometimes deliberately and sometimes as a side effect. And as the Internet of Things ushers in an era of more sensors and more data—and more algorithms—we need to ensure that we reap the benefits while avoiding the harms.

Right now, the Chinese government is watching how companies use "social credit" scores in state-approved pilot projects. The most prominent one is Sesame Credit, and it's much more than a financial scoring system.

Citizens are judged not only by conventional financial criteria, but by their actions and associations. Rumors abound about how this system works. Various news sites are speculating that your score will go up if you share a link from a state-sponsored news agency and go down if you post pictures of Tiananmen Square. Similarly, your score will go up if you purchase local agricultural products and down if you purchase Japanese anime. Right now the worst fears seem overblown, but could certainly come to pass in the future.

This story has spread because it's just the sort of behavior you'd expect from the authoritarian government in China. But there's little about the scoring systems used by Sesame Credit that's unique to China. All of us are being categorized and judged by similar algorithms, both by companies and by governments. While the aim of these systems might not be social control, it's often the byproduct. And if we're not careful, the creepy results we imagine for the Chinese will be our lot as well.

Sesame Credit is largely based on a US system called FICO. That's the system that determines your credit score. You actually have a few dozen different ones, and they determine whether you can get a mortgage, car loan or credit card, and what sorts of interest rates you're offered. The exact algorithm is secret, but we know in general what goes into a FICO score: how much debt you have, how good you've been at repaying your debt, how long your credit history is and so on.

There's nothing about your social network, but that might change. In August, Facebook was awarded a patent on using a borrower's social network to help determine if he or she is a good credit risk. Basically, your creditworthiness becomes dependent on the creditworthiness of your friends. Associate with deadbeats, and you're more likely to be judged as one.

Your associations can be used to judge you in other ways as well. It's now common for employers to use social media sites to screen job applicants. This manual process is increasingly being outsourced and automated; companies like Social Intelligence, Evolv and First Advantage automatically process your social networking activity and provide hiring recommendations for employers. The dangers of this type of system—from discriminatory biases resulting from the data to an obsession with scores over more social measures—are too many.

The company Klout tried to make a business of measuring your online influence, hoping its proprietary system would become an industry standard used for things like hiring and giving out free product samples.

The US government is judging you as well. Your social media postings could get you on the terrorist watch list, affecting your ability to fly on an airplane and even get a job. In 2012, a British tourist's tweet caused the US to deny him entry into the country. We know that the National Security Agency uses complex computer algorithms to sift through the Internet data it collects on both Americans and foreigners.

All of these systems, from Sesame Credit to the NSA's secret algorithms, are made possible by computers and data. A couple of generations ago, you would apply for a home mortgage at a bank that knew you, and a bank manager would make a determination of your creditworthiness. Yes, the system was prone to all sorts of abuses, ranging from discrimination to an old-boy network of friends helping friends. But the system also couldn't scale. It made no sense for a bank across the state to give you a loan, because they didn't know you. Loans stayed local.

FICO scores changed that. Now, a computer crunches your credit history and produces a number. And you can take that number to any mortgage lender in the country. They don't need to know you; your score is all they need to decide whether you're trustworthy.

This score enabled the home mortgage, car loan, credit card and other lending industries to explode, but it brought with it other problems. People who don't conform to the financial norm—having and using credit cards, for example—can have trouble getting loans when they need them. The automatic nature of the system enforces conformity.

The secrecy of the algorithms further pushes people toward conformity. If you are worried that the US government will classify you as a potential terrorist, you're less likely to friend Muslims on Facebook. If you know that your Sesame Credit score is partly based on your not buying "subversive" products or being friends with dissidents, you're more likely to overcompensate by not buying anything but the most innocuous books or corresponding with the most boring people.

Uber is an example of how this works. Passengers rate drivers and drivers rate passengers; both risk getting booted out of the system if their rankings get too low. This weeds out bad drivers and passengers, but also results in marginal people being blocked from the system, and everyone else trying to not make any special requests, avoid controversial conversation topics, and generally behave like good corporate citizens.

Many have documented a chilling effect among American Muslims, with them avoiding certain discussion topics lest they be taken the wrong way. Even if nothing would happen because of it, their free speech has been curtailed because of the secrecy surrounding government surveillance. How many of you are reluctant to Google "pressure cooker bomb"? How many are a bit worried that I used it in this essay?

This is what social control looks like in the Internet age. The Cold-War-era methods of undercover agents, informants living in your neighborhood, and agents provocateur is too labor-intensive and inefficient. These automatic algorithms make possible a wholly new way to enforce conformity. And by accepting algorithmic classification into our lives, we're paving the way for the same sort of thing China plans to put into place.

It doesn't have to be this way. We can get the benefits of automatic algorithmic systems while avoiding the dangers. It's not even hard.

The first step is to make these algorithms public. Companies and governments both balk at this, fearing that people will deliberately try to game them, but the alternative is much worse.

The second step is for these systems to be subject to oversight and accountability. It's already illegal for these algorithms to have discriminatory outcomes, even if they're not deliberately designed in. This concept needs to be expanded. We as a society need to understand what we expect out of the algorithms that automatically judge us and ensure that those expectations are met.

We also need to provide manual systems for people to challenge their classifications. Automatic algorithms are going to make mistakes, whether it's by giving us bad credit scores or flagging us as terrorists. We need the ability to clear our names if this happens, through a process that restores human judgment.

Sesame Credit sounds like a dystopia because we can easily imagine how the Chinese government can use a system like this to enforce conformity and stifle dissent. Our own systems seem safer, because we don't believe the corporations and governments that run them are malevolent. But the dangers are inherent in the technologies. As we move into a world where we are increasingly judged by algorithms, we need to ensure that they do so fairly and properly.

Class Breaks

Originally published in Edge.org *as part of their annual question:* "What scientific term or concept ought to be more widely known?", *December 30, 2016*

There's a concept from computer security known as a class break. It's a particular security vulnerability that breaks not just one system, but an entire class of systems. Examples might be a vulnerability in a particular operating system that allows an attacker to take remote control of every computer that runs on that system's software. Or a vulnerability in Internet-enabled digital video recorders and webcams that allow an attacker to recruit those devices into a massive botnet.

It's a particular way computer systems can fail, exacerbated by the characteristics of computers and software. It only takes one smart person to figure out how to attack the system. Once he does that, he can write software that automates his attack. He can do it over the Internet, so he doesn't have to be near his victim. He can automate his attack so it works while he sleeps. And then he can pass the ability to someone—or to lots of people—without the skill. This changes the nature of security failures, and completely upends how we need to defend against them.

An example: Picking a mechanical door lock requires both skill and time. Each lock is a new job, and success at one lock doesn't guarantee success with another of the same design. Electronic door locks, like the ones you now find in hotel rooms, have different vulnerabilities. An attacker can find a flaw in the design that allows him to create a key card that opens every door. If he publishes his attack software, not just the attacker, but anyone can now open every lock. And if those locks are connected to the Internet, attackers could potentially open door locks remotely—they could open every door lock remotely at the same time. That's a class break.

It's how computer systems fail, but it's not how we think about failures. We still think about automobile security in terms of individual car thieves manually stealing cars. We don't think of hackers remotely taking control of cars over the Internet. Or, remotely disabling every car over the Internet. We think about voting fraud as unauthorized individuals trying to vote. We don't think about a single person or organization remotely manipulating thousands of Internet-connected voting machines.

In a sense, class breaks are not a new concept in risk management. It's the difference between home burglaries and fires, which happen occasionally to different houses in a neighborhood over the course of the year, and floods and earthquakes, which either happen to everyone in the neighborhood or no one. Insurance companies can handle both types of risk, but they are inherently different. The increasing computerization of everything is moving us from a burglary/fire risk model to a flood/earthquake model, which a given threat either affects everyone in town or doesn't happen at all.

But there's a key difference between floods/earthquakes and class breaks in computer systems: the former are random natural phenomena, while the latter is human-directed. Floods don't change their behavior to maximize their damage based on the types of defenses we build. Attackers do that to computer systems. Attackers examine our systems, looking for class breaks. And once one of them finds one, they'll exploit it again and again until the vulnerability is fixed.

As we move into the world of the Internet of Things, where computers permeate our lives at every level, class breaks will become increasingly important. The combination of automation and action at a distance will give attackers more power and leverage than they have ever had before. Security notions like the precautionary principle—where the potential of harm is so great that we err on the side of not deploying a new technology without proofs of security—will become more important in a world where an attacker can open all of the door locks or hack all of the power plants. It's not an inherently less secure world, but it's a differently secure world. It's a world where driverless cars are much safer than people-driven cars, until suddenly they're not. We need to build systems that assume the possibility of class breaks—and maintain security despite them.

5 Elections and Voting

Candidates Won't Hesitate to Use Manipulative Advertising to Score Votes

Originally published in the Guardian, *February 4, 2016*

This presidential election, prepare to be manipulated.

In politics, as in the marketplace, you are the consumer. But you only have one vote to "spend" per election, and in November you'll almost always only have two possible candidates on which to spend it.

In every election, both of those candidates are going to pull every trick in the surveillance-driven, highly personalized internet advertising world to get you to vote for them. Or, if they think you'll vote for the other candidate, to stay home and not vote.

In 2012, Barack Obama deftly used both social media and his own database of supporters to outmaneuver Mitt Romney, spending $47 milion on social media advertising—10 times more than his challenger. The Republicans have learned from that race, and are now just as sophisticated.

Over the past eight years, everyone has learned from the latest research in advertising manipulation. Their data can better determine your political affiliation, and level of engagement, than ever before. You'll see personalized ads precisely targeted to your interests and opinions, based on the things you've written and articles you've read.

There are hundreds of companies that collect data about you and your behavior, online and offline, primarily for advertising purposes.

Those companies categorize you by dozens of different variables and sell your information to companies that want to sell things to you. This is why searching for a Hawaiian vacation results in ads for those vacations on site after site, and why a clothing item you purchase follows you around on internet banner ads for days.

This year, both parties are going to spend more money on personalized advertising, and they're going to spend it more effectively. Candidates are going to take their own data and their party's data and correlate with additional data they buy.

They're going to know where you live and where you work, and persuade you to attend local events. They're going to attempt to manipulate you into sharing, liking and retweeting their messages. And they're going to do everything they can to make sure you vote for them.

Already we've seen one skirmish surrounding voter information: Bernie Sanders's campaign improperly accessed Hillary Clinton's supporters from the Democrats' master database.

During the 2012 election, Facebook ran an experiment in voter manipulation. Users were able to post an "I Voted" icon, much like the real stickers many of us get at polling places after voting. What Facebook did was randomly manipulate who could see that icon. They found that there was a bandwagon effect with respect to voting: you are more likely to vote if you believe your friends are voting. In Facebook's experiment, this manipulation had the effect of increasing voter turnout 0.14%—enough to sway a close election.

Every candidate's goal is, essentially, to selectively manipulate the visibility of that icon. They're going to want to make sure their supporters see the icon a lot, and that the supporters of every other candidate don't see it at all. Similarly, they are going to want to buy advertising space on Google to display positive links for themselves and negative links for their rivals.

Research also shows that public pressure and even shame increases voter turnout. One 2006 study in Michigan showed an 8% increase. Last week Ted Cruz sent Iowa supporters a "report card" on their voting record, hoping to shame them into action. He got bad press for it, but it was undoubtedly effective.

There are even more manipulative techniques. Multiple new studies show that we are more receptive to an advertising message if it's delivered by someone who looks like us. Already some advertisements are produced in multiple versions, with people of different ethnicities, genders and ages, for use in different markets; it's not uncommon in the Asian market. Tagged image databases will allow advertisers to go much further on the internet, creating an individualized image by automatically morphing an image of you with another image. You won't consciously recognize the image, but you will trust that face more. Will some candidate do this? Sooner or later, probably.

Everyone expects the 2016 presidential election to be fought on social media platforms like Facebook, Twitter and Instagram. It'll be highly personalized, and it'll be very manipulative.

Recognize it when it happens. It's your best defense against being manipulated. After all, you want to vote for the candidates you think are best for the country—not the ones with the most effective psychological tricks.

The Security of Our Election Systems

Originally published in the Washington Post, *July 27, 2016*

Russia was behind the hacks into the Democratic National Committee's computer network that led to the release of thousands of internal emails just before the party's convention began, US intelligence agencies have reportedly concluded.

The FBI is investigating. WikiLeaks promises there is more data to come. The political nature of this cyberattack means that Democrats and Republicans are trying to spin this as much as possible. Even so, we have to accept that someone is attacking our nation's computer systems in an apparent attempt to influence a presidential election. This kind of cyberattack targets the very core of our democratic process. And it points to the possibility of an even worse problem in November—that our election systems and our voting machines could be vulnerable to a similar attack.

If the intelligence community has indeed ascertained that Russia is to blame, our government needs to decide what to do in response. This is difficult because the attacks are politically partisan, but it is essential. If foreign governments learn that they can influence our elections with impunity, this opens the door for future manipulations, both document thefts and dumps like this one that we see and more subtle manipulations that we don't see.

Retaliation is politically fraught and could have serious consequences, but this is an attack against our democracy. We need to confront Russian President Vladimir Putin in some way—politically, economically or in cyberspace—and make it clear that we will not tolerate this kind of interference by any government. Regardless of your political leanings this time, there's no guarantee the next country that tries to manipulate our elections will share your preferred candidates.

Even more important, we need to secure our election systems before autumn. If Putin's government has already used a cyberattack to attempt to help Trump win, there's no reason to believe he won't do it again—especially now that Trump is inviting the "help."

Over the years, more and more states have moved to electronic voting machines and have flirted with Internet voting. These systems are insecure and vulnerable to attack.

But while computer security experts like me have sounded the alarm for many years, states have largely ignored the threat, and the machine manufacturers have thrown up enough obfuscating babble that election officials are largely mollified.

We no longer have time for that. We must ignore the machine manufacturers' spurious claims of security, create tiger teams to test the machines' and systems' resistance to attack, drastically increase their cyber-defenses and take them offline if we can't guarantee their security online.

Longer term, we need to return to election systems that are secure from manipulation. This means voting machines with voter-verified paper audit trails, and no Internet voting. I know it's slower and less convenient to stick to the old-fashioned way, but the security risks are simply too great.

There are other ways to attack our election system on the Internet besides hacking voting machines or changing vote tallies: deleting voter records, hijacking candidate or party websites, targeting and intimidating campaign workers or donors. There have already been multiple instances of political doxing—publishing personal information and documents about a person or organization—and we could easily see more of it in this election cycle. We need to take these risks much more seriously than before.

Government interference with foreign elections isn't new, and in fact, that's something the United States itself has repeatedly done in recent history. Using cyberattacks to influence elections is newer but has been done before, too—most notably in Latin America. Hacking of voting machines isn't new, either. But what is new is a foreign government interfering with a US national election on a large scale. Our democracy cannot tolerate it, and we as citizens cannot accept it.

Last April, the Obama administration issued an executive order outlining how we as a nation respond to cyberattacks against our critical infrastructure. While our election technology was not explicitly mentioned, our political process is certainly critical. And while they're a hodgepodge of separate state-run systems, together their security affects every one of us. After everyone has voted, it is essential that both sides believe the election was fair and the results accurate. Otherwise, the election has no legitimacy.

Election security is now a national security issue; federal officials need to take the lead, and they need to do it quickly.

Election Security

Originally published in the New York Times,
November 9, 2016

It's over. The voting went smoothly. As of the time of writing, there are no serious fraud allegations, nor credible evidence that anyone tampered with voting rolls or voting machines. And most important, the results are not in doubt.

While we may breathe a collective sigh of relief about that, we can't ignore the issue until the next election. The risks remain.

As computer security experts have been saying for years, our newly computerized voting systems are vulnerable to attack by both individual hackers and government-sponsored cyberwarriors. It is only a matter of time before such an attack happens.

Electronic voting machines can be hacked, and those machines that do not include a paper ballot that can verify each voter's choice can be hacked undetectably. Voting rolls are also vulnerable; they are all computerized databases whose entries can be deleted or changed to sow chaos on Election Day.

The largely ad hoc system in states for collecting and tabulating individual voting results is vulnerable as well. While the difference between theoretical if demonstrable vulnerabilities and an actual attack on Election Day is considerable, we got lucky this year. Not just presidential elections are at risk, but state and local elections, too.

To be very clear, this is not about voter fraud. The risks of ineligible people voting, or people voting twice, have been repeatedly shown to be virtually nonexistent, and "solutions" to this problem are largely voter-suppression measures. Election fraud, however, is both far more feasible and much more worrisome.

Here's my worry. On the day after an election, someone claims that a result was hacked. Maybe one of the candidates points to a wide discrepancy between the most recent polls and the actual results. Maybe an anonymous person announces that he hacked a particular brand of voting machine, describing in detail how. Or maybe it's a system failure during Election Day: voting machines recording significantly fewer votes than there were voters, or zero votes for one candidate or another. (These are not theoretical occurrences; they have both happened in the United States before, though because of error, not malice.)

We have no procedures for how to proceed if any of these things happen. There's no manual, no national panel of experts, no regulatory body to steer us through this crisis. How do we figure out if someone hacked the vote? Can we recover the true votes, or are they lost? What do we do then?

First, we need to do more to secure our elections system. We should declare our voting systems to be critical national infrastructure. This is largely symbolic, but it demonstrates a commitment to secure elections and makes funding and other resources available to states.

We need national security standards for voting machines, and funding for states to procure machines that comply with those standards. Voting-security experts can deal with the technical details, but such machines must include a paper ballot that provides a record verifiable by voters. The simplest and most reliable way to do that is already practiced in 37 states: optical-scan paper ballots, marked by the voters, counted by computer but recountable by hand. And we need a system of pre-election and postelection security audits to increase confidence in the system.

Second, election tampering, either by a foreign power or by a domestic actor, is inevitable, so we need detailed procedures to follow—both technical procedures to figure out what happened, and legal procedures to figure out what to do—that will efficiently get us to a fair and equitable election resolution. There should be a board of independent computer-security experts to unravel what happened, and a board of independent election officials, either at the Federal Election Commission or elsewhere, empowered to determine and put in place an appropriate response.

In the absence of such impartial measures, people rush to defend their candidate and their party. Florida in 2000 was a perfect example. What could have been a purely technical issue of determining the intent of every voter became a battle for who would win the presidency. The debates about hanging chads and spoiled ballots and how broad the recount should be were contested by people angling for a particular outcome. In the same way, after a hacked election, partisan politics will place tremendous pressure on officials to make decisions that override fairness and accuracy.

That is why we need to agree on policies to deal with future election fraud. We need procedures to evaluate claims of voting-machine hacking. We need a fair and robust vote-auditing process. And we need all of this in place before an election is hacked and battle lines are drawn.

In response to Florida, the Help America Vote Act of 2002 required each state to publish its own guidelines on what constitutes a vote. Some states—Indiana, in particular—set up a "war room" of public and private cybersecurity experts ready to help if anything did occur. While the Department of Homeland Security is assisting some states with election security, and the F.B.I. and the Justice Department made some preparations this year, the approach is too piecemeal.

Elections serve two purposes. First, and most obvious, they are how we choose a winner. But second, and equally important, they convince the loser—and all the supporters—that he or she lost. To achieve the first purpose, the voting system must be fair and accurate. To achieve the second one, it must be *shown* to be fair and accurate.

We need to have these conversations before something happens, when everyone can be calm and rational about the issues. The integrity of our elections is at stake, which means our democracy is at stake.

Hacking and the 2016 Presidential Election

Originally published in the Washington Post,
November 23, 2016

Was the 2016 presidential election hacked? It's hard to tell. There were no obvious hacks on Election Day, but new reports have raised the question of whether voting machines were tampered with in three states that Donald Trump won this month: Wisconsin, Michigan and Pennsylvania.

The researchers behind these reports include voting rights lawyer John Bonifaz and J. Alex Halderman, the director of the University of Michigan Center for Computer Security and Society, both respected in the community. They have been talking with Hillary Clinton's campaign, but their analysis is not yet public.

According to a report in New York magazine, the share of votes received by Clinton was significantly lower in precincts that used a particular type of voting machine: The magazine story suggested that Clinton had received 7 percent fewer votes in Wisconsin counties that used electronic machines, which could be hacked, than in counties that used paper ballots. That is exactly the sort of result we would expect to see if there had been some sort of voting machine hack. There are many different types of voting machines, and attacks against one type would not work against the others. So a voting anomaly correlated to machine type could be a red flag, although Trump did better across the entire Midwest than pre-election polls expected, and there are also some correlations between voting machine type and the demographics of the various precincts. Even Halderman wrote early Wednesday morning that "the most likely explanation is that the polls were systematically wrong, rather than that the election was hacked."

What the allegations, and the ripples they're causing on social media, really show is how fundamentally untrustworthy our hodge-podge election system is.

Accountability is a major problem for U.S. elections. The candidates are the ones required to petition for recounts, and we throw the matter into the courts when we can't figure it out. This all happens after an election, and because the battle lines have already been drawn, the process is intensely political. Unlike many other countries, we don't have an independent body empowered to investigate these matters. There is no government agency empowered to verify these researchers' claims, even if it would be merely to reassure voters that the election count was accurate.

Instead, we have a patchwork of voting systems: different rules, different machines, different standards. I've seen arguments that there is security in this setup—an attacker can't broadly attack the entire country—but the downsides of this system are much more critical. National standards would significantly improve our voting process.

Further investigation of the claims raised by the researchers would help settle this particular question. Unfortunately, time is of the essence—underscoring another problem with how we conduct elections. For anything to happen, Clinton has to call for a recount and investigation. She has until Friday to do it in Wisconsin, until Monday in Pennsylvania and until next Wednesday in Michigan. I don't expect the research team to have any better data before then. Without changes to the system, we're telling future hackers that they can be successful as long as they're able to hide their attacks for a few weeks until after the recount deadlines pass.

Computer forensics investigations are not easy, and they're not quick. They require access to the machines. They involve analysis of Internet traffic. If we suspect a foreign country like Russia, the National Security Agency will analyze what they've intercepted from that country. This could easily take weeks, perhaps even months. And in the end, we might not even get a definitive answer. And even if we do end up with evidence that the voting machines were hacked, we don't have rules about what to do next.

Although winning those three states would flip the election, I predict Clinton will do nothing (her campaign, after all, has reportedly been aware of the researchers' work for nearly a week). Not because she does not believe the researchers—although she might not—but because she doesn't want to throw the post-election process into turmoil by starting a highly politicized process whose eventual outcome will have little to do with computer forensics and a lot to do with which party has more power in the three states.

But we only have two years until the next national elections, and it's time to start fixing things if we don't want to be wondering the same things about hackers in 2018. The risks are real: Electronic voting machines that don't use a paper ballot are vulnerable to hacking.

Clinton supporters are seizing on this story as their last lifeline of hope. I sympathize with them. When I wrote about vote-hacking the day after the election, I said: "Elections serve two purposes. First, and most obvious, they are how we choose a winner. But second, and equally important, they convince the loser—and all the supporters—that he or she lost." If the election system fails to do the second, we risk undermining the legitimacy of our democratic process. Clinton's supporters deserve to know whether this apparent statistical anomaly is the result of a hack against our election system or a spurious correlation. They deserve an election that is demonstrably fair and accurate. Our patchwork, ad hoc system means they may never feel confident in the outcome. And that will further erode the trust we have in our election systems.

6 Privacy and Surveillance

Restoring Trust in Government and the Internet

Originally published in CNN.com, *July 31, 2013*

In July 2012, responding to allegations that the video-chat service Skype—owned by Microsoft—was changing its protocols to make it possible for the government to eavesdrop on users, Corporate Vice President Mark Gillett took to the company's blog to deny it.

Turns out that wasn't quite true.

Or at least he—or the company's lawyers—carefully crafted a statement that could be defended as true while completely deceiving the reader. You see, Skype wasn't changing its protocols to make it possible for the government to eavesdrop on users, because the government was already able to eavesdrop on users.

At a Senate hearing in March, Director of National Intelligence James Clapper assured the committee that his agency didn't collect data on hundreds of millions of Americans. He was lying, too. He later defended his lie by inventing a new definition of the word "collect," an excuse that didn't even pass the laugh test.

As Edward Snowden's documents reveal more about the NSA's activities, it's becoming clear that we can't trust anything anyone official says about these programs.

Google and Facebook insist that the NSA has no "direct access" to their servers. Of course not; the smart way for the NSA to get all the data is through sniffers.

Apple says it's never heard of PRISM. Of course not; that's the internal name of the NSA database. Companies are publishing reports purporting to show how few requests for customer-data access they've received, a meaningless number when a single Verizon request can cover all of their customers. The Guardian reported that Microsoft secretly worked with the NSA to subvert the security of Outlook, something it carefully denies. Even President Obama's justifications and denials are phrased with the intent that the listener will take his words very literally and not wonder what they really mean.

NSA Director Gen. Keith Alexander has claimed that the NSA's massive surveillance and data mining programs have helped stop more than 50 terrorist plots, 10 inside the US. Do you believe him? I think it depends on your definition of "helped." We're not told whether these programs were instrumental in foiling the plots or whether they just happened to be of minor help because the data was there. It also depends on your definition of "terrorist plots." An examination of plots that the FBI claims to have foiled since 9/11 reveals that would-be terrorists have commonly been delusional, and most have been egged on by FBI undercover agents or informants.

Left alone, few were likely to have accomplished much of anything.

Both government agencies and corporations have cloaked themselves in so much secrecy that it's impossible to verify anything they say; revelation after revelation demonstrates that they've been lying to us regularly and tell the truth only when there's no alternative.

There's much more to come. Right now, the press has published only a tiny percentage of the documents Snowden took with him. And Snowden's files are only a tiny percentage of the number of secrets our government is keeping, awaiting the next whistleblower.

Ronald Reagan once said "trust but verify." That works only if we can verify. In a world where everyone lies to us all the time, we have no choice but to trust blindly, and we have no reason to believe that anyone is worthy of blind trust. It's no wonder that most people are ignoring the story; it's just too much cognitive dissonance to try to cope with it.

This sort of thing can destroy our country. Trust is essential in our society. And if we can't trust either our government or the corporations that have intimate access into so much of our lives, society suffers. Study after study demonstrates the value of living in a high-trust society and the costs of living in a low-trust one.

Rebuilding trust is not easy, as anyone who has betrayed or been betrayed by a friend or lover knows, but the path involves transparency, oversight and accountability. Transparency first involves coming clean. Not a little bit at a time, not only when you have to, but complete disclosure about everything. Then it involves continuing disclosure. No more secret rulings by secret courts about secret laws. No more secret programs whose costs and benefits remain hidden.

Oversight involves meaningful constraints on the NSA, the FBI and others. This will be a combination of things: a court system that acts as a third-party advocate for the rule of law rather than a rubber-stamp organization, a legislature that understands what these organizations are doing and regularly debates requests for increased power, and vibrant public-sector watchdog groups that analyze and debate the government's actions.

Accountability means that those who break the law, lie to Congress or deceive the American people are held accountable. The NSA has gone rogue, and while it's probably not possible to prosecute people for what they did under the enormous veil of secrecy it currently enjoys, we need to make it clear that this behavior will not be tolerated in the future. Accountability also means voting, which means voters need to know what our leaders are doing in our name.

This is the only way we can restore trust. A market economy doesn't work unless consumers can make intelligent buying decisions based on accurate product information. That's why we have agencies like the FDA, truth-in-packaging laws and prohibitions against false advertising.

In the same way, democracy can't work unless voters know what the government is doing in their name. That's why we have open-government laws. Secret courts making secret rulings on secret laws, and companies flagrantly lying to consumers about the insecurity of their products and services, undermine the very foundations of our society.

Since the Snowden documents became public, I have been receiving emails from people seeking advice on whom to trust. As a security and privacy expert, I'm expected to know which companies protect their users' privacy and which encryption programs the NSA can't break. The truth is, I have no idea. No one outside the classified government world does. I tell people that they have no choice but to decide whom they trust and to then trust them as a matter of faith. It's a lousy answer, but until our government starts down the path of regaining our trust, it's the only thing we can do.

The NSA Is Commandeering the Internet

Originally published in TheAtlantic.com, *August 12, 2013*

It turns out that the NSA's domestic and world-wide surveillance apparatus is even more extensive than we thought. Bluntly: The government has commandeered the Internet. Most of the largest Internet companies provide information to the NSA, betraying their users. Some, as we've learned, fight and lose. Others cooperate, either out of patriotism or because they believe it's easier that way.

I have one message to the executives of those companies: fight.

Do you remember those old spy movies, when the higher ups in government decide that the mission is more important than the spy's life? It's going to be the same way with you. You might think that your friendly relationship with the government means that they're going to protect you, but they won't. The NSA doesn't care about you or your customers, and will burn you the moment it's convenient to do so.

We're already starting to see that. Google, Yahoo, Microsoft and others are pleading with the government to allow them to explain details of what information they provided in response to National Security Letters and other government demands. They've lost the trust of their customers, and explaining what they do—and don't do—is how to get it back. The government has refused; they don't care.

It will be the same with you. There are lots more high-tech companies who have cooperated with the government. Most of those company names are somewhere in the thousands of documents that Edward Snowden took with him, and sooner or later they'll be released to the public. The NSA probably told you that your cooperation would forever remain secret, but they're sloppy. They'll put your company name on presentations delivered to thousands of people: government employees, contractors, probably even foreign nationals. If Snowden doesn't have a copy, the next whistleblower will.

This is why you have to fight. When it becomes public that the NSA has been hoovering up all of your users' communications and personal files, what's going to save you in the eyes of those users is whether or not you fought. Fighting will cost you money in the short term, but capitulating will cost you more in the long term.

Already companies are taking their data and communications out of the US.

The extreme case of fighting is shutting down entirely. The secure email service Lavabit did that last week, abruptly. Ladar Levison, that site's owner, wrote on his homepage: "I have been forced to make a difficult decision: to become complicit in crimes against the American people or walk away from nearly ten years of hard work by shutting down Lavabit. After significant soul searching, I have decided to suspend operations. I wish that I could legally share with you the events that led to my decision."

The same day, Silent Circle followed suit, shutting down their email service in advance of any government strong-arm tactics: "We see the writing the wall, and we have decided that it is best for us to shut down Silent Mail now. We have not received subpoenas, warrants, security letters, or anything else by any government, and this is why we are acting now." I realize that this is extreme. Both of those companies can do it because they're small. Google or Facebook couldn't possibly shut themselves off rather than cooperate with the government. They're too large; they're public. They have to do what's economically rational, not what's moral.

But they can fight. You, an executive in one of those companies, can fight. You'll probably lose, but you need to take the stand. And you might win. It's time we called the government's actions what they really are: commandeering. Commandeering is a practice we're used to in wartime, where commercial ships are taken for military use, or production lines are converted to military production. But now it's happening in peacetime. Vast swaths of the Internet are being commandeered to support this surveillance state.

If this is happening to your company, do what you can to isolate the actions. Do you have employees with security clearances who can't tell you what they're doing? Cut off all automatic lines of communication with them, and make sure that only specific, required, authorized acts are being taken on behalf of government. Only then can you look your customers and the public in the face and say that you don't know what is going on—that your company has been commandeered.

Journalism professor Jeff Jarvis recently wrote in the *Guardian*: "Technology companies: now is the moment when you must answer for us, your users, whether you are collaborators in the US government's efforts to 'collect it all—our every move on the Internet—or whether you, too, are victims of its overreach."

So while I'm sure it's cool to have a secret White House meeting with President Obama—I'm talking to you, Google, Apple, AT&T, and whoever else was in the room—resist. Attend the meeting, but fight the secrecy. Whose side are you on?

The NSA isn't going to remain above the law forever. Already public opinion is changing, against the government and their corporate collaborators. If you want to keep your users' trust, demonstrate that you were on their side.

Conspiracy Theories and the NSA

Originally published in TheAtlantic.com, *September 4, 2013*

I've recently seen two articles speculating on the NSA's capability, and practice, of spying on members of Congress and other elected officials. The evidence is all circumstantial and smacks of conspiracy thinking—and I have no idea whether any of it is true or not—but it's a good illustration of what happens when trust in a public institution fails.

The NSA has repeatedly lied about the extent of its spying program. James R. Clapper, the director of national intelligence, has lied about it to Congress. Top-secret documents provided by Edward Snowden, and reported on by the *Guardian* and other newspapers, repeatedly show that the NSA's surveillance systems are monitoring the communications of American citizens. The DEA has used this information to apprehend drug smugglers, then lied about it in court. The IRS has used this information to find tax cheats, then lied about it. It's even been used to arrest a copyright violator. It seems that every time there is an allegation against the NSA, no matter how outlandish, it turns out to be true.

Guardian reporter Glenn Greenwald has been playing this well, dribbling the information out one scandal at a time. It's looking more and more as if the NSA doesn't know what Snowden took. It's hard for someone to lie convincingly if he doesn't know what the opposition actually knows.

All of this denying and lying results in us not trusting anything the NSA says, anything the president says about the NSA, or anything companies say about their involvement with the NSA. We know secrecy corrupts, and we see that corruption. There's simply no credibility, and—the real problem—no way for us to verify anything these people might say.

It's a perfect environment for conspiracy theories to take root: no trust, assuming the worst, no way to verify the facts. Think JFK assassination theories. Think 9/11 conspiracies. Think UFOs. For all we know, the NSA *might* be spying on elected officials. Edward Snowden said that he had the ability to spy on anyone in the US, in real time, from his desk. His remarks were belittled, but it turns out he was right.

This is not going to improve anytime soon. Greenwald and other reporters are still poring over Snowden's documents, and will continue to report stories about NSA overreach, lawbreaking, abuses, and privacy violations well into next year. The "independent" review that Obama promised of these surveillance programs will not help, because it will lack both the power to discover everything the NSA is doing and the ability to relay that information to the public.

It's time to start cleaning up this mess. We need a special prosecutor, one not tied to the military, the corporations complicit in these programs, or the current political leadership, whether Democrat or Republican. This prosecutor needs free rein to go through the NSA's files and discover the full extent of what the agency is doing, as well as enough technical staff who have the capability to understand it. He needs the power to subpoena government officials and take their sworn testimony. He needs the ability to bring criminal indictments where appropriate. And, of course, he needs the requisite security clearance to see it all.

We also need something like South Africa's Truth and Reconciliation Commission, where both government and corporate employees can come forward and tell their stories about NSA eavesdropping without fear of reprisal.

Yes, this will overturn the paradigm of keeping everything the NSA does secret, but Snowden and the reporters he's shared documents with have already done that. The secrets are going to come out, and the journalists doing the outing are not going to be sympathetic to the NSA. If the agency were smart, it'd realize that the best thing it could do would be to get ahead of the leaks.

The result needs to be a public report about the NSA's abuses, detailed enough that public watchdog groups can be convinced that everything is known. Only then can our country go about cleaning up the mess: shutting down programs, reforming the Foreign Intelligence Surveillance Act system, and reforming surveillance law to make it absolutely clear that even the NSA cannot eavesdrop on Americans without a warrant.

Comparisons are springing up between today's NSA and the FBI of the 1950s and 1960s, and between NSA Director Keith Alexander and J. Edgar Hoover. We never managed to rein in Hoover's FBI—it took his death for change to occur. I don't think we'll get so lucky with the NSA. While Alexander has enormous personal power, much of his power comes from the institution he leads. When he is replaced, that institution will remain.

Trust is essential for society to function. Without it, conspiracy theories naturally take hold. Even worse, without it we fail as a country and as a culture. It's time to reinstitute the ideals of democracy: The government works for the people, open government is the best way to protect against government abuse, and a government keeping secrets from its people is a rare exception, not the norm.

How to Remain Secure against the NSA

Originally published in the Guardian, *September 6, 2013*

Now that we have enough details about how the NSA eavesdrops on the Internet, including today's disclosures of the NSA's deliberate weakening of cryptographic systems, we can finally start to figure out how to protect ourselves.

For the past two weeks, I have been working with the Guardian on NSA stories, and have read hundreds of top-secret NSA documents provided by whistleblower Edward Snowden. I wasn't part of today's story—it was in process well before I showed up—but everything I read confirms what the Guardian is reporting.

At this point, I feel I can provide some advice for keeping secure against such an adversary.

The primary way the NSA eavesdrops on Internet communications is in the network. That's where their capabilities best scale. They have invested in enormous programs to automatically collect and analyze network traffic. Anything that requires them to attack individual end-point computers is significantly more costly and risky for them, and they will do those things carefully and sparingly.

Leveraging its secret agreements with telecommunications companies—all the US and UK ones, and many other "partners" around the world—the NSA gets access to the communications trunks that move Internet traffic. In cases where it doesn't have that sort of friendly access, it does its best to surreptitiously monitor communications channels: tapping undersea cables, intercepting satellite communications, and so on.

That's an enormous amount of data, and the NSA has equivalently enormous capabilities to quickly sift through it all, looking for interesting traffic. "Interesting" can be defined in many ways: by the source, the destination, the content, the individuals involved, and so on. This data is funneled into the vast NSA system for future analysis.

The NSA collects much more metadata about Internet traffic: who is talking to whom, when, how much, and by what mode of communication. Metadata is a lot easier to store and analyze than content. It can be extremely personal to the individual, and is enormously valuable intelligence.

The Systems Intelligence Directorate is in charge of data collection, and the resources it devotes to this is staggering. I read status report after status report about these programs, discussing capabilities, operational details, planned upgrades, and so on. Each individual problem—recovering electronic signals from fiber, keeping up with the terabyte streams as they go by, filtering out the interesting stuff—has its own group dedicated to solving it. Its reach is global.

The NSA also attacks network devices directly: routers, switches, firewalls, etc. Most of these devices have surveillance capabilities already built in; the trick is to surreptitiously turn them on. This is an especially fruitful avenue of attack; routers are updated less frequently, tend not to have security software installed on them, and are generally ignored as a vulnerability.

The NSA also devotes considerable resources to attacking endpoint computers. This kind of thing is done by its TAO—Tailored Access Operations—group. TAO has a menu of exploits it can serve up against your computer—whether you're running Windows, Mac OS, Linux, iOS, or something else—and a variety of tricks to get them on to your computer. Your anti-virus software won't detect them, and you'd have trouble finding them even if you knew where to look. These are hacker tools designed by hackers with an essentially unlimited budget. What I took away from reading the Snowden documents was that if the NSA wants in to your computer, it's in. Period.

The NSA deals with any encrypted data it encounters more by subverting the underlying cryptography than by leveraging any secret mathematical breakthroughs. First, there's a lot of bad cryptography out there. If it finds an Internet connection protected by MS-CHAP, for example, that's easy to break and recover the key. It exploits poorly chosen user passwords, using the same dictionary attacks hackers use in the unclassified world.

As was revealed today, the NSA also works with security product vendors to ensure that commercial encryption products are broken in secret ways that only it knows about. We know this has happened historically: CryptoAG and Lotus Notes are the most public examples, and there is evidence of a back door in Windows. A few people have told me some recent stories about their experiences, and I plan to write about them soon. Basically, the NSA asks companies to subtly change their products in undetectable ways: making the random number generator less random, leaking the key somehow, adding a common exponent to a public-key exchange protocol, and so on. If the back door is discovered, it's explained away as a mistake. And as we now know, the NSA has enjoyed enormous success from this program.

TAO also hacks into computers to recover long-term keys. So if you're running a VPN that uses a complex shared secret to protect your data and the NSA decides it cares, it might try to steal that secret. This kind of thing is only done against high-value targets.

How do you communicate securely against such an adversary? Snowden said it in an online Q&A soon after he made his first document public: "Encryption works. Properly implemented strong crypto systems are one of the few things that you can rely on."

I believe this is true, despite today's revelations and tantalizing hints of "groundbreaking cryptanalytic capabilities" made by James Clapper, the director of national intelligence in another top-secret document. Those capabilities involve deliberately weakening the cryptography.

Snowden's follow-on sentence is equally important: "Unfortunately, endpoint security is so terrifically weak that NSA can frequently find ways around it."

Endpoint means the software you're using, the computer you're using it on, and the local network you're using it in. If the NSA can modify the encryption algorithm or drop a Trojan on your computer, all the cryptography in the world doesn't matter at all. If you want to remain secure against the NSA, you need to do your best to ensure that the encryption can operate unimpeded.

With all this in mind, I have five pieces of advice:

1. **Hide in the network**. Implement hidden services. Use Tor to anonymize yourself. Yes, the NSA targets Tor users, but it's work for them. The less obvious you are, the safer you are.

2. **Encrypt your communications**. Use TLS. Use IPsec. Again, while it's true that the NSA targets encrypted connections—and it may have explicit exploits against these protocols—you're much better protected than if you communicate in the clear.

3. **Assume that while your computer can be compromised, it would take work and risk on the part of the NSA—so it probably isn't**. If you have something really important, use an air gap. Since I started working with the Snowden documents, I bought a new computer that has *never* been connected to the Internet. If I want to transfer a file, I encrypt the file on the secure computer and walk it over to my Internet computer, using a USB stick. To decrypt something, I reverse the process. This might not be bulletproof, but it's pretty good.

4. **Be suspicious of commercial encryption software, especially from large vendors**. My guess is that most encryption products from large US companies have NSA-friendly back doors, and many foreign ones probably do as well. It's prudent to assume that foreign products also have foreign-installed backdoors.

Closed-source software is easier for the NSA to backdoor than open-source software. Systems relying on master secrets are vulnerable to the NSA, through either legal or more clandestine means.

5. **Try to use public-domain encryption that has to be compatible with other implementations**. For example, it's harder for the NSA to backdoor TLS than BitLocker, because any vendor's TLS has to be compatible with every other vendor's TLS, while BitLocker only has to be compatible with itself, giving the NSA a lot more freedom to make changes. And because BitLocker is proprietary, it's far less likely those changes will be discovered. Prefer symmetric cryptography over public-key cryptography. Prefer conventional discrete-log-based systems over elliptic-curve systems; the latter have constants that the NSA influences when they can.

Since I started working with Snowden's documents, I have been using GPG, Silent Circle, Tails, OTR, TrueCrypt, BleachBit, and a few other things I'm not going to write about. There's an undocumented encryption feature in my Password Safe program from the command line; I've been using that as well.

I understand that most of this is impossible for the typical Internet user. Even I don't use all these tools for most everything I am working on. And I'm still primarily on Windows, unfortunately. Linux would be safer.

The NSA has turned the fabric of the Internet into a vast surveillance platform, but they are not magical. They're limited by the same economic realities as the rest of us, and our best defense is to make surveillance of us as expensive as possible.

Trust the math. Encryption is your friend. Use it well, and do your best to ensure that nothing can compromise it. That's how you can remain secure even in the face of the NSA.

Air Gaps

Originally published in Wired.com, *October 7, 2013*

Since I started working with Snowden's documents, I have been using a number of tools to try to stay secure from the NSA. The advice I shared included using Tor, preferring certain cryptography over others, and using public-domain encryption wherever possible.

I also recommended using an air gap, which physically isolates a computer or local network of computers from the Internet. (The name comes from the literal gap of air between the computer and the Internet; the word predates wireless networks.)

But this is more complicated than it sounds, and requires explanation.

Since we know that computers connected to the Internet are vulnerable to outside hacking, an air gap should protect against those attacks. There are a lot of systems that use—or should use—air gaps: classified military networks, nuclear power plant controls, medical equipment, avionics, and so on.

Osama Bin Laden used one. I hope human rights organizations in repressive countries are doing the same.

Air gaps might be conceptually simple, but they're hard to maintain in practice. The truth is that nobody wants a computer that never receives files from the Internet and never sends files out into the Internet. What they want is a computer that's not directly connected to the Internet, albeit with some secure way of moving files on and off.

But every time a file moves back or forth, there's the potential for attack.

And air gaps *have* been breached. Stuxnet was a US and Israeli military-grade piece of malware that attacked the Natanz nuclear plant in Iran. It successfully jumped the air gap and penetrated the Natanz network. Another piece of malware named agent.btz, probably Chinese in origin, successfully jumped the air gap protecting US military networks.

These attacks work by exploiting security vulnerabilities in the removable media used to transfer files on and off the air-gapped computers.

Since working with Snowden's NSA files, I have tried to maintain a single air-gapped computer. It turned out to be harder than I expected, and I have ten rules for anyone trying to do the same:

1. When you set up your computer, connect it to the Internet as little as possible. It's impossible to completely avoid connecting the computer to the Internet, but try to configure it all at once and as anonymously as possible. I purchased my computer off-the-shelf in a big box store, then went to a friend's network and downloaded everything I needed in a single session. (The ultra-paranoid way to do this is to buy two identical computers, configure one using

the above method, upload the results to a cloud-based anti-virus checker, and transfer the results of *that* to the air gap machine using a one-way process.)

2. Install the minimum software set you need to do your job, and disable all operating system services that you won't need. The less software you install, the less an attacker has available to exploit. I downloaded and installed OpenOffice, a PDF reader, a text editor, TrueCrypt, and BleachBit. That's all. (No, I don't have any inside knowledge about TrueCrypt, and there's a lot about it that makes me suspicious. But for Windows full-disk encryption it's that, Microsoft's BitLocker, or Symantec's PGPDisk—and I am more worried about large US corporations being pressured by the NSA than I am about TrueCrypt.)

3. Once you have your computer configured, never directly connect it to the Internet again. Consider physically disabling the wireless capability so it doesn't get turned on by accident.

4. If you need to install new software, download it anonymously from a random network, put it on some removable media, and then manually transfer it to the air-gapped computer. This is by no means perfect, but it's an attempt to make it harder for the attacker to target your computer.

5. Turn off all autorun features. This should be standard practice for all the computers you own, but it's especially important for an air-gapped computer. Agent.btz used autorun to infect US military computers.

6. Minimize the amount of executable code you move onto the air-gapped computer. Text files are best. Microsoft Office files and PDFs are more dangerous, since they might have embedded macros. Turn off all macro capabilities you can on the air-gapped computer. Don't worry too much about patching your system; in general, the risk of the executable code is worse than the risk of not having your patches up to date. You're not on the Internet, after all.

7. Only use trusted media to move files on and off air-gapped computers. A USB stick you purchase from a store is safer than one given to you by someone you don't know—or one you find in a parking lot.

8. For file transfer, a writable optical disk (CD or DVD) is safer than a USB stick. Malware can silently write data to a USB stick, but it

can't spin the CD-R up to 1000 rpm without your noticing. This means that the malware can only write to the disk when you write to the disk. You can also verify how much data has been written to the CD by physically checking the back of it. If you've only written one file but it looks like three-quarters of the CD was burned, you have a problem. Note: the first company to market a USB stick with a light that indicates a write operation—not read *or* write; I've got one of those—wins a prize.

9. When moving files on and off your air-gapped computer, use the absolute smallest storage device you can. And fill up the entire device with random files. If an air-gapped computer is compromised, the malware is going to try to sneak data off it using that media. While malware can easily hide stolen files from you, it can't break the laws of physics. So if you use a tiny transfer device, it can only steal a very small amount of data at a time. If you use a large device, it can take that much more. Business-card-sized mini-CDs can have capacity as low as 30 MB. I still see 1-GB USB sticks for sale.

10. Consider encrypting everything you move on and off the air-gapped computer. Sometimes you'll be moving public files and it won't matter, but sometimes you won't be, and it will. And if you're using optical media, those disks will be impossible to erase. Strong encryption solves these problems. And don't forget to encrypt the computer as well; whole-disk encryption is the best.

One thing I didn't do, although it's worth considering, is use a stateless operating system like Tails. You can configure Tails with a persistent volume to save your data, but no operating system changes are ever saved. Booting Tails from a read-only DVD—you can keep your data on an encrypted USB stick—is even more secure. Of course, this is not foolproof, but it greatly reduces the potential avenues for attack.

Yes, all this is advice for the paranoid. And it's probably impossible to enforce for any network more complicated than a single computer with a single user. But if you're thinking about setting up an air-gapped computer, you already believe that some very powerful attackers are after you personally. If you're going to use an air gap, use it properly.

Of course you can take things further. I have met people who have physically removed the camera, microphone, and wireless capability altogether. But that's too much paranoia for me right now.

Why the NSA's Defense of Mass Data Collection Makes No Sense

Originally published in the Atlantic, *October 21, 2013*

The basic government defense of the NSA's bulk-collection programs— whether it be the list of all the telephone calls you made, your email address book and IM buddy list, or the messages you send your friends—is that what the agency is doing is perfectly legal, and doesn't really count as surveillance, until a human being looks at the data.

It's what Director of National Intelligence James R. Clapper meant when he lied to Congress. When asked, "Does the NSA collect any type of data at all on millions or hundreds of millions of Americans?" he replied, "No sir, not wittingly." To him, the definition of "collect" requires that a human look at it. So when the NSA collects—using the dictionary definition of the word—data on hundreds of millions of Americans, it's not *really* collecting it, because only computers process it.

The NSA maintains that we shouldn't worry about human processing, either, because it has rules about accessing all that data. General Keith Alexander, director of the NSA, said that in a recent *New York Times* interview: "The agency is under rules preventing it from investigating that so-called haystack of data unless it has a 'reasonable, articulable' justification, involving communications with terrorists abroad, he added."

There are lots of things wrong with this defense.

First, it doesn't match up with U.S. law. Wiretapping is legally defined as acquisition by device, with no requirement that a human look at it. This has been the case since 1968, amended in 1986.

Second, it's unconstitutional. The Fourth Amendment prohibits general warrants: warrants that don't describe "the place to be searched, and the persons or things to be seized." The sort of indiscriminate search and seizure the NSA is conducting is exactly the sort of general warrant that the Constitution forbids, in addition to it being a search by any reasonable definition of the term. The NSA has tried to secretly redefine the word "search," but it's forgotten about the seizure part. When it collects data on all of us, it's seizing it.

Third, this assertion leads to absurd conclusions. Mandatory cameras in bedrooms could become okay, as long as there were rules governing when the government could look at the recordings. Being required to wear a police-issued listening device 24/7 could become okay, as long as those same rules were in place. If you're uncomfortable with these notions, it's because you realize that data collection matters, regardless of whether someone looks at it.

Fourth, creating such an attractive target is reckless. The NSA claims to be one of the biggest victims of foreign hacking attempts, and it's holding all of this information on us? Yes, the NSA is good at security, but it's ridiculous to assume it can survive all attacks by foreign governments, criminals, and hackers—especially when a single insider was able to walk out of the door with pretty much all their secrets.

Finally, and most importantly: Even if you are not bothered by the speciousness of the legal justifications, or you are already desensitized to government invasion of your privacy, there is a danger grounded in everything we have learned about how humans respond when put in positions of unchecked power. Assuming the NSA follows its own rules—which even it admits it doesn't always—rules can change quickly. The NSA says it only looks at such data when investigating terrorism, but the definition of that term has broadened considerably. The NSA is constantly pushing the law to allow more and more surveillance. Even Representative Jim Sensenbrenner, the author of the Patriot Act, says that it doesn't allow what the NSA claims it allows.

A massive trove of surveillance data on everyone is incredibly tempting for all parts of government to use. Once we have everyone's data, it'll be hard to prevent it from being used to solve conventional crimes and for all sorts of things. It's a totalitarian government's wet dream.

The NSA's claim that it only looks when it's investigating terrorism is already false. We already know the NSA passes data to the DEA and IRS with instructions to lie about its origins in court—"parallel construction" is the term being used. What else is done with that data? What else *could* be?

It doesn't make sense to build systems that could facilitate a future police state.

This sort of surveillance isn't new. We even have a word for it: It's the Panopticon. The Panopticon was a prison design created by 18th-century philosopher Jeremy Bentham, and has been a metaphor for a surveillance state ever since. The basic idea is that prisoners live under the constant threat of surveillance. It's not that they are watched all the time—it's that they never know when they're being watched. It's the basis of Orwell's *1984* dystopia: Winston Smith never knew if he was being watched, but always knew it was a possibility. It's why online surveillance works so well in China to deter behavior; no one knows if and when it will detect their actions online.

Panopticon-like surveillance—intermittent, but always possible—changes human behavior. It makes us more compliant, less individual. It reduces liberty and freedom. Philosopher Michael P. Lynch recently wrote about how it dehumanizes us: "when we lose the very capacity to have privileged access to our psychological information—the capacity for self-knowledge, so to speak, we literally lose our selves.... To the extent we risk the loss of privacy we risk, in a very real sense, the loss of our very status as subjective, autonomous persons."

George Dyson recently wrote that a system that "is granted (or assumes) the absolute power to protect itself against dangerous ideas will of necessity also be defensive against original and creative thoughts." That's what living in a Panopticon gets you.

Already, many of us avoid using "dangerous" words and phrases online, even innocuously. Or making nervous jokes about it when we do.

By ceding the NSA the ability to conduct ubiquitous surveillance on everybody, we cede to it an enormous amount of control over our own lives. Once the NSA takes a copy of your data, you no longer control it. You can't delete it. You can't change it. You might not even know when the rules under which it uses your data change. And until Edward Snowden leaked documents that show what the NSA is doing, you didn't even know that the government had taken it.

What else don't we know that the NSA has or does?

Defending Against Crypto Backdoors ━━━

Originally published in Wired.com, *October 16, 2013*

We already know the NSA wants to eavesdrop on the Internet. It has secret agreements with telcos to get direct access to bulk Internet traffic. It has massive systems like TUMULT, TURMOIL, and TURBULENCE to sift through it all. And it can identify ciphertext—encrypted information—and figure out which programs could have created it.

But what the NSA wants is to be able to read that encrypted information in as close to real-time as possible. It wants backdoors, just like the cybercriminals and less benevolent governments do.

And we have to figure out how to make it harder for them, or anyone else, to insert those backdoors.

How the NSA Gets Its Backdoors

The FBI tried to get backdoor access embedded in an AT&T secure telephone system in the mid-1990s. The Clipper Chip included something called a LEAF: a Law Enforcement Access Field. It was the key used to encrypt the phone conversation, itself encrypted in a special key known to the FBI, and it was transmitted along with the phone conversation. An FBI eavesdropper could intercept the LEAF and decrypt it, then use the data to eavesdrop on the phone call.

But the Clipper Chip faced severe backlash, and became defunct a few years after being announced.

Having lost that public battle, the NSA decided to get its backdoors through subterfuge: by asking nicely, pressuring, threatening, bribing, or mandating through secret order. The general name for this program is BULLRUN.

Defending against these attacks is difficult. We know from subliminal channel and kleptography research that it's pretty much impossible to guarantee that a complex piece of software isn't leaking secret information. We know from Ken Thompson's famous talk on "trusting trust" (first delivered in the ACM Turing Award Lectures) that you can never be totally sure if there's a security flaw in your software.

Since BULLRUN became public last month, the security community has been examining security flaws discovered over the past several years, looking for signs of deliberate tampering. The Debian random number flaw was probably not deliberate, but the 2003 Linux security vulnerability probably was. The DUAL_EC_DRBG random number generator may or may not have been a backdoor. The SSL 2.0 flaw was probably an honest mistake. The GSM A5/1 encryption algorithm was almost certainly deliberately weakened. All the common RSA moduli out there in the wild: we don't know. Microsoft's _NSAKEY looks like a smoking gun, but honestly, we don't know.

How the NSA Designs Backdoors

While a separate program that sends our data to some IP address somewhere is certainly how any hacker—from the lowliest script kiddie up to the NSA—spies on our computers, it's too labor-intensive to work in the general case.

For government eavesdroppers like the NSA, subtlety is critical. In particular, three characteristics are important:

- *Low discoverability.* The less the backdoor affects the normal operations of the program, the better. Ideally, it shouldn't affect functionality at all. The smaller the backdoor is, the better. Ideally, it should just look like normal functional code. As a blatant example, an email encryption backdoor that appends a plaintext copy to the encrypted copy is much less desirable than a backdoor that reuses most of the key bits in a public IV (initialization vector).
- *High deniability.* If discovered, the backdoor should look like a mistake. It could be a single opcode change. Or maybe a "mistyped" constant. Or "accidentally" reusing a single-use key multiple times. This is the main reason I am skeptical about _NSAKEY as a deliberate backdoor, and why so many people don't believe the DUAL_EC_DRBG backdoor is real: they're both too obvious.
- *Minimal conspiracy.* The more people who know about the backdoor, the more likely the secret is to get out. So any good backdoor should be known to very few people. That's why the recently described potential vulnerability in Intel's random

number generator worries me so much; one person could make this change during mask generation, and no one else would know.

These characteristics imply several things:

- A closed-source system is safer to subvert, because an open-source system comes with a greater risk of that subversion being discovered. On the other hand, a big open-source system with a lot of developers and sloppy version control is easier to subvert.
- If a software system only has to interoperate with itself, then it is easier to subvert. For example, a closed VPN encryption system only has to interoperate with other instances of that same proprietary system. This is easier to subvert than an industry-wide VPN standard that has to interoperate with equipment from other vendors.
- A commercial software system is easier to subvert, because the profit motive provides a strong incentive for the company to go along with the NSA's requests.
- Protocols developed by large open standards bodies are harder to influence, because a lot of eyes are paying attention. Systems designed by closed standards bodies are easier to influence, especially if the people involved in the standards don't really understand security.
- Systems that send seemingly random information in the clear are easier to subvert. One of the most effective ways of subverting a system is by leaking key information—recall the LEAF—and modifying random nonces or header information is the easiest way to do that.

Design Strategies for Defending against Backdoors

With these principles in mind, we can list design strategies. None of them is foolproof, but they are all useful. I'm sure there's more; this list isn't meant to be exhaustive, nor the final word on the topic. It's simply a starting place for discussion. But it won't work unless customers start demanding software with this sort of transparency.

- *Vendors should make their encryption code public*, including the protocol specifications. This will allow others to examine the code for vulnerabilities. It's true we won't know for sure if the code we're seeing is the code that's actually used in the application, but surreptitious substitution is hard to do, forces the company to outright lie, and increases the number of people required for the conspiracy to work.

- *The community should create independent compatible versions* of encryption systems, to verify they are operating properly. I envision companies paying for these independent versions, and universities accepting this sort of work as good practice for their students. And yes, I know this can be very hard in practice.

- *There should be no master secrets.* These are just too vulnerable.

- *All random number generators should conform to published and accepted standards.* Breaking the random number generator is the easiest difficult-to-detect method of subverting an encryption system. A corollary: we need better published and accepted RNG standards.

- *Encryption protocols* should be designed so as not to leak any random information. Nonces should be considered part of the key or public predictable counters if possible. Again, the goal is to make it harder to subtly leak key bits in this information.

This is a hard problem. We don't have any technical controls that protect users from the authors of their software.

And the current state of software makes the problem even harder: Modern apps chatter endlessly on the Internet, providing noise and cover for covert communications. Feature bloat provides a greater "attack surface" for anyone wanting to install a backdoor.

In general, what we need is assurance: methodologies for ensuring that a piece of software does what it's supposed to do and nothing more. Unfortunately, we're terrible at this. Even worse, there's not a lot of practical research in this area—and it's hurting us badly right now.

Yes, we need legal prohibitions against the NSA trying to subvert authors and deliberately weaken cryptography. But this isn't just about the NSA, and legal controls won't protect against those who don't follow the law and ignore international agreements. We need to make their job harder by increasing their risk of discovery. Against a risk-averse adversary, it might be good enough.

A Fraying of the Public/Private Surveillance Partnership

Originally published in TheAtlantic.com, *November 8, 2013*

The public/private surveillance partnership between the NSA and corporate data collectors is starting to fray. The reason is sunlight. The publicity resulting from the Snowden documents has made companies think twice before allowing the NSA access to their users' and customers' data.

Pre-Snowden, there was no downside to cooperating with the NSA. If the NSA asked you for copies of all your Internet traffic, or to put backdoors into your security software, you could assume that your cooperation would forever remain secret. To be fair, not every corporation cooperated willingly. Some fought in court. But it seems that a lot of them, telcos and backbone providers especially, were happy to give the NSA unfettered access to everything. Post-Snowden, this is changing. Now that many companies' cooperation has become public, they're facing a PR backlash from customers and users who are upset that their data is flowing to the NSA. And this is costing those companies business.

How much is unclear. In July, right after the PRISM revelations, the Cloud Security Alliance reported that US cloud companies could lose $35 billion over the next three years, mostly due to losses of foreign sales. Surely that number has increased as outrage over NSA spying continues to build in Europe and elsewhere. There is no similar report for software sales, although I have attended private meetings where several large US software companies complained about the loss of foreign sales. On the hardware side, IBM is losing business in China. The US telecom companies are also suffering: AT&T is losing business worldwide.

This is the new reality. The rules of secrecy are different, and companies have to assume that their responses to NSA data demands will become public. This means there is now a significant cost to cooperating, and a corresponding benefit to fighting.

Over the past few months, more companies have woken up to the fact that the NSA is basically treating them as adversaries, and are responding as such. In mid-October, it became public that the NSA was collecting email address books and buddy lists from Internet users logging into different service providers. Yahoo, which didn't encrypt those user connections by default, allowed the NSA to collect much more of its data than Google, which did. That same day, Yahoo announced that it would implement SSL encryption by default for all of its users. Two weeks later, when it became public that the NSA was collecting data on Google users by eavesdropping on the company's trunk connections between its data centers, Google announced that it would encrypt those connections.

We recently learned that Yahoo fought a government order to turn over data. Lavabit fought its order as well. Apple is now tweaking the government. And we think better of those companies because of it.

Now Lavabit, which closed down its email service rather than comply with the NSA's request for the master keys that would compromise all of its customers, has teamed with Silent Circle to develop a secure email standard that is resistant to these kinds of tactics.

The Snowden documents made it clear how much the NSA relies on corporations to eavesdrop on the Internet. The NSA didn't build a massive Internet eavesdropping system from scratch. It noticed that the corporate world was already eavesdropping on every Internet user—surveillance is the business model of the Internet, after all—and simply got copies for itself.

Now, that secret ecosystem is breaking down. Supreme Court Justice Louis Brandeis wrote about transparency, saying "Sunlight is said to be the best of disinfectants." In this case, it seems to be working.

These developments will only help security. Remember that while Edward Snowden has given us a window into the NSA's activities, these sorts of tactics are probably also used by other intelligence services around the world. And today's secret NSA programs become tomorrow's PhD theses, and the next day's criminal hacker tools. It's impossible to build an Internet where the good guys can eavesdrop and the bad guys cannot. We have a choice between an Internet that is vulnerable to all attackers or an Internet that is safe from all attackers. And a safe and secure Internet is in everyone's best interests, including the US's.

Surveillance as a Business Model

Originally published in CNN.com, *November 20, 2013*

Google recently announced that it would start including individual users' names and photos in some ads. This means that if you rate some product positively, your friends may see ads for that product with your name and photo attached—without your knowledge or consent. Meanwhile, Facebook is eliminating a feature that allowed people to retain some portions of their anonymity on its website.

These changes come on the heels of Google's move to explore replacing tracking cookies with something that users have even less control over. Microsoft is doing something similar by developing its own tracking technology.

More generally, lots of companies are evading the "Do Not Track" rules, meant to give users a say in whether companies track them. Turns out the whole "Do Not Track" legislation has been a sham.

It shouldn't come as a surprise that big technology companies are tracking us on the Internet even more aggressively than before.

If these features don't sound particularly beneficial to you, it's because you're not the customer of any of these companies. You're the product, and you're being improved for their actual customers: their advertisers.

This is nothing new. For years, these sites and others have systematically improved their "product" by reducing user privacy. This excellent infographic, for example, illustrates how Facebook has done so over the years.

The "Do Not Track" law serves as a sterling example of how bad things are. When it was proposed, it was supposed to give users the right to demand that Internet companies not track them. Internet companies fought hard against the law, and when it was passed, they fought to ensure that it didn't have any benefit to users. Right now, complying is entirely voluntary, meaning that no Internet company has to follow the law. If a company does, because it wants the PR benefit of seeming to take user privacy seriously, it can still track its users.

Really: if you tell a "Do Not Track"–enabled company that you don't want to be tracked, it will stop showing you personalized ads. But your activity will be tracked—and your personal information collected, sold and used—just like everyone else's. It's best to think of it as a "track me in secret" law.

Of course, people don't think of it that way. Most people aren't fully aware of how much of their data is collected by these sites. And, as the "Do Not Track" story illustrates, Internet companies are doing their best to keep it that way.

The result is a world where our most intimate personal details are collected and stored. I used to say that Google has a more intimate picture of what I'm thinking of than my wife does. But that's not far enough: Google has a more intimate picture than I do. The company knows exactly what I am thinking about, how much I am thinking about it, and when I stop thinking about it: all from my Google searches. And it remembers all of that forever.

As the Edward Snowden revelations continue to expose the full extent of the National Security Agency's eavesdropping on the Internet, it has become increasingly obvious how much of that has been enabled by the corporate world's existing eavesdropping on the Internet.

The public/private surveillance partnership is fraying, but it's largely alive and well. The NSA didn't build its eavesdropping system from scratch; it got itself a copy of what the corporate world was already collecting.

There are a lot of reasons why Internet surveillance is so prevalent and pervasive.

One, users like free things, and don't realize how much value they're giving away to get it. We know that "free" is a special price that confuses peoples' thinking.

Google's 2013 third quarter profits were nearly $3 billion; that profit is the difference between how much our privacy is worth and the cost of the services we receive in exchange for it.

Two, Internet companies deliberately make privacy not salient. When you log onto Facebook, you don't think about how much personal information you're revealing to the company; you're chatting with your friends. When you wake up in the morning, you don't think about how you're going to allow a bunch of companies to track you throughout the day; you just put your cell phone in your pocket.

And three, the Internet's winner-takes-all market means that privacy-preserving alternatives have trouble getting off the ground. How many of you know that there is a Google alternative called Duck-DuckGo that doesn't track you? Or that you can use cut-out sites to anonymize your Google queries? I have opted out of Facebook, and I know it affects my social life.

There are two types of changes that need to happen in order to fix this. First, there's the market change. We need to become actual customers of these sites so we can use purchasing power to force them to take our privacy seriously. But that's not enough. Because of the market failures surrounding privacy, a second change is needed. We need government regulations that protect our privacy by limiting what these sites can do with our data.

Surveillance is the business model of the Internet—Al Gore recently called it a "stalker economy." All major websites run on advertising, and the more personal and targeted that advertising is, the more revenue the site gets for it. As long as we users remain the product, there is minimal incentive for these companies to provide any real privacy.

Finding People's Locations Based on Their Activities in Cyberspace

Originally published in TheAtlantic.com, *February 11, 2014*

Glenn Greenwald is back reporting about the NSA, now with Pierre Omidyar's news organization FirstLook and its introductory publication, the *Intercept*. Writing with national security reporter Jeremy Scahill, his first article covers how the NSA helps target individuals for assassination by drone.

Leaving aside the extensive political implications of the story, the article and the NSA source documents reveal additional information about how the agency's programs work. From this and other articles, we can now piece together how the NSA tracks individuals in the real world through their actions in cyberspace.

Its techniques to locate someone based on their electronic activities are straightforward, although they require an enormous capability to monitor data networks. One set of techniques involves the cell phone network, and the other the Internet.

Tracking Locations with Cell Towers

Every cell-phone network knows the approximate location of all phones capable of receiving calls. This is necessary to make the system work; if the system doesn't know what cell you're in, it isn't able to route calls to your phone. We already know that the NSA conducts physical surveillance on a massive scale using this technique.

By triangulating location information from different cell phone towers, cell phone providers can geolocate phones more accurately. This is often done to direct emergency services to a particular person, such as someone who has made a 911 call. The NSA can get this data either by network eavesdropping with the cooperation of the carrier or by intercepting communications between the cell phones and the towers. A previously released Top Secret NSA document says this: "GSM Cell Towers can be used as a physical-geolocation point in relation to a GSM handset of interest."

This technique becomes even more powerful if you can employ a drone. Greenwald and Scahill write:

> The agency also equips drones and other aircraft with devices known as "virtual base-tower transceivers"—creating, in effect, a fake cell phone tower that can force a targeted person's device to lock onto the NSA's receiver without their knowledge.

The drone can do this multiple times as it flies around the area, measuring the signal strength—and inferring distance—each time. Again from the *Intercept* article:

> The NSA geolocation system used by JSOC is known by the code name GILGAMESH. Under the program, a specially constructed device is attached to the drone. As the drone circles, the device locates the SIM card or handset that the military believes is used by the target.

The Top Secret source document associated with the *Intercept* story says:

> As part of the GILGAMESH (PREDATOR-based active geo-location) effort, this team used some advanced mathematics to develop a new geolocation algorithm intended for operational use on unmanned aerial vehicle (UAV) flights.

This is at least part of that advanced mathematics.

None of this works if the target turns his phone off or exchanges SMS cards often with his colleagues, which Greenwald and Scahill write is routine. It won't work in much of Yemen, which isn't on any cell phone network. Because of this, the NSA also tracks people based on their actions on the Internet.

Finding You from Your Web Connection

A surprisingly large number of Internet applications leak location data. Applications on your smart phone can transmit location data from your GPS receiver over the Internet. We already know that the NSA collects this data to determine location. Also, many applications transmit the IP address of the network the computer is connected to. If the NSA has a database of IP addresses and locations, it can use that to locate users.

According to a previously released Top Secret NSA document, that program is code named HAPPYFOOT: "The HAPPYFOOT analytic aggregated leaked location-based service / location-aware application data to infer IP geo-locations."

Another way to get this data is to collect it from the geographical area you're interested in. Greenwald and Scahill talk about exactly this:

> In addition to the GILGAMESH system used by
> JSOC, the CIA uses a similar NSA platform known as
> SHENANIGANS. The operation—previously undisclosed—
> utilizes a pod on aircraft that vacuums up massive amounts
> of data from any wireless routers, computers, smart phones
> or other electronic devices that are within range.

And again from an NSA document associated with the FirstLook story: "Our mission (VICTORYDANCE) mapped the Wi-Fi fingerprint of nearly every major town in Yemen." In the hacker world, this is known as war-driving, and has even been demonstrated from drones.

Another story from the Snowden documents describes a research effort to locate individuals based on the location of wifi networks they log into.

This is how the NSA can find someone, even when their cell phone is turned off and their SIM card is removed. If they're at an Internet café and they log into an account that identifies them, the NSA can locate them—because the NSA already knows where that Wi-Fi network is.

This also explains the drone assassination of Hassan Guhl, also reported in the *Washington Post* last October. In the story, Guhl was at an Internet cafe when he read an email from his wife. Although the article doesn't describe how that email was intercepted by the NSA, the NSA was able to use it to determine his location.

There's almost certainly more. NSA surveillance is robust, and they almost certainly have several different ways of identifying individuals on cell phone and Internet connections. For example, they can hack individual smart phones and force them to divulge location information.

As fascinating as the technology is, the critical policy question—and the one discussed extensively in the FirstLook article—is how reliable all this information is. While much of the NSA's capabilities to locate someone in the real world by their network activity piggy-backs on corporate surveillance capabilities, there's a critical difference: False positives are much more expensive. If Google or Facebook gets a physical location wrong, they show someone an ad for a restaurant they're nowhere near. If the NSA gets a physical location wrong, they call a drone strike on innocent people.

As we move to a world where all of us are tracked 24/7, these are the sorts of trade-offs we need to keep in mind.

Surveillance by Algorithm

Originally published in the Guardian, *February 27, 2014*

Increasingly, we are watched not by people but by algorithms. Amazon and Netflix track the books we buy and the movies we stream, and suggest other books and movies based on our habits. Google and Facebook watch what we do and what we say, and show us advertisements based on our behavior. Google even modifies our web search results based on our previous behavior. Smartphone navigation apps watch us as we drive, and update suggested route information based on traffic congestion. And the National Security Agency, of course, monitors our phone calls, emails and locations, then uses that information to try to identify terrorists.

Documents provided by Edward Snowden and revealed by the Guardian today show that the UK spy agency GHCQ, with help from the NSA, has been collecting millions of webcam images from innocent Yahoo users. And that speaks to a key distinction in the age of algorithmic surveillance: is it really okay for a computer to monitor you online, and for that data collection and analysis only to count as a potential privacy invasion when a person sees it? I say it's not, and the latest Snowden leaks only make more clear how important this distinction is.

The robots-vs.-spies divide is especially important as we decide what to do about NSA and GCHQ surveillance. The spy community and the Justice Department have reported back early on President Obama's request for changing how the NSA "collects" your data, but the potential reforms—FBI monitoring, holding on to your phone records and more—still largely depend on what the meaning of "collects" is.

Indeed, ever since Snowden provided reporters with a trove of top secret documents, we've been subjected to all sorts of NSA word games. And the word "collect" has a very special definition, according to the Department of Defense (DoD). A 1982 procedures manual (pdf; page 15) says: "information shall be considered as 'collected' only when it has been received for use by an employee of a DoD intelligence component in the course of his official duties." And "data acquired by electronic means is 'collected' only when it has been processed into intelligible form."

Director of National Intelligence James Clapper likened the NSA's accumulation of data to a library. All those books are stored on the shelves, but very few are actually read. "So the task for us in the interest of preserving security and preserving civil liberties and privacy," says Clapper, "is to be as precise as we possibly can be when we go in that library and look for the books that we need to open up and actually read." Only when an individual book is read does it count as "collection," in government parlance.

So, think of that friend of yours who has thousands of books in his house. According to the NSA, he's not actually "collecting" books. He's doing something else with them, and the only books he can claim to have "collected" are the ones he's actually read.

This is why Clapper claims—to this day—that he didn't lie in a Senate hearing when he replied "no" to this question: "Does the NSA collect any type of data at all on millions or hundreds of millions of Americans?"

If the NSA collects—I'm using the everyday definition of the word here—all of the contents of everyone's email, it doesn't count it as being collected in NSA terms until someone reads it. And if it collects—I'm sorry, but that's really the correct word—everyone's phone records or location information and stores it in an enormous database, that doesn't count as being collected—NSA definition—until someone looks at it. If the agency uses computers to search those emails for keywords, or correlates that location information for relationships between people, it doesn't count as collection, either. Only when those computers spit out a particular person has the data—in NSA terms—actually been collected.

If the modern spy dictionary has you confused, maybe dogs can help us understand why this legal workaround, by big tech companies and the government alike, is still a serious invasion of privacy.

Back when Gmail was introduced, this was Google's defense, too, about its context-sensitive advertising. Google's computers examine each individual email and insert an advertisement nearby, related to the contents of your email. But no person at Google reads any Gmail messages; only a computer does. In the words of one Google executive: "Worrying about a computer reading your email is like worrying about your dog seeing you naked."

But now that we have an example of a spy agency seeing people naked—there are a surprising number of sexually explicit images in the newly revealed Yahoo image collection—we can more viscerally understand the difference.

To wit: when you're watched by a dog, you know that what you're doing will go no further than the dog. The dog can't remember the details of what you've done. The dog can't tell anyone else. When you're watched by a computer, that's not true. You might be told that the computer isn't saving a copy of the video, but you have no assurance that that's true. You might be told that the computer won't alert a person if it perceives something of interest, but you can't know if that's true. You do know that the computer is making decisions based on what it receives, and you have no way of confirming that no human being will access that decision.

When a computer stores your data, there's always a risk of exposure. There's the risk of accidental exposure, when some hacker or criminal breaks in and steals the data. There's the risk of purposeful exposure, when the organization that has your data uses it in some manner. And there's the risk that another organization will demand access to the data. The FBI can serve a National Security Letter on Google, demanding details on your email and browsing habits. There isn't a court order in the world that can get that information out of your dog.

Of course, any time we're judged by algorithms, there's the potential for false positives. You are already familiar with this; just think of all the irrelevant advertisements you've been shown on the Internet, based on some algorithm misinterpreting your interests. In advertising, that's okay. It's annoying, but there's little actual harm, and you were busy reading your email anyway, right? But that harm increases as the accompanying judgments become more important: our credit ratings depend on algorithms; how we're treated at airport security does, too. And most alarming of all, drone targeting is partly based on algorithmic surveillance.

The primary difference between a computer and a dog is that the computer interacts with other people in the real world, and the dog does not. If someone could isolate the computer in the same way a dog is isolated, we wouldn't have any reason to worry about algorithms crawling around in our data. But we can't. Computer algorithms are intimately tied to people. And when we think of computer algorithms surveilling us or analyzing our personal data, we need to think about the people behind those algorithms. Whether or not anyone actually looks at our data, the very fact that they even could is what makes it surveillance.

This is why Yahoo called GCHQ's webcam-image collection "a whole new level of violation of our users' privacy." This is why we're not mollified by attempts from the UK equivalent of the NSA to apply facial recognition algorithms to the data, or to limit how many people viewed the sexually explicit images. This is why Google's eavesdropping is different than a dog's eavesdropping and why the NSA's definition of "collect" makes no sense whatsoever.

Metadata = Surveillance

Originally published in the March/April 2014 issue of
IEEE Security and Privacy

Ever since reporters began publishing stories about NSA activities, based on documents provided by Edward Snowden, we've been repeatedly assured by government officials that it's "only metadata." This might fool the average person, but it shouldn't fool those of us in the security field. Metadata equals surveillance data, and collecting metadata on people means putting them under surveillance.

An easy thought experiment demonstrates this. Imagine that you hired a private detective to eavesdrop on a subject. That detective would plant a bug in that subject's home, office, and car. He would eavesdrop on his computer. He would listen in on that subject's conversations, both face to face and remotely, and you would get a report on what was said in those conversations. (This is what President Obama repeatedly reassures us isn't happening with our phone calls. But am I the only one who finds it suspicious that he always uses very specific words? "The NSA is not listening in on your phone calls." This leaves open the possibility that the NSA is recording, transcribing, and analyzing your phone calls—and very occasionally reading them. This is far more likely to be true, and something a pedantically minded president could claim he wasn't lying about.)

Now imagine that you asked that same private detective to put a subject under constant surveillance. You would get a different report, one that included things like where he went, what he did, who he spoke to—and for how long—who he wrote to, what he read, and what he purchased. This is all metadata, data we know the NSA is collecting. So when the president says that it's only metadata, what you should really hear is that we're all under constant and ubiquitous surveillance.

What's missing from much of the discussion about the NSA's activities is what they're doing with all of this surveillance data. The newspapers focus on what's being collected, not on how it's being analyzed—with the singular exception of the *Washington Post* story on cell phone location collection. By their nature, cell phones are tracking devices. For a network to connect calls, it needs to know which cell the phone is located in. In an urban area, this narrows a phone's location to a few blocks. GPS data, transmitted across the network by far too many apps, locates a phone even more precisely. Collecting this data in bulk, which is what the NSA does, effectively puts everyone under physical surveillance.

This is new. Police could always tail a suspect, but now they can tail everyone—suspect or not. And once they're able to do that, they can perform analyses that weren't otherwise possible. The *Washington Post* reported two examples. One, you can look for pairs of phones that move toward each other, turn off for an hour or so, and then turn themselves back on while moving away from each other. In other words, you can look for secret meetings. Two, you can locate specific phones of interest and then look for other phones that move geographically in synch with those phones. In other words, you can look for someone physically tailing someone else. I'm sure there are dozens of other clever analyses you can perform with a database like this. We need more researchers thinking about the possibilities. I can assure you that the world's intelligence agencies are conducting this research.

How could a secret police use other surveillance databases: everyone's calling records, everyone's purchasing habits, everyone's browsing history, everyone's Facebook and Twitter history? How could these databases be combined in interesting ways? We need more research on the emergent properties of ubiquitous electronic surveillance.

We can't protect against what we don't understand. And whatever you think of the NSA or the other 5-Eyes countries, these techniques aren't solely theirs. They're being used by many countries to intimidate and control their populations. In a few years, they'll be used by corporations for psychological manipulation—persuasion or advertising—and even sooner by cybercriminals for more illicit purposes.

Everyone Wants You to Have Security, But Not from Them

Originally published in Forbes.com, *February 23, 2015*

In December, Google's Executive Chairman Eric Schmidt was interviewed at the CATO Institute Surveillance Conference. One of the things he said, after talking about some of the security measures his company has put in place post-Snowden, was: "If you have important information, the safest place to keep it is in Google. And I can assure you that the safest place to not keep it is anywhere else."

The surprised me, because Google collects all of your information to show you more targeted advertising. Surveillance is the business model of the Internet, and Google is one of the most successful companies at that. To claim that Google protects your privacy better than anyone else is to profoundly misunderstand why Google stores your data for free in the first place.

I was reminded of this last week when I appeared on Glenn Beck's show along with cryptography pioneer Whitfield Diffie. Diffie said:

> You can't have privacy without security, and I think we have glaring failures in computer security in problems that we've been working on for 40 years. You really should not live in fear of opening an attachment to a message. It ought to be confined; your computer ought to be able to handle it. And the fact that we have persisted for decades without solving these problems is partly because they're very difficult, but partly because there are lots of people who want you to be secure against everyone but them. And that includes all of the major computer manufacturers who, roughly speaking, want to manage your computer for you. The trouble is, I'm not sure of any practical alternative.

That neatly explains Google. Eric Schmidt does want your data to be secure. He wants Google to be the safest place for your data—as long as you don't mind the fact that Google has access to your data. Facebook wants the same thing: to protect your data from everyone except Facebook. Hardware companies are no different. Last week, we learned that Lenovo computers shipped with a piece of adware called Superfish that broke users' security to spy on them for advertising purposes.

Governments are no different. The FBI wants people to have strong encryption, but it wants backdoor access so it can get at your data. UK Prime Minister David Cameron wants you to have good security, just as long as it's not so strong as to keep the UK government out. And, of course, the NSA spends a lot of money ensuring that there's no security it can't break.

Corporations want access to your data for profit; governments want it for security purposes, be they benevolent or malevolent. But Diffie makes an even stronger point: we give lots of companies access to our data because it makes our lives easier.

I wrote about this in my latest book, *Data and Goliath*:

> *Convenience is the other reason we willingly give highly personal data to corporate interests, and put up with becoming objects of their surveillance. As I keep saying, surveillance-based services are useful and valuable. We like it when we can access our address book, calendar, photographs, documents, and everything else on any device we happen to be near. We like services like Siri and Google Now, which work best when they know tons about you. Social networking apps make it easier to hang out with our friends. Cell phone apps like Google Maps, Yelp, Weather, and Uber work better and faster when they know our location. Letting apps like Pocket or Instapaper know what we're reading feels like a small price to pay for getting everything we want to read in one convenient place. We even like it when ads are targeted to exactly what we're interested in. The benefits of surveillance in these and other applications are real, and significant.*

Like Diffie, I'm not sure there is any practical alternative. The reason the Internet is a worldwide mass-market phenomenon is that all the technological details are hidden from view. Someone else is taking care of it. We want strong security, but we also want companies to have access to our computers, smart devices, and data. We want someone else to manage our computers and smart phones, organize our email and photos, and help us move data between our various devices.

Those "someones" will necessarily be able to violate our privacy, either by deliberately peeking at our data or by having such lax security that they're vulnerable to national intelligence agencies, cyber-criminals, or both. Last week, we learned that the NSA broke into the Dutch company Gemalto and stole the encryption keys for billions—yes, billions—of cell phones worldwide. That was possible because we consumers don't want to do the work of securely generating those keys and setting up our own security when we get our phones; we want it done automatically by the phone manufacturers. We want our data to be secure, but we want someone to be able to recover it all when we forget our password.

We'll never solve these security problems as long as we're our own worst enemy. That's why I believe that any long-term security solution will not only be technological, but political as well. We need laws that will protect our privacy from those who obey the laws, and to punish those who break the laws. We need laws that require those entrusted with our data to protect our data. Yes, we need better security technologies, but we also need laws mandating the use of those technologies.

Why We Encrypt

Originally published in Securing Safe Spaces Online, *June 1, 2015*

Encryption protects our data. It protects our data when it's sitting on our computers and in data centers, and it protects it when it's being transmitted around the Internet. It protects our conversations, whether video, voice, or text. It protects our privacy. It protects our anonymity. And sometimes, it protects our lives.

This protection is important for everyone. It's easy to see how encryption protects journalists, human rights defenders, and political activists in authoritarian countries. But encryption protects the rest of us as well. It protects our data from criminals. It protects it from competitors, neighbors, and family members. It protects it from malicious attackers, and it protects it from accidents.

Encryption works best if it's ubiquitous and automatic. The two forms of encryption you use most often—https URLs on your browser, and the handset-to-tower link for your cell phone calls—work so well because you don't even know they're there.

Encryption should be enabled for everything by default, not a feature you turn on only if you're doing something you consider worth protecting.

This is important. If we only use encryption when we're working with important data, then encryption signals that data's importance. If only dissidents use encryption in a country, that country's authorities have an easy way of identifying them. But if everyone uses it all of the time, encryption ceases to be a signal. No one can distinguish simple chatting from deeply private conversation. The government can't tell the dissidents from the rest of the population. Every time you use encryption, you're protecting someone who needs to use it to stay alive.

It's important to remember that encryption doesn't magically convey security. There are many ways to get encryption wrong, and we regularly see them in the headlines. Encryption doesn't protect your computer or phone from being hacked, and it can't protect metadata, such as email addresses that need to be unencrypted so your mail can be delivered.

But encryption is the most important privacy-preserving technology we have, and one that is uniquely suited to protect against bulk surveillance—the kind done by governments looking to control their populations and criminals looking for vulnerable victims. By forcing both to target their attacks against individuals, we protect society.

Today, we are seeing government pushback against encryption. Many countries, from States like China and Russia to more democratic governments like the United States and the United Kingdom, are either talking about or implementing policies that limit strong encryption. This is dangerous, because it's technically impossible, and the attempt will cause incredible damage to the security of the Internet.

There are two morals to all of this. One, we should push companies to offer encryption to everyone, by default. And two, we should resist demands from governments to weaken encryption. Any weakening, even in the name of legitimate law enforcement, puts us all at risk. Even though criminals benefit from strong encryption, we're all much more secure when we all have strong encryption.

Automatic Face Recognition and Surveillance

Originally published in Forbes.com, *September 29, 2015*

ID checks were a common response to the terrorist attacks of 9/11, but they'll soon be obsolete. You won't have to show your ID, because you'll be identified automatically. A security camera will capture your face, and it'll be matched with your name and a whole lot of other information besides. Welcome to the world of automatic facial recognition. Those who have access to databases of identified photos will have the power to identify us. Yes, it'll enable some amazing personalized services; but it'll also enable whole new levels of surveillance. The underlying technologies are being developed today, and there are currently no rules limiting their use.

Walk into a store, and the salesclerks will know your name. The store's cameras and computers will have figured out your identity, and looked you up in both their store database and a commercial marketing database they've subscribed to. They'll know your name, salary, interests, what sort of sales pitches you're most vulnerable to, and how profitable a customer you are. Maybe they'll have read a profile based on your tweets and know what sort of mood you're in. Maybe they'll know your political affiliation or sexual identity, both predictable by your social media activity. And they're going to engage with you accordingly, perhaps by making sure you're well taken care of or possibly by trying to make you so uncomfortable that you'll leave.

Walk by a policeman, and she will know your name, address, criminal record, and with whom you routinely are seen. The potential for discrimination is enormous, especially in low-income communities where people are routinely harassed for things like unpaid parking tickets and other minor violations. And in a country where people are arrested for their political views, the use of this technology quickly turns into a nightmare scenario.

The critical technology here is computer face recognition. Traditionally it has been pretty poor, but it's slowly improving. A computer is now as good as a person. Already Google's algorithms can accurately match child and adult photos of the same person, and Facebook has an algorithm that works by recognizing hair style, body shape, and body language—and works even when it can't see faces. And while we humans are pretty much as good at this as we're ever going to get, computers will continue to improve. Over the next years, they'll continue to get more accurate, making better matches using even worse photos.

Matching photos with names also requires a database of identified photos, and we have plenty of those too. Driver's license databases are a gold mine: all shot face forward, in good focus and even light, with accurate identity information attached to each photo. The enormous photo collections of social media and photo archiving sites are another. They contain photos of us from all sorts of angles and in all sorts of lighting conditions, and we helpfully do the identifying step for the companies by tagging ourselves and our friends. Maybe this data will appear on handheld screens. Maybe it'll be automatically displayed on computer-enhanced glasses. Imagine salesclerks—or politicians—being able to scan a room and instantly see wealthy customers highlighted in green, or policemen seeing people with criminal records highlighted in red.

Science fiction writers have been exploring this future in both books and movies for decades. Ads followed people from billboard to billboard in the movie *Minority Report*. In John Scalzi's recent novel *Lock In*, characters scan each other like the salesclerks I described above.

This is no longer fiction. High-tech billboards can target ads based on the gender of who's standing in front of them. In 2011, researchers at Carnegie Mellon pointed a camera at a public area on campus and were able to match live video footage with a public database of tagged photos in real time. Already government and commercial authorities have set up facial recognition systems to identify and monitor people at sporting events, music festivals, and even churches. The Dubai police are working on integrating facial recognition into Google Glass, and more US local police forces are using the technology.

Facebook, Google, Twitter, and other companies with large databases of tagged photos know how valuable their archives are. They see all kinds of services powered by their technologies—services they can sell to businesses like the stores you walk into and the governments you might interact with.

Other companies will spring up whose business models depend on capturing our images in public and selling them to whoever has use for them. If you think this is farfetched, consider a related technology that's already far down that path: license-plate capture.

Today in the US there's a massive but invisible industry that records the movements of cars around the country. Cameras mounted on cars and tow trucks capture license places along with date/time/location information, and companies use that data to find cars that are scheduled for repossession. One company, Vigilant Solutions, claims to collect 70 million scans in the US every month. The companies that engage in this business routinely share that data with the police, giving the police a steady stream of surveillance information on innocent people that they could not legally collect on their own. And the companies are already looking for other profit streams, selling that surveillance data to anyone else who thinks they have a need for it.

This could easily happen with face recognition. Finding bail jumpers could even be the initial driving force, just as finding cars to repossess was for license plate capture.

Already the FBI has a database of 52 million faces, and describes its integration of facial recognition software with that database as "fully operational." In 2014, FBI Director James Comey told Congress that the database would not include photos of ordinary citizens, although the FBI's own documents indicate otherwise. And just last month, we learned that the FBI is looking to buy a system that will collect facial images of anyone an officer stops on the street.

In 2013, Facebook had a quarter of a trillion user photos in its database. There's currently a class-action lawsuit in Illinois alleging that the company has over a billion "face templates" of people, collected without their knowledge or consent.

Last year, the US Department of Commerce tried to prevail upon industry representatives and privacy organizations to write a voluntary code of conduct for companies using facial recognition technologies. After 16 months of negotiations, all of the consumer-focused privacy organizations pulled out of the process because industry representatives were unable to agree on any limitations on something as basic as nonconsensual facial recognition.

When we talk about surveillance, we tend to concentrate on the problems of data collection: CCTV cameras, tagged photos, purchasing habits, our writings on sites like Facebook and Twitter. We think much less about data analysis. But effective and pervasive surveillance is just as much about analysis. It's sustained by a combination of cheap and ubiquitous cameras, tagged photo databases, commercial databases of our actions that reveal our habits and personalities, and—most of all—fast and accurate face recognition software.

Don't expect to have access to this technology for yourself anytime soon. This is not facial recognition for all. It's just for those who can either demand or pay for access to the required technologies—most importantly, the tagged photo databases. And while we can easily imagine how this might be misused in a totalitarian country, there are dangers in free societies as well. Without meaningful regulation, we're moving into a world where governments and corporations will be able to identify people both in real time and backwards in time, remotely and in secret, without consent or recourse.

Despite protests from industry, we need to regulate this budding industry. We need limitations on how our images can be collected without our knowledge or consent, and on how they can be used. The technologies aren't going away, and we can't uninvent these capabilities. But we can ensure that they're used ethically and responsibly, and not just as a mechanism to increase police and corporate power over us.

The Internet of Things that Talk about You behind Your Back

Originally published in Vice Motherboard, *January 8, 2016*

SilverPush is an Indian startup that's trying to figure out all the different computing devices you own. It embeds inaudible sounds into the webpages you read and the television commercials you watch. Software secretly embedded in your computers, tablets, and smartphones picks up the signals, and then uses cookies to transmit that information back to SilverPush. The result is that the company can track you across your different devices. It can correlate the television commercials you watch with the web searches you make. It can link the things you do on your tablet with the things you do on your work computer.

Your computerized things are talking about you behind your back, and for the most part you can't stop them—or even learn what they're saying.

This isn't new, but it's getting worse.

Surveillance is the business model of the Internet, and the more these companies know about the intimate details of your life, the more they can profit from it. Already there are dozens of companies that secretly spy on you as you browse the Internet, connecting your behavior on different sites and using that information to target advertisements. You know it when you search for something like a Hawaiian vacation, and ads for similar vacations follow you around the Internet for weeks. Companies like Google and Facebook make an enormous profit connecting the things you write about and are interested in with companies trying to sell you things.

Cross-device tracking is the latest obsession for Internet marketers. You probably use multiple Internet devices: your computer, your smartphone, your tablet, maybe your Internet-enabled television—and, increasingly, "Internet of Things" devices like smart thermostats and appliances. All of these devices are spying on you, but the different spies are largely unaware of each other. Start-up companies like SilverPush, 4Info, Drawbridge, Flurry, and Cross Screen Consultants, as well as the big players like Google, Facebook, and Yahoo, are all experimenting with different technologies to "fix" this problem.

Retailers want this information very much. They want to know whether their television advertising causes people to search for their products on the Internet. They want to correlate people's web searching on their smartphones with their buying behavior on their computers. They want to track people's locations using the surveillance capabilities of their smartphones, and use that information to send geographically targeted ads to their computers. They want the surveillance data from smart appliances correlated with everything else.

This is where the Internet of Things makes the problem worse. As computers get embedded into more of the objects we live with and use, and permeate more aspects of our lives, more companies want to use them to spy on us without our knowledge or consent.

Technically, of course, we did consent. The license agreement we didn't read but legally agreed to when we unthinkingly clicked "I agree" on a screen, or opened a package we purchased, gives all of those companies the legal right to conduct all of this surveillance. And the way US privacy law is currently written, they own all of that data and don't need to allow us to see it.

We accept all of this Internet surveillance because we don't really think about it. If there were a dozen people from Internet marketing companies with pens and clipboards peering over our shoulders as we sent our Gmails and browsed the Internet, most of us would object immediately. If the companies that made our smartphone apps actually followed us around all day, or if the companies that collected our license plate data could be seen as we drove, we would demand they stop. And if our televisions, computer, and mobile devices talked about us and coordinated their behavior in a way we could hear, we would be creeped out.

The Federal Trade Commission is looking at cross-device tracking technologies, with an eye to regulating them. But if recent history is a guide, any regulations will be minor and largely ineffective at addressing the larger problem.

We need to do better. We need to have a conversation about the privacy implications of cross-device tracking, but—more importantly—we need to think about the ethics of our surveillance economy. Do we want companies knowing the intimate details of our lives, and being able to store that data forever? Do we truly believe that we have no rights to see the data that's collected about us, to correct data that's wrong, or to have data deleted that's personal or embarrassing? At a minimum, we need limits on the behavioral data that can legally be collected about us and how long it can be stored, a right to download data collected about us, and a ban on third-party ad tracking. The last one is vital: it's the companies that spy on us from website to website, or from device to device, that are doing the most damage to our privacy.

The Internet surveillance economy is less than 20 years old, and emerged because there was no regulation limiting any of this behavior. It's now a powerful industry, and it's expanding past computers and smartphones into every aspect of our lives. It's long past time we set limits on what these computers, and the companies that control them, can say about us and do to us behind our backs.

Security vs. Surveillance

This essay previously appeared as part of the paper "Don't Panic: Making Progress on the 'Going Dark' Debate." It was reprinted on Lawfare. A modified version was reprinted by the *MIT Technology Review*. (*February 1, 2016*)

Both the "going dark" metaphor of FBI Director James Comey and the contrasting "golden age of surveillance" metaphor of privacy law professor Peter Swire focus on the value of data to law enforcement. As framed in the media, encryption debates are about whether law enforcement should have surreptitious access to data, or whether companies should be allowed to provide strong encryption to their customers.

It's a myopic framing that focuses only on one threat—criminals, including domestic terrorists—and the demands of law enforcement and national intelligence. This obscures the most important aspects of the encryption issue: the security it provides against a much wider variety of threats.

Encryption secures our data and communications against eavesdroppers like criminals, foreign governments, and terrorists. We use it every day to hide our cell phone conversations from eavesdroppers, and to hide our Internet purchasing from credit card thieves. Dissidents in China and many other countries use it to avoid arrest. It's a vital tool for journalists to communicate with their sources, for NGOs to protect their work in repressive countries, and for attorneys to communicate with their clients.

Many technological security failures of today can be traced to failures of encryption. In 2014 and 2015, unnamed hackers—probably the Chinese government—stole 21.5 million personal files of US government employees and others. They wouldn't have obtained this data if it had been encrypted. Many large-scale criminal data thefts were made either easier or more damaging because data wasn't encrypted: Target, TJ Maxx, Heartland Payment Systems, and so on. Many countries are eavesdropping on the unencrypted communications of their own citizens, looking for dissidents and other voices they want to silence.

Adding backdoors will only exacerbate the risks. As technologists, we can't build an access system that only works for people of a certain citizenship, or with a particular morality, or only in the presence of a specified legal document. If the FBI can eavesdrop on your text messages or get at your computer's hard drive, so can other governments. So can criminals. So can terrorists. This is not theoretical; again and again, backdoor accesses built for one purpose have been surreptitiously used for another. Vodafone built backdoor access into Greece's cell phone network for the Greek government; it was used against the

Greek government in 2004–2005. Google kept a database of backdoor accesses provided to the US government under CALEA; the Chinese breached that database in 2009.

We're not being asked to choose between security and privacy. We're being asked to choose between less security and more security.

This trade-off isn't new. In the mid-1990s, cryptographers argued that escrowing encryption keys with central authorities would weaken security. In 2013, cybersecurity researcher Susan Landau published her excellent book *Surveillance or Security?*, which deftly parsed the details of this trade-off and concluded that security is far more important.

Ubiquitous encryption protects us much more from bulk surveillance than from targeted surveillance. For a variety of technical reasons, computer security is extraordinarily weak. If a sufficiently skilled, funded, and motivated attacker wants in to your computer, they're in. If they're not, it's because you're not high enough on their priority list to bother with. Widespread encryption forces the listener—whether a foreign government, criminal, or terrorist—to target. And this hurts repressive governments much more than it hurts terrorists and criminals.

Of course, criminals and terrorists have used, are using, and will use encryption to hide their planning from the authorities, just as they will use many aspects of society's capabilities and infrastructure: cars, restaurants, telecommunications. In general, we recognize that such things can be used by both honest and dishonest people. Society thrives nonetheless because the honest so outnumber the dishonest. Compare this with the tactic of secretly poisoning all the food at a restaurant. Yes, we might get lucky and poison a terrorist before he strikes, but we'll harm all the innocent customers in the process. Weakening encryption for everyone is harmful in exactly the same way.

The Value of Encryption

Originally published in the Ripon Forum, *April 1, 2016*

In today's world of ubiquitous computers and networks, it's hard to overstate the value of encryption. Quite simply, encryption keeps you safe. Encryption protects your financial details and passwords when you bank online. It protects your cell phone conversations from eavesdroppers. If you encrypt your laptop—and I hope you do—it protects your data if your computer is stolen. It protects your money and your privacy.

Encryption protects the identity of dissidents all over the world. It's a vital tool to allow journalists to communicate securely with their sources, NGOs to protect their work in repressive countries, and attorneys to communicate privately with their clients.

Encryption protects our government. It protects our government systems, our lawmakers, and our law enforcement officers. Encryption protects our officials working at home and abroad. During the whole Apple vs. FBI debate, I wondered if Director James Comey realized how many of his own agents used iPhones and relied on Apple's security features to protect them.

Encryption protects our critical infrastructure: our communications network, the national power grid, our transportation infrastructure, and everything else we rely on in our society. And as we move to the Internet of Things with its interconnected cars and thermostats and medical devices, all of which can destroy life and property if hacked and misused, encryption will become even more critical to our personal and national security.

Security is more than encryption, of course. But encryption is a critical component of security. While it's mostly invisible, you use strong encryption every day, and our Internet-laced world would be a far riskier place if you did not.

When it's done right, strong encryption is unbreakable encryption. Any weakness in encryption will be exploited—by hackers, criminals, and foreign governments. Many of the hacks that make the news can be attributed to weak or—even worse—nonexistent encryption.

The FBI wants the ability to bypass encryption in the course of criminal investigations. This is known as a "backdoor," because it's a way to access the encrypted information that bypasses the normal encryption mechanisms. I am sympathetic to such claims, but as a technologist I can tell you that there is no way to give the FBI that capability without weakening the encryption against all adversaries as well. This is critical to understand. I can't build an access technology that only works with proper legal authorization, or only for people with a particular citizenship or the proper morality. The technology just doesn't work that way.

If a backdoor exists, then anyone can exploit it. All it takes is knowledge of the backdoor and the capability to exploit it. And while it might temporarily be a secret, it's a fragile secret. Backdoors are one of the primary ways to attack computer systems.

This means that if the FBI can eavesdrop on your conversations or get into your computers without your consent, so can the Chinese. Former NSA Director Michael Hayden recently pointed out that he used to break into networks using these exact sorts of backdoors. Backdoors weaken us against all sorts of threats.

Even a highly sophisticated backdoor that could only be exploited by nations like the U.S. and China today will leave us vulnerable to cybercriminals tomorrow. That's just the way technology works: things become easier, cheaper, more widely accessible. Give the FBI the ability to hack into a cell phone today, and tomorrow you'll hear reports that a criminal group used that same ability to hack into our power grid.

Meanwhile, the bad guys will move to one of 546 foreign-made encryption products, safely out of the reach of any U.S. law.

Either we build encryption systems to keep everyone secure, or we build them to leave everybody vulnerable.

The FBI paints this as a trade-off between security and privacy. It's not. It's a trade-off between more security and less security. Our national security needs strong encryption. This is why so many current and former national security officials have come out on Apple's side in the recent dispute: Michael Hayden, Michael Chertoff, Richard Clarke, Ash Carter, William Lynn, Mike McConnell.

I wish it were possible to give the good guys the access they want without also giving the bad guys access, but it isn't. If the FBI gets its way and forces companies to weaken encryption, all of us—our data, our networks, our infrastructure, our society—will be at risk.

The FBI isn't going dark. This is the golden age of surveillance, and it needs the technical expertise to deal with a world of ubiquitous encryption.

Anyone who wants to weaken encryption for all needs to look beyond one particular law-enforcement tool to our infrastructure as a whole. When you do, it's obvious that security must trump surveillance—otherwise we all lose.

Congress Removes FCC Privacy Protections on Your Internet Usage

Originally published in the Guardian, *March 13, 2017*

Think about all of the websites you visit every day. Now imagine if the likes of Time Warner, AT&T, and Verizon collected *all* of your browsing history and sold it on to the highest bidder. That's what will probably happen if Congress has its way.

This week, lawmakers voted to allow Internet service providers to violate your privacy for their own profit. Not only have they voted to repeal a rule that protects your privacy, they are also trying to make it illegal for the Federal Communications Commission to enact other rules to protect your privacy online.

That this is not provoking greater outcry illustrates how much we've ceded any willingness to shape our technological future to for-profit companies and are allowing them to do it for us.

There are a lot of reasons to be worried about this. Because your Internet service provider controls your connection to the Internet, it is in a position to see everything you do on the Internet. Unlike a search engine or social networking platform or news site, you can't easily switch to a competitor. And there's not a lot of competition in the market, either. If you have a choice between two high-speed providers in the US, consider yourself lucky.

What can telecom companies do with this newly granted power to spy on everything you're doing? Of course they can sell your data to marketers—and the inevitable criminals and foreign governments who also line up to buy it. But they can do more creepy things as well.

They can snoop through your traffic and insert their own ads. They can deploy systems that remove encryption so they can better eavesdrop. They can redirect your searches to other sites. They can install surveillance software on your computers and phones. None of these are hypothetical.

They're all things Internet service providers have done before, and they are some of the reasons the FCC tried to protect your privacy in the first place. And now they'll be able to do all of these things in secret, without your knowledge or consent. And, of course, governments worldwide will have access to these powers. And all of that data will be at risk of hacking, either by criminals and other governments.

Telecom companies have argued that other Internet players already have these creepy powers—although they didn't use the word "creepy"—so why should they not have them as well? It's a valid point.

Surveillance is already the business model of the Internet, and literally hundreds of companies spy on your Internet activity against your interests and for their own profit.

Your email provider already knows everything you write to your family, friends, and colleagues. Google already knows our hopes, fears, and interests, because that's what we search for.

Your cellular provider already tracks your physical location at all times: it knows where you live, where you work, when you go to sleep at night, when you wake up in the morning, and—because everyone has a smartphone—who you spend time with and who you sleep with.

And some of the things these companies do with that power is no less creepy. Facebook has run experiments in manipulating your mood by changing what you see on your news feed. Uber used its ride data to identify one-night stands. Even Sony once installed spyware on customers' computers to try and detect if they copied music files.

Aside from spying for profit, companies can spy for other purposes. Uber has already considered using data it collects to intimidate a journalist. Imagine what an Internet service provider can do with the data it collects: against politicians, against the media, against rivals.

Of course the telecom companies want a piece of the surveillance capitalism pie. Despite dwindling revenues, increasing use of ad blockers, and increases in clickfraud, violating our privacy is still a profitable business—especially if it's done in secret.

The bigger question is: why do we allow for-profit corporations to create our technological future in ways that are optimized for their profits and anathema to our own interests?

When markets work well, different companies compete on price and features, and society collectively rewards better products by purchasing them. This mechanism fails if there is no competition, or if rival companies choose not to compete on a particular feature. It fails when customers are unable to switch to competitors. And it fails when what companies do remains secret.

Unlike service providers like Google and Facebook, telecom companies are infrastructure that requires government involvement and regulation. The practical impossibility of consumers learning the extent of surveillance by their Internet service providers, combined with the difficulty of switching them, means that the decision about whether to be spied on should be with the consumer and not a telecom giant. That this new bill reverses that is both wrong and harmful.

Today, technology is changing the fabric of our society faster than at any other time in history. We have big questions that we need to tackle: not just privacy, but questions of freedom, fairness, and liberty. Algorithms are making decisions about policing, healthcare.

Driverless vehicles are making decisions about traffic and safety. Warfare is increasingly being fought remotely and autonomously. Censorship is on the rise globally. Propaganda is being promulgated more efficiently than ever. These problems won't go away. If anything, the Internet of things and the computerization of every aspect of our lives will make it worse.

In today's political climate, it seems impossible that Congress would legislate these things to our benefit. Right now, regulatory agencies such as the FTC and FCC are our best hope to protect our privacy and security against rampant corporate power. That Congress has decided to reduce that power leaves us at enormous risk.

It's too late to do anything about this bill—Trump will certainly sign it—but we need to be alert to future bills that reduce our privacy and security.

Infrastructure Vulnerabilities Make Surveillance Easy

Originally published in Al Jazeera, *April 11, 2017*

Governments want to spy on their citizens for all sorts of reasons. Some countries do it to help solve crimes or to try to find "terrorists" before they act.

Others do it to find and arrest reporters or dissidents. Some only target individuals, others attempt to spy on everyone all the time.

Many countries spy on the citizens of other countries: for reasons of national security, for advantages in trade negotiations, or to steal intellectual property.

None of this is new. What is new, however, is how easy it has all become. Computers naturally produce data about their activities, which means they're constantly producing surveillance data about us as we interact with them.

Corporations are doing it for their own purposes; collecting and using this data has become the dominant business model of the internet. Increasingly, governments around the world are ensuring that they too have access to the data, either by mandating that the companies give it to them or surreptitiously grabbing their own copy.

Since Edward Snowden revealed to the world the extent of the NSA's global surveillance network, there has been a vigorous debate in the technological community about what its limits should be.

Less discussed is how many of these same surveillance techniques are used by other—smaller and poorer—more totalitarian countries to spy on political opponents, dissidents, human rights defenders; the press in Toronto has documented some of the many abuses, by countries like Ethiopia, the UAE, Iran, Syria, Kazakhstan, Sudan, Ecuador, Malaysia, and China.

That these countries can use network surveillance technologies to violate human rights is a shame on the world, and there's a lot of blame to go around.

We can point to the governments that are using surveillance against their own citizens.

We can certainly blame the cyberweapons arms manufacturers that are selling those systems, and the countries—mostly European—that allow those arms manufacturers to sell those systems.

There's a lot more the global internet community could do to limit the availability of sophisticated internet and telephony surveillance equipment to totalitarian governments. But I want to focus on another contributing cause to this problem: the fundamental insecurity of our digital systems that makes this a problem in the first place.

Exploiting Existing Vulnerabilities

IMSI catchers are fake mobile phone towers. They allow someone to impersonate a cell network and collect information about phones in the vicinity of the device and they're used to create lists of people who were at a particular event or near a particular location.

Fundamentally, the technology works because the phone in your pocket automatically trusts any cell tower to which it connects. There's no security in the connection protocols between the phones and the towers.

IP intercept systems are used to eavesdrop on what people do on the internet. Unlike the surveillance that happens at the sites you visit, by companies like Facebook and Google, this surveillance happens at the point where your computer connects to the internet. Here, someone can eavesdrop on everything you do.

This system also exploits existing vulnerabilities in the underlying internet communications protocols. Most of the traffic between your computer and the internet is unencrypted, and what is encrypted is often vulnerable to man-in-the-middle attacks because of insecurities in both the internet protocols and the encryption protocols that protect it.

There are many other examples. What they all have in common is that they are vulnerabilities in our underlying digital communications systems that allow someone—whether it's a country's secret police, a rival national intelligence organization, or criminal group—to break or bypass what security there is and spy on the users of these systems.

These insecurities exist for two reasons. First, they were designed in an era where computer hardware was expensive and inaccessibility was a reasonable proxy for security. When the mobile phone network was designed, faking a cell tower was an incredibly difficult technical exercise, and it was reasonable to assume that only legitimate cell providers would go to the effort of creating such towers.

At the same time, computers were less powerful and software was much slower, so adding security into the system seemed like a waste of resources. Fast forward to today: computers are cheap and software is fast, and what was impossible only a few decades ago is now easy.

The second reason is that governments use these surveillance capabilities for their own purposes. The FBI has used IMSI-catchers for years to investigate crimes. The NSA uses IP interception systems to collect foreign intelligence. Both of these agencies, as well as their counterparts in other countries, have put pressure on the standards bodies that create these systems to not implement strong security.

Of course, technology isn't static. With time, things become cheaper and easier. What was once a secret NSA interception program or a secret FBI investigative tool becomes usable by less-capable governments and cybercriminals.

"Wrongheaded and Dangerous"

Man-in-the-middle attacks against internet connections are a common criminal tool to steal credentials from users and hack their accounts.

IMSI-catchers are used by criminals, too. Right now, you can go onto Alibaba.com and buy your own IMSI catcher for under $2,000.

Despite their uses by democratic governments for legitimate purposes, our security would be much better served by fixing these vulnerabilities in our infrastructures.

These systems are not only used by dissidents in totalitarian countries, they're also used by legislators, corporate executives, critical infrastructure providers, and many others in the US and elsewhere.

That we allow people to remain insecure and vulnerable is both wrongheaded and dangerous.

Earlier this month, two American legislators—Senator Ron Wyden and Rep Ted Lieu—sent a letter to the chairman of the Federal Communications Commission, demanding that he do something about the country's insecure telecommunications infrastructure.

They pointed out that not only are insecurities rampant in the underlying protocols and systems of the telecommunications infrastructure, but also that the FCC knows about these vulnerabilities and isn't doing anything to force the telcos to fix them.

Wyden and Lieu make the point that fixing these vulnerabilities is a matter of US national security, but it's also a matter of international human rights. All modern communications technologies are global, and anything the US does to improve its own security will also improve security worldwide.

Yes, it means that the FBI and the NSA will have a harder job spying, but it also means that the world will be a safer and more secure place.

7 Business and Economics of Security

More on Feudal Security

Originally published in the Harvard Business Review website, *June 6, 2013*

Facebook regularly abuses the privacy of its users. Google has stopped supporting its popular RSS feeder. Apple prohibits all iPhone apps that are political or sexual. Microsoft might be cooperating with some governments to spy on Skype calls, but we don't know which ones. Both Twitter and LinkedIn have recently suffered security breaches that affected the data of hundreds of thousands of their users.

If you've started to think of yourself as a hapless peasant in a *Game of Thrones* power struggle, you're more right than you may realize. These are not traditional companies, and we are not traditional customers. These are feudal lords, and we are their vassals, peasants, and serfs.

Power has shifted in IT, in favor of both cloud-service providers and closed-platform vendors. This power shift affects many things, and it profoundly affects security.

Traditionally, computer security was the user's responsibility. Users purchased their own antivirus software and firewalls, and any breaches were blamed on their inattentiveness. It's kind of a crazy business model. Normally we expect the products and services we buy to be safe and secure, but in IT we tolerated lousy products and supported an enormous aftermarket for security.

Now that the IT industry has matured, we expect more security "out of the box." This has become possible largely because of two technology trends: cloud computing and vendor-controlled platforms. The first means that most of our data resides on other networks: Google Docs, Salesforce.com, Facebook, Gmail. The second means that our new Internet devices are both closed and controlled by the vendors, giving us limited configuration control: iPhones, ChromeBooks, Kindles, BlackBerry PDAs. Meanwhile, our relationship with IT has changed. We used to use our computers to do things. We now use our vendor-controlled computing devices to go places. All of these places are owned by someone.

The new security model is that someone else takes care of it—without telling us any of the details. I have no control over the security of my Gmail or my photos on Flickr. I can't demand greater security for my presentations on Prezi or my task list on Trello, no matter how confidential they are. I can't audit any of these cloud services. I can't delete cookies on my iPad or ensure that files are securely erased. Updates on my Kindle happen automatically, without my knowledge or consent. I have so little visibility into the security of Facebook that I have no idea what operating system they're using.

There are a lot of good reasons why we're all flocking to these cloud services and vendor-controlled platforms. The benefits are enormous, from cost to convenience to reliability to security itself. But it is inherently a feudal relationship. We cede control of our data and computing platforms to these companies and trust that they will treat us well and protect us from harm. And if we pledge complete allegiance to them—if we let them control our email and calendar and address book and photos and everything—we get even more benefits. We become their vassals; or, on a bad day, their serfs.

There are a lot of feudal lords out there. Google and Apple are the obvious ones, but Microsoft is trying to control both user data and the end-user platform as well. Facebook is another lord, controlling much of the socializing we do on the Internet. Other feudal lords are smaller and more specialized—Amazon, Yahoo, Verizon, and so on—but the model is the same.

To be sure, feudal security has its advantages. These companies are much better at security than the average user. Automatic backup has saved a lot of data after hardware failures, user mistakes, and malware infections. Automatic updates have increased security dramatically. This is also true for small organizations; they are more secure than they would be if they tried to do it themselves. For large corporations with dedicated IT security departments, the benefits are less clear. Sure, even large companies outsource critical functions like tax preparation and cleaning services, but large companies have specific requirements for security, data retention, audit, and so on—and that's just not possible with most of these feudal lords.

Feudal security also has its risks. Vendors can, and do, make security mistakes affecting hundreds of thousands of people. Vendors can lock people into relationships, making it hard for them to take their data and leave. Vendors can act arbitrarily, against our interests; Facebook regularly does this when it changes people's defaults, implements new features, or modifies its privacy policy. Many vendors give our data to the government without notice, consent, or a warrant; almost all sell it for profit. This isn't surprising, really; companies should be expected to act in their own self-interest and not in their users' best interest.

The feudal relationship is inherently based on power. In Medieval Europe, people would pledge their allegiance to a feudal lord in exchange for that lord's protection. This arrangement changed as the lords realized that they had all the power and could do whatever they wanted. Vassals were used and abused; peasants were tied to their land and became serfs.

It's the Internet lords' popularity and ubiquity that enable them to profit; laws and government relationships make it easier for them to hold onto power. These lords are vying with each other for profits and power. By spending time on their sites and giving them our personal information—whether through search queries, emails, status updates, likes, or simply our behavioral characteristics—we are providing the raw material for that struggle. In this way we are like serfs, toiling the land for our feudal lords. If you don't believe me, try to take your data with you when you leave Facebook. And when war breaks out among the giants, we become collateral damage.

So how do we survive? Increasingly, we have little alternative but to trust someone, so we need to decide who we trust—and who we don't—and then act accordingly. This isn't easy; our feudal lords go out of their way not to be transparent about their actions, their security, or much of anything. Use whatever power you have—as individuals, none; as large corporations, more—to negotiate with your lords. And, finally, don't be extreme in any way: politically, socially, culturally. Yes, you can be shut down without recourse, but it's usually those on the edges that are affected. Not much solace, I agree, but it's something.

On the policy side, we have an action plan. In the short term, we need to keep circumvention—the ability to modify our hardware, software, and data files—legal and preserve net neutrality. Both of these things limit how much the lords can take advantage of us, and they increase the possibility that the market will force them to be more benevolent. The last thing we want is the government—that's us—spending resources to enforce one particular business model over another and stifling competition.

In the longer term, we all need to work to reduce the power imbalance. Medieval feudalism evolved into a more balanced relationship in which lords had responsibilities as well as rights. Today's Internet feudalism is both ad hoc and one-sided. We have no choice but to trust the lords, but we receive very few assurances in return. The lords have a lot of rights, but few responsibilities or limits. We need to balance this relationship, and government intervention is the only way we're going to get it. In medieval Europe, the rise of the centralized state and the rule of law provided the stability that feudalism lacked. The Magna Carta first forced responsibilities on governments and put humans on the long road toward government by the people and for the people.

We need a similar process to rein in our Internet lords, and it's not something that market forces are likely to provide. The very definition of power is changing, and the issues are far bigger than the Internet and our relationships with our IT providers.

The Public/Private Surveillance Partnership

Originally published in Bloomberg.com, *July 31, 2013*

Imagine the government passed a law requiring all citizens to carry a tracking device. Such a law would immediately be found unconstitutional. Yet we all carry mobile phones.

If the National Security Agency required us to notify it whenever we made a new friend, the nation would rebel. Yet we notify Facebook. If the Federal Bureau of Investigation demanded copies of all our conversations and correspondence, it would be laughed at. Yet we provide copies of our email to Google, Microsoft or whoever our mail host is; we provide copies of our text messages to Verizon, AT&T and

Sprint; and we provide copies of other conversations to Twitter, Facebook, LinkedIn, or whatever other site is hosting them.

The primary business model of the Internet is built on mass surveillance, and our government's intelligence-gathering agencies have become addicted to that data. Understanding how we got here is critical to understanding how we undo the damage.

Computers and networks inherently produce data, and our constant interactions with them allow corporations to collect an enormous amount of intensely personal data about us as we go about our daily lives. Sometimes we produce this data inadvertently simply by using our phones, credit cards, computers and other devices. Sometimes we give corporations this data directly on Google, Facebook, Apple Inc.'s iCloud and so on in exchange for whatever free or cheap service we receive from the Internet in return.

The NSA is also in the business of spying on everyone, and it has realized it's far easier to collect all the data from these corporations rather than from us directly. In some cases, the NSA asks for this data nicely. In other cases, it makes use of subtle threats or overt pressure. If that doesn't work, it uses tools like national security letters.

The result is a corporate-government surveillance partnership, one that allows both the government and corporations to get away with things they couldn't otherwise.

There are two types of laws in the US, each designed to constrain a different type of power: constitutional law, which places limitations on government, and regulatory law, which constrains corporations. Historically, these two areas have largely remained separate, but today each group has learned how to use the other's laws to bypass their own restrictions. The government uses corporations to get around its limits, and corporations use the government to get around their limits.

This partnership manifests itself in various ways. The government uses corporations to circumvent its prohibitions against eavesdropping domestically on its citizens. Corporations rely on the government to ensure that they have unfettered use of the data they collect.

Here's an example: It would be reasonable for our government to debate the circumstances under which corporations can collect and use our data, and to provide for protections against misuse. But if the government is using that very data for its own surveillance purposes, it has an incentive to oppose any laws to limit data collection. And because corporations see no need to give consumers any choice in this matter—because it would only reduce their profits—the market isn't going to protect consumers, either.

Our elected officials are often supported, endorsed and funded by these corporations as well, setting up an incestuous relationship between corporations, lawmakers and the intelligence community.

The losers are us, the people, who are left with no one to stand up for our interests. Our elected government, which is supposed to be responsible to us, is not. And corporations, which in a market economy are supposed to be responsive to our needs, are not. What we have now is death to privacy—and that's very dangerous to democracy and liberty.

The simple answer is to blame consumers, who shouldn't use mobile phones, credit cards, banks or the Internet if they don't want to be tracked. But that argument deliberately ignores the reality of today's world. Everything we do involves computers, even if we're not using them directly. And by their nature, computers produce tracking data. We can't go back to a world where we don't use computers, the Internet or social networking. We have no choice but to share our personal information with these corporations, because that's how our world works today.

Curbing the power of the corporate-private surveillance partnership requires limitations on both what corporations can do with the data we choose to give them and restrictions on how and when the government can demand access to that data. Because both of these changes go against the interests of corporations and the government, we have to demand them as citizens and voters. We can lobby our government to operate more transparently—disclosing the opinions of the Foreign Intelligence Surveillance Court would be a good start—and hold our lawmakers accountable when it doesn't. But it's not going to be easy. There are strong interests doing their best to ensure that the steady stream of data keeps flowing.

Should Companies Do Most of Their Computing in the Cloud?

Originally published in the Economist website, *June 5, 2015*

Yes. No. Yes. Maybe. Yes. Okay, it's complicated.

The economics of cloud computing are compelling. For companies, the lower operating costs, the lack of capital expenditure, the ability to quickly scale and the ability to outsource maintenance are just some of the benefits. Computing is infrastructure, like cleaning, payroll, tax preparation and legal services. All of these are outsourced. And computing is becoming a utility, like power and water. Everyone does their power generation and water distribution "in the cloud." Why should IT be any different?

Two reasons. The first is that IT is complicated: it is more like payroll services than like power generation. What this means is that you have to choose your cloud providers wisely, and make sure you have good contracts in place with them. You want to own your data, and be able to download that data at any time. You want assurances that your data will not disappear if the cloud provider goes out of business or discontinues your service. You want reliability and availability assurances, tech support assurances, whatever you need.

The downside is that you will have limited customization options. Cloud computing is cheaper because of economics of scale, and—like any outsourced task—you tend to get what you get. A restaurant with a limited menu is cheaper than a personal chef who can cook anything you want. Fewer options at a much cheaper price: it's a feature, not a bug.

The second reason that cloud computing is different is security. This is not an idle concern. IT security is difficult under the best of circumstances, and security risks are one of the major reasons it has taken so long for companies to embrace the cloud. And here it really gets complicated.

On the pro-cloud side, cloud providers have the potential to be far more secure than the corporations whose data they are holding. It is the same economies of scale. For most companies, the cloud provider is likely to have better security than them—by a lot. All but the largest companies benefit from the concentration of security expertise at the cloud provider.

On the anti-cloud side, the cloud provider might not meet your legal needs. You might have regulatory requirements that the cloud provider cannot meet. Your data might be stored in a country with laws you do not like—or cannot legally use. Many foreign companies are thinking twice about putting their data inside America, because of laws allowing the government to get at that data in secret. Other countries around the world have even more draconian government-access rules.

Also on the anti-cloud side, a large cloud provider is a juicier target. Whether or not this matters depends on your threat profile. Criminals already steal far more credit card numbers than they can monetize; they are more likely to go after the smaller, less-defended networks. But a national intelligence agency will prefer the one-stop shop a cloud provider affords. That is why the NSA broke into Google's data centers.

Finally, the loss of control is a security risk. Moving your data into the cloud means that someone else is controlling that data. This is fine if they do a good job, but terrible if they do not. And for free cloud services, that loss of control can be critical. The cloud provider can delete your data on a whim, if it believes you have violated some term of service that you never even knew existed. And you have no recourse.

As a business, you need to weigh the benefits against the risks. And that will depend on things like the type of cloud service you're considering, the type of data that's involved, how critical the service is, how easily you could do it in house, the size of your company and the regulatory environment, and so on.

Let me start by describing two approaches to the cloud.

Most of the students I meet at Harvard University live their lives in the cloud. Their email, documents, contacts, calendars, photos and everything else are stored on servers belonging to large Internet companies in America and elsewhere. They use cloud services for everything. They converse and share on Facebook and Instagram and Twitter. They seamlessly switch among their laptops, tablets and phones. It wouldn't be a stretch to say that they don't really care where their computers end and the Internet begins, and they are used to having immediate access to all of their data on the closest screen available.

In contrast, I personally use the cloud as little as possible. My email is on my own computer—I am one of the last Eudora users—and not at a web service like Gmail or Hotmail. I don't store my contacts or calendar in the cloud. I don't use cloud backup. I don't have personal accounts on social networking sites like Facebook or Twitter. (This makes me a freak, but highly productive.) And I don't use many software and hardware products that I would otherwise really like, because they force you to keep your data in the cloud: Trello, Evernote, Fitbit.

Why don't I embrace the cloud in the same way my younger colleagues do? There are three reasons, and they parallel the trade-offs corporations faced with the same decisions are going to make.

The first is control. I want to be in control of my data, and I don't want to give it up. I have the ability to keep control by running my own services my way. Most of those students lack the technical expertise, and have no choice. They also want services that are only available on the cloud, and have no choice. I have deliberately made my life harder, simply to keep that control. Similarly, companies are going to decide whether or not they want to—or even can—keep control of their data.

The second is security. I talked about this at length in my opening statement. Suffice it to say that I am extremely paranoid about cloud security, and think I can do better. Lots of those students don't care very much. Again, companies are going to have to make the same decision about who is going to do a better job, and depending on their own internal resources, they might make a different decision.

The third is the big one: trust. I simply don't trust large corporations with my data. I know that, at least in America, they can sell my data at will and disclose it to whomever they want. It can be made public inadvertently by their lax security. My government can get access to it without a warrant. Again, lots of those students don't care. And again, companies are going to have to make the same decisions.

Like any outsourcing relationship, cloud services are based on trust. If anything, that is what you should take away from this exchange. Try to do business only with trustworthy providers, and put contracts in place to ensure their trustworthiness. Push for government regulations that establish a baseline of trustworthiness for cases where you don't have that negotiation power. Fight laws that give governments secret access to your data in the cloud. Cloud computing is the future of computing; we need to ensure that it is secure and reliable.

Despite my personal choices, my belief is that, in most cases, the benefits of cloud computing outweigh the risks. My company, Resilient Systems, uses cloud services both to run the business and to host our own products that we sell to other companies. For us it makes the most sense. But we spend a lot of effort ensuring that we use only trustworthy cloud providers, and that we are a trustworthy cloud provider to our own customers.

Cloud computing is the future of computing. Specialization and outsourcing make society more efficient and scalable, and computing isn't any different.

But why aren't we there yet? Why don't we, in Simon Crosby's words, "get on with it"? I have discussed some reasons: loss of control, new and unquantifiable security risks, and—above all—a lack of trust. It is not enough to simply discount them, as the number of companies not embracing the cloud shows. It is more useful to consider what we need to do to bridge the trust gap.

A variety of mechanisms can create trust. When I outsourced my food preparation to a restaurant last night, it never occurred to me to worry about food safety. That blind trust is largely created by government regulation. It ensures that our food is safe to eat, just as it ensures our paint will not kill us and our planes are safe to fly. It is all well and good for Mr. Crosby to write that cloud companies "will invest heavily to ensure that they can satisfy complex...regulations," but this presupposes that we have comprehensive regulations. Right now, it is largely a free-for-all out there, and it can be impossible to see how security in the cloud works. When robust consumer-safety regulations underpin outsourcing, people can trust the systems.

This is true for any kind of outsourcing. Attorneys, tax preparers and doctors are licensed and highly regulated, by both governments and professional organizations. We trust our doctors to cut open our bodies because we know they are not just making it up. We need a similar professionalism in cloud computing.

Reputation is another big part of trust. We rely on both word-of-mouth and professional reviews to decide on a particular car or restaurant. But none of that works without considerable transparency. Security is an example. Mr Crosby writes: "Cloud providers design security into their systems and dedicate enormous resources to protect their customers." Maybe some do; many certainly do not. Without more transparency, as a cloud customer you cannot tell the difference. Try asking either Amazon Web Services or Salesforce.com to see the details of their security arrangements, or even to indemnify you for data breaches on their networks. It is even worse for free consumer cloud services like Gmail and iCloud.

We need to trust cloud computing's performance, reliability and security. We need open standards, rules about being able to remove our data from cloud services, and the assurance that we can switch cloud services if we want to.

We also need to trust who has access to our data, and under what circumstances. One commenter wrote: "After Snowden, the idea of doing your computing in the cloud is preposterous." He isn't making a technical argument: a typical corporate data center isn't any better defended than a cloud-computing one. He is making a legal argument. Under American law—and similar laws in other countries—the government can force your cloud provider to give up your data without your knowledge and consent. If your data is in your own data center, you at least get to see a copy of the court order.

Corporate surveillance matters, too. Many cloud companies mine and sell your data or use it to manipulate you into buying things. Blocking broad surveillance by both governments and corporations is critical to trusting the cloud, as is eliminating secret laws and orders regarding data access.

In the future, we will do all our computing in the cloud: both commodity computing and computing that requires personalized expertise. But this future will only come to pass when we manage to create trust in the cloud.

Security Economics of the Internet of Things

Originally published in Vice Motherboard, *October 6, 2016*

Brian Krebs is a popular reporter on the cybersecurity beat. He regularly exposes cybercriminals and their tactics, and consequently is regularly a target of their ire. Last month, he wrote about an online attack-for-hire service that resulted in the arrest of the two proprietors. In the aftermath, his site was taken down by a massive DDoS attack.

In many ways, this is nothing new. Distributed denial-of-service attacks are a family of attacks that cause websites and other Internet-connected systems to crash by overloading them with traffic. The "distributed" part means that other insecure computers on the Internet—sometimes in the millions—are recruited to a botnet to unwittingly participate in the attack. The tactics are decades old; DDoS attacks are perpetrated by lone hackers trying to be annoying, criminals trying to extort money, and governments testing their tactics. There are defenses, and there are companies that offer DDoS mitigation services for hire.

Basically, it's a size vs. size game. If the attackers can cobble together a fire hose of data bigger than the defender's capability to cope with, they win. If the defenders can increase their capability in the face of attack, they win.

What was new about the Krebs attack was both the massive scale and the particular devices the attackers recruited. Instead of using traditional computers for their botnet, they used CCTV cameras, digital video recorders, home routers, and other embedded computers attached to the Internet as part of the Internet of Things.

Much has been written about how the IoT is wildly insecure. In fact, the software used to attack Krebs was simple and amateurish. What this attack demonstrates is that the economics of the IoT mean that it will remain insecure unless government steps in to fix the problem. This is a market failure that can't get fixed on its own.

Our computers and smartphones are as secure as they are because there are teams of security engineers working on the problem. Companies like Microsoft, Apple, and Google spend a lot of time testing their code before it's released, and quickly patch vulnerabilities when they're discovered. Those companies can support such teams because those companies make a huge amount of money, either directly or indirectly, from their software—and, in part, compete on its security. This isn't true of embedded systems like digital video recorders or home routers. Those systems are sold at a much lower margin, and are often built by offshore third parties. The companies involved simply don't have the expertise to make them secure.

Even worse, most of these devices don't have any way to be patched. Even though the source code to the botnet that attacked Krebs has been made public, we can't update the affected devices. Microsoft delivers security patches to your computer once a month. Apple does it just as regularly, but not on a fixed schedule. But the only way for you to update the firmware in your home router is to throw it away and buy a new one.

The security of our computers and phones also comes from the fact that we replace them regularly. We buy new laptops every few years. We get new phones even more frequently. This isn't true for all of the embedded IoT systems. They last for years, even decades. We might buy a new DVR every five or ten years. We replace our refrigerator every 25 years. We replace our thermostat approximately never. Already the banking industry is dealing with the security problems of

Windows 95 embedded in ATMs. This same problem is going to occur all over the Internet of Things.

The market can't fix this because neither the buyer nor the seller cares. Think of all the CCTV cameras and DVRs used in the attack against Brian Krebs. The owners of those devices don't care. Their devices were cheap to buy, they still work, and they don't even know Brian. The sellers of those devices don't care: they're now selling newer and better models, and the original buyers only cared about price and features. There is no market solution because the insecurity is what economists call an externality: it's an effect of the purchasing decision that affects other people. Think of it kind of like invisible pollution.

What this all means is that the IoT will remain insecure unless government steps in and fixes the problem. When we have market failures, government is the only solution. The government could impose security regulations on IoT manufacturers, forcing them to make their devices secure even though their customers don't care. They could impose liabilities on manufacturers, allowing people like Brian Krebs to sue them. Any of these would raise the cost of insecurity and give companies incentives to spend money making their devices secure.

Of course, this would only be a domestic solution to an international problem. The Internet is global, and attackers can just as easily build a botnet out of IoT devices from Asia as from the United States. Long term, we need to build an Internet that is resilient against attacks like this. But that's a long time coming. In the meantime, you can expect more attacks that leverage insecure IoT devices.

8 Human Aspects of Security

Human-Machine Trust Failures

Originally published in the Sept/Oct 2013 issue of
IEEE Security & Privacy

I jacked a visitor's badge from the Eisenhower Executive Office Building in Washington, DC, last month. The badges are electronic; they're enabled when you check in at building security. You're supposed to wear it on a chain around your neck at all times and drop it through a slot when you leave.

I kept the badge. I used my body as a shield, and the chain made a satisfying noise when it hit bottom. The guard let me through the gate.

The person after me had problems, though. Some part of the system knew something was wrong, and wouldn't let her out. Eventually, the guard had to manually override something.

My point in telling this story is not to demonstrate how I beat the EEOB's security—I'm sure the badge was quickly deactivated and showed up in some missing-badge log next to my name—but to illustrate how security vulnerabilities can result from human/machine trust failures. Something went wrong between when I went through the gate and when the person after me did. The system knew it but couldn't adequately explain it to the guards. The guards knew it but didn't know the details. Because the failure occurred when the person after me tried to leave the building, they assumed she was the problem. And when they cleared her of wrongdoing, they blamed the system.

In any hybrid security system, the human portion needs to trust the machine portion. To do so, both must understand the expected behavior for every state—how the system can fail and what those failures look like. The machine must be able to communicate its state and have the capacity to alert the humans when an expected state transition doesn't happen as expected. Things will go wrong, either by accident or as the result of an attack, and the humans are going to need to troubleshoot the system in real time—that requires understanding on both parts. Each time things go wrong, and the machine portion doesn't communicate well, the human portion trusts it a little less.

This problem is not specific to security systems, but inducing this sort of confusion is a good way to attack systems. When the attackers understand the system—especially the machine part—better than the humans in the system do, they can create a failure to exploit. Many social engineering attacks fall into this category. Failures also happen the other way. We've all experienced trust without understanding, when the human part of the system defers to the machine, even though it makes no sense: "The computer is always right."

Humans and machines have different strengths. Humans are flexible and can do creative thinking in ways that machines cannot. But they're easily fooled. Machines are more rigid and can handle state changes and process flows much better than humans can. But they're bad at dealing with exceptions. If humans are to serve as security sensors, they need to understand what is being sensed. (That's why "if you see something, say something" fails so often.) If a machine automatically processes input, it needs to clearly flag anything unexpected.

The more machine security is automated, and the more the machine is expected to enforce security without human intervention, the greater the impact of a successful attack. If this sounds like an argument for interface simplicity, it is. The machine design will be necessarily more complicated: more resilience, more error handling, and more internal checking. But the human/computer communication needs to be clear and straightforward. That's the best way to give humans the trust and understanding they need in the machine part of any security system.

Government Secrecy and the Generation Gap

Originally published in the Financial Times,
September 5, 2013

Big-government secrets require a lot of secret-keepers. As of October 2012, almost 5m people in the US have security clearances, with 1.4m at the top-secret level or higher, according to the Office of the Director of National Intelligence.

Most of these people do not have access to as much information as Edward Snowden, the former National Security Agency contractor turned leaker, or even Chelsea Manning, the former US army soldier previously known as Bradley who was convicted for giving material to WikiLeaks. But a lot of them do—and that may prove the Achilles heel of government. Keeping secrets is an act of loyalty as much as anything else, and that sort of loyalty is becoming harder to find in the younger generations. If the NSA and other intelligence bodies are going to survive in their present form, they are going to have to figure out how to reduce the number of secrets.

As the writer Charles Stross has explained, the old way of keeping intelligence secrets was to make it part of a life-long culture. The intelligence world would recruit people early in their careers and give them jobs for life. It was a private club, one filled with code words and secret knowledge.

You can see part of this in Mr Snowden's leaked documents. The NSA has its own lingo—the documents are riddled with codename—its own conferences, its own awards and recognitions. An intelligence career meant that you had access to a new world, one to which "normal" people on the outside were completely oblivious. Membership of the private club meant people were loyal to their organisations, which were in turn loyal back to them.

Those days are gone. Yes, there are still the codenames and the secret knowledge, but a lot of the loyalty is gone. Many jobs in intelligence are now outsourced, and there is no job-for-life culture in the corporate world any more. Workforces are flexible, jobs are interchangeable and people are expendable.

Sure, it is possible to build a career in the classified world of government contracting, but there are no guarantees. Younger people grew up knowing this: there are no employment guarantees anywhere. They see it in their friends. They see it all around them.

Many will also believe in openness, especially the hacker types the NSA needs to recruit. They believe that information wants to be free, and that security comes from public knowledge and debate. Yes, there are important reasons why some intelligence secrets need to be secret, and the NSA culture reinforces secrecy daily. But this is a crowd that is used to radical openness. They have been writing about themselves on the Internet for years. They have said very personal things on Twitter; they have had embarrassing photographs of themselves posted on Facebook. They have been dumped by a lover in public. They have overshared in the most compromising ways—and they have got through it. It is a tougher sell convincing this crowd that government secrecy trumps the public's right to know.

Psychologically, it is hard to be a whistleblower. There is an enormous amount of pressure to be loyal to our peer group: to conform to their beliefs, and not to let them down. Loyalty is a natural human trait; it is one of the social mechanisms we use to thrive in our complex social world. This is why good people sometimes do bad things at work.

When someone becomes a whistleblower, he or she is deliberately eschewing that loyalty. In essence, they are deciding that allegiance to society at large trumps that to peers at work. That is the difficult part. They know their work buddies by name, but "society at large" is amorphous and anonymous. Believing that your bosses ultimately do not care about you makes that switch easier.

Whistleblowing is the civil disobedience of the information age. It is a way that someone without power can make a difference. And in the information age—the fact that everything is stored on computers and potentially accessible with a few keystrokes and mouse clicks—whistleblowing is easier than ever.

Mr Snowden is 30 years old; Manning 25. They are members of the generation we taught not to expect anything long-term from their employers. As such, employers should not expect anything long-term from them. It is still hard to be a whistleblower, but for this generation it is a whole lot easier.

A lot has been written about the problem of over-classification in US government. It has long been thought of as anti-democratic and a barrier to government oversight. Now we know that it is also a security risk. Organizations such as the NSA need to change their culture of secrecy, and concentrate their security efforts on what truly needs to remain secret. Their default practice of classifying everything is not going to work any more.

Hey, NSA, you've got a problem.

Choosing Secure Passwords

Originally published in Boing Boing, *February 25, 2014*

As insecure as passwords generally are, they're not going away anytime soon. Every year you have more and more passwords to deal with, and every year they get easier and easier to break. You need a strategy.

The best way to explain how to choose a good password is to explain how they're broken. The general attack model is what's known as an offline password-guessing attack. In this scenario, the attacker gets a file of encrypted passwords from somewhere people want to authenticate to. His goal is to turn that encrypted file into unencrypted passwords he can use to authenticate himself. He does this by guessing passwords, and then seeing if they're correct. He can try guesses as fast as his computer will process them—and he can parallelize the attack—and gets immediate confirmation if he guesses correctly. Yes, there are ways to foil this attack, and that's why we can still have four-digit PINs on ATM cards, but it's the correct model for breaking passwords.

There are commercial programs that do password cracking, sold primarily to police departments. There are also hacker tools that do the same thing. And they're *really* good.

The efficiency of password cracking depends on two largely independent things: power and efficiency.

Power is simply computing power. As computers have become faster, they're able to test more passwords per second; one program advertises eight million per second. These crackers might run for days, on many machines simultaneously. For a high-profile police case, they might run for months.

Efficiency is the ability to guess passwords cleverly. It doesn't make sense to run through every eight-letter combination from "aaaaaaaa" to "zzzzzzzz" in order. That's 200 billion possible passwords, most of them very unlikely. Password crackers try the most common passwords first.

A typical password consists of a root plus an appendage. The root isn't necessarily a dictionary word, but it's usually something pronounceable. An appendage is either a suffix (90% of the time) or a prefix (10% of the time). One cracking program I saw started with a dictionary of about 1,000 common passwords, things like "letmein," "temp," "123456," and so on. Then it tested them each with about 100 common suffix appendages: "1," "4u," "69," "abc," "!," and so on. It recovered about a quarter of all passwords with just these 100,000 combinations.

Crackers use different dictionaries: English words, names, foreign words, phonetic patterns and so on for roots; two digits, dates, single symbols and so on for appendages. They run the dictionaries with various capitalizations and common substitutions: "$" for "s", "@" for "a," "1" for "l" and so on. This guessing strategy quickly breaks about two-thirds of all passwords.

Modern password crackers combine different words from their dictionaries:

> *What was remarkable about all three cracking sessions were the types of plains that got revealed. They included passcodes such as "k1araj0hns0n," "Sh1alabe0uf," "Apr!l221973," "Qbesancon321," "DG091101%," "@Yourmom69," "ilovetofunot," "windermere2313," "tmdmmj17," and "BandGeek2014." Also included in the list: "all of the lights" (yes, spaces are allowed on many sites), "i hate hackers," "allineedislove," "ilovemySister31," "iloveyousomuch," "Philippians4:13," "Philippians4:6-7," and "qeadzcwrsfxv1331." "gonefishing1125" was another password Steube saw appear on his computer screen. Seconds after it was cracked, he noted, "You won't ever find it using brute force."*

This is why the oft-cited XKCD scheme for generating passwords—string together individual words like "correcthorsebatterystaple"—is no longer good advice. The password crackers are on to this trick.

The attacker will feed any personal information he has access to about the password creator into the password crackers. A good password cracker will test names and addresses from the address book, meaningful dates, and any other personal information it has. Postal codes are common appendages. If it can, the guesser will index the target hard drive and create a dictionary that includes every printable string, including deleted files. If you ever saved an email with your password, or kept it in an obscure file somewhere, or if your program ever stored it in memory, this process will grab it. And it will speed the process of recovering your password.

Last year, Ars Technica gave three experts a 16,000-entry encrypted password file, and asked them to break as many as possible. The winner got 90% of them, the loser 62%—in a few hours. It's the same sort of thing we saw in 2012, 2007, and earlier. If there's any new news, it's that this kind of thing is getting easier faster than people think.

Pretty much anything that can be remembered can be cracked.

There's still one scheme that works. Back in 2008, I described the "Schneier scheme":

> So if you want your password to be hard to guess, you should choose something that this process will miss. My advice is to take a sentence and turn it into a password. Something like "This little piggy went to market" might become "tlpWENT2m". That nine-character password won't be in anyone's dictionary. Of course, don't use this one, because I've written about it. Choose your own sentence—something personal.

Here are some examples:

- WIw7,mstmsritt... = When I was seven, my sister threw my stuffed rabbit in the toilet.
- Wow...doestcst = Wow, does that couch smell terrible.
- Ltime@go-inag~faaa! = Long time ago in a galaxy not far away at all.
- uTVM,TPw55:utvm,tpwstillsecure = Until this very moment, these passwords were still secure.

You get the idea. Combine a personally memorable sentence with some personally memorable tricks to modify that sentence into a password to create a lengthy password. Of course, the site has to accept all of those non-alpha-numeric characters and an arbitrarily long password. Otherwise, it's much harder.

Even better is to use random unmemorable alphanumeric passwords (with symbols, if the site will allow them), and a password manager like Password Safe to create and store them. Password Safe includes a random password generation function. Tell it how many characters you want—twelve is my default—and it'll give you passwords like y.)v_|.7)7Bl, B3h4_[%}kgv), and QG6,FN4nFAm_. The program supports cut and paste, so you're not actually typing those characters very much. I'm recommending Password Safe for Windows because I wrote the first version, know the person currently in charge of the code, and trust its security. There are ports of Password Safe to other OSs, but I had nothing to do with those. There are also other password managers out there, if you want to shop around.

There's more to passwords than simply choosing a good one:

1. Never reuse a password you care about. Even if you choose a secure password, the site it's for could leak it because of its own incompetence. You don't want someone who gets your password for one application or site to be able to use it for another.

2. Don't bother updating your password regularly. Sites that require 90-day—or whatever—password upgrades do more harm than good. Unless you think your password might be compromised, don't change it.

3. Beware the "secret question." You don't want a backup system for when you forget your password to be easier to break than your password. Really, it's smart to use a password manager. Or to write your passwords down on a piece of paper and *secure that piece of paper.*

4. One more piece of advice: if a site offers two-factor authentication, seriously consider using it. It's almost certainly a security improvement.

The Human Side of Heartbleed

Originally published in the Mark News, *May 19, 2014*

The announcement on April 7 was alarming. A new Internet vulnerability called Heartbleed could allow hackers to steal your logins and passwords. It affected a piece of security software that is used on half a million websites worldwide. Fixing it would be hard: It would strain our security infrastructure and the patience of users everywhere.

It was a software insecurity, but the problem was entirely human.

Software has vulnerabilities because it's written by people, and people make mistakes—thousands of mistakes. This particular mistake was made in 2011 by a German graduate student who was one of the unpaid volunteers working on a piece of software called OpenSSL. The update was approved by a British consultant.

In retrospect, the mistake should have been obvious, and it's amazing that no one caught it. But even though thousands of large companies around the world used this critical piece of software for free, no one took the time to review the code after its release.

The mistake was discovered around March 21, 2014, and was reported on April 1 by Neel Mehta of Google's security team, who quickly realized how potentially devastating it was. Two days later, in an odd coincidence, researchers at a security company called Codenomicon independently discovered it.

When a researcher discovers a major vulnerability in a widely used piece of software, he generally discloses it responsibly. Why? As soon as a vulnerability becomes public, criminals will start using it to hack systems, steal identities, and generally create mayhem, so we have to work together to fix the vulnerability quickly after it's announced.

The researchers alerted some of the larger companies quietly so that they could fix their systems before the public announcement. (Who to tell early is another very human problem: If you tell too few, you're not really helping, but if you tell too many, the secret could get out.) Then Codenomicon announced the vulnerability.

One of the biggest problems we face in the security community is how to communicate these sorts of vulnerabilities. The story is technical, and people often don't know how to react to the risk. In this case, the Codenomicon researchers did well. They created a public website explaining (in simple terms) the vulnerability and how to fix it, and they created a logo—a red bleeding heart—that every news outlet used for coverage of the story.

The first week of coverage varied widely, as some people panicked and others downplayed the threat. This wasn't surprising: There was a lot of uncertainty about the risk, and it wasn't immediately obvious how disastrous the vulnerability actually was.

The major Internet companies were quick to patch vulnerable systems. Individuals were less likely to update their passwords, but by and large, that was OK.

True to form, hackers started exploiting the vulnerability within minutes of the announcement. We assume that governments also exploited the vulnerability while they could. I'm sure the US National Security Agency had advance warning.

By now, it's largely over. There are still lots of unpatched systems out there. (Many of them are embedded hardware systems that can't be patched.) The risk of attack is still there, but minimal. In the end, the actual damage was also minimal, although the expense of restoring security was great.

The question that remains is this: What should we expect in the future—are there more Heartbleeds out there?

Yes. Yes there are. The software we use contains thousands of mistakes—many of them security vulnerabilities. Lots of people are looking for these vulnerabilities: Researchers are looking for them. Criminals and hackers are looking for them. National intelligence agencies in the United States, the United Kingdom, China, Russia, and elsewhere are looking for them. The software vendors themselves are looking for them.

What happens when a vulnerability is found depends on who finds it. If the vendor finds it, it quietly fixes it. If a researcher finds it, he or she alerts the vendor and then reports it to the public. If a national intelligence agency finds the vulnerability, it either quietly uses it to spy on others or—if we're lucky—alerts the vendor. If criminals and hackers find it, they use it until a security company notices and alerts the vendor, and then it gets fixed—usually within a month.

Heartbleed was unique because there was no single fix. The software had to be updated, and then websites had to regenerate their encryption keys and get new public-key certificates. After that, people had to update their passwords. This multi-stage process had to take place publicly, which is why the announcement happened the way it did.

Yes, it'll happen again. But most of the time, it'll be easier to deal with than this.

The Security of Data Deletion

Originally published in ArsTechnica.com, *January 12, 2015*

Thousands of articles have called the December attack against Sony Pictures a wake-up call to industry. Regardless of whether the attacker was the North Korean government, a disgruntled former employee, or a group of random hackers, the attack showed how vulnerable a large organization can be and how devastating the publication of its private correspondence, proprietary data, and intellectual property can be.

But while companies are supposed to learn that they need to improve their security against attack, there's another equally important but much less discussed lesson here: companies should have an aggressive deletion policy.

One of the social trends of the computerization of our business and social communications tools is the loss of the ephemeral. Things we used to say in person or on the phone we now say in email, by text message, or on social networking platforms. Memos we used to read and then throw away now remain in our digital archives. Big data initiatives mean that we're saving everything we can about our customers on the remote chance that it might be useful later.

Everything is now digital, and storage is cheap—why not save it all?

Sony illustrates the reason why not. The hackers published old emails from company executives that caused enormous public embarrassment to the company. They published old emails by employees that caused less-newsworthy personal embarrassment to those employees, and these messages are resulting in class-action lawsuits against the company. They published old documents. They published everything they got their hands on.

Saving data, especially email and informal chats, is a liability.

It's also a security risk: the risk of exposure. The exposure could be accidental. It could be the result of data theft, as happened to Sony. Or it could be the result of litigation. Whatever the reason, the best security against these eventualities is not to have the data in the first place.

If Sony had had an aggressive data deletion policy, much of what was leaked couldn't have been stolen and wouldn't have been published.

An organization-wide deletion policy makes sense. Customer data should be deleted as soon as it isn't immediately useful. Internal emails can probably be deleted after a few months, IM chats even more quickly, and other documents in one to two years. There are exceptions, of course, but they should be exceptions. Individuals should need to deliberately flag documents and correspondence for longer retention. But unless there are laws requiring an organization to save a particular type of data for a prescribed length of time, deletion should be the norm.

This has always been true, but many organizations have forgotten it in the age of big data. In the wake of the devastating leak of terabytes of sensitive Sony data, I hope we'll all remember it now.

Living in a Code Yellow World

Originally published in Fusion.net, *September 22, 2015*

In the 1980s, handgun expert Jeff Cooper invented something called the Color Code to describe what he called the "combat mind-set." Here is his summary:

> In **White** you are unprepared and unready to take lethal action. If you are attacked in White you will probably die unless your adversary is totally inept.
>
> In **Yellow** you bring yourself to the understanding that your life may be in danger and that you may have to do something about it.
>
> In **Orange** you have determined upon a specific adversary and are prepared to take action which may result in his death, but you are not in a lethal mode.
>
> In **Red** you are in a lethal mode and will shoot if circumstances warrant.

Cooper talked about remaining in Code Yellow over time, but he didn't write about its psychological toll. It's significant. Our brains can't be on that alert level constantly. We need downtime. We need to relax. This is why we have friends around whom we can let our guard down and homes where we can close our doors to outsiders. We only want to visit Yellowland occasionally.

Since 9/11, the US has increasingly become Yellowland, a place where we assume danger is imminent. It's damaging to us individually and as a society.

I don't mean to minimize actual danger. Some people really do live in a Code Yellow world, due to the failures of government in their home countries. Even there, we know how hard it is for them to maintain a constant level of alertness in the face of constant danger. Psychologist Abraham Maslow wrote about this, making safety a basic level in his hierarchy of needs. A lack of safety makes people anxious and tense, and the long-term effects are debilitating.

The same effects occur when we believe we're living in an unsafe situation even if we're not. The psychological term for this is hypervigilance. Hypervigilance in the face of imagined danger causes stress and anxiety. This, in turn, alters how your hippocampus functions, and causes an excess of cortisol in your body. Now cortisol is great in small and infrequent doses, and helps you run away from tigers. But it destroys your brain and body if you marinate in it for extended periods of time.

Not only does trying to live in Yellowland harm you physically, it changes how you interact with your environment and it impairs your judgment. You forget what's normal and start seeing the enemy everywhere. Terrorism actually relies on this kind of reaction to succeed.

Here's an example from *The Washington Post* last year: "I was taking pictures of my daughters. A stranger thought I was exploiting them." A father wrote about his run-in with an off-duty DHS agent, who interpreted an innocent family photoshoot as something nefarious and proceeded to harass and lecture the family. That the parents were white and the daughters Asian added a racist element to the encounter.

At the time, people wrote about this as an example of worst-case thinking, saying that as a DHS agent, "he's paid to suspect the worst at all times and butt in." While, yes, it was a "disturbing reminder of how the mantra of 'see something, say something' has muddied the waters of what constitutes suspicious activity," I think there's a deeper story here. The agent is trying to live his life in Yellowland, and it caused him to see predators where there weren't any.

I call these "movie-plot threats," scenarios that would make great action movies but that are implausible in real life. Yellowland is filled with them.

Last December former DHS director Tom Ridge wrote about the security risks of building a NFL stadium near the Los Angeles Airport. His report is full of movie-plot threats, including terrorists shooting down a plane and crashing it into a stadium. His conclusion, that it is simply too dangerous to build a sports stadium within a few miles of the airport, is absurd. He's been living too long in Yellowland.

That our brains aren't built to live in Yellowland makes sense, because actual attacks are rare. The person walking towards you on the street isn't an attacker. The person doing something unexpected over there isn't a terrorist. Crashing an airplane into a sports stadium is more suitable to a *Die Hard* movie than real life. And the white man taking pictures of two Asian teenagers on a ferry isn't a sex slaver. (I mean, really?)

Most of us, that DHS agent included, are complete amateurs at knowing the difference between something benign and something that's actually dangerous. Combine this with the rarity of attacks, and you end up with an overwhelming number of false alarms. This is the ultimate problem with programs like "see something, say something." They waste an enormous amount of time and money.

Those of us fortunate enough to live in a Code White society are much better served acting like we do. This is something we need to learn at all levels, from our personal interactions to our national policy. Since the terrorist attacks of 9/11, many of our counterterrorism policies have helped convince people they're not safe, and that they need to be in a constant state of readiness. We need our leaders to lead us out of Yellowland, not to perpetuate it.

This essay previously appeared on Fusion.net.

Security Design: Stop Trying to Fix the User

Originally published in the Sep/Oct 2016 issue of
IEEE Security & Privacy

Every few years, a researcher replicates a security study by littering USB sticks around an organization's grounds and waiting to see how many people pick them up and plug them in, causing the autorun function to install innocuous malware on their computers. These studies are great for making security professionals feel superior. The researchers get to demonstrate their security expertise and use the results as "teachable moments" for others. "If only everyone was more security aware and had more security training," they say, "the Internet would be a much safer place."

Enough of that. The problem isn't the users: it's that we've designed our computer systems' security so badly that we demand the user do all of these counterintuitive things. Why can't users choose easy-to-remember passwords? Why can't they click on links in emails with wild abandon? Why can't they plug a USB stick into a computer without facing a myriad of viruses? Why are we trying to fix the user instead of solving the underlying security problem?

Traditionally, we've thought about security and usability as a trade-off: a more secure system is less functional and more annoying, and a more capable, flexible, and powerful system is less secure. This "either/or" thinking results in systems that are neither usable nor secure.

Our industry is littered with examples. First: security warnings. Despite researchers' good intentions, these warnings just inure people to them. I've read dozens of studies about how to get people to pay attention to security warnings. We can tweak their wording, highlight them in red, and jiggle them on the screen, but nothing works because users know the warnings are invariably meaningless. They don't see "the certificate has expired; are you sure you want to go to this webpage?" They see, "I'm an annoying message preventing you from reading a webpage. Click here to get rid of me."

Next: passwords. It makes no sense to force users to generate passwords for websites they only log in to once or twice a year. Users realize this: they store those passwords in their browsers, or they never even bother trying to remember them, using the "I forgot my password" link as a way to bypass the system completely—effectively falling back on the security of their email account.

And finally: phishing links. Users are free to click around the Web until they encounter a link to a phishing website. Then everyone wants to know how to train the user not to click on suspicious links. But you can't train users not to click on links when you've spent the past two decades teaching them that links are there to be clicked.

We must stop trying to fix the user to achieve security. We'll never get there, and research toward those goals just obscures the real problems. Usable security does not mean "getting people to do what we want." It means creating security that works, given (or despite) what people do. It means security solutions that deliver on users' security goals without—as the 19th-century Dutch cryptographer Auguste Kerckhoffs aptly put it—"stress of mind, or knowledge of a long series of rules."

I've been saying this for years. Security usability guru (and one of the guest editors of this issue) M. Angela Sasse has been saying it even longer. People—and developers—are finally starting to listen. Many security updates happen automatically so users don't have to remember to manually update their systems. Opening a Word or Excel document inside Google Docs isolates it from the user's system so they don't have to worry about embedded malware. And programs can run in sandboxes that don't compromise the entire computer. We've come a long way, but we have a lot further to go.

"Blame the victim" thinking is older than the Internet, of course. But that doesn't make it right. We owe it to our users to make the Information Age a safe place for everyone—not just those with "security awareness."

Security Orchestration and Incident Response

Originally published in the Security Intelligence blog, *March 21, 2017*

Last month at the RSA Conference, I saw a lot of companies selling security incident response automation. Their promise was to replace people with computers—sometimes with the addition of machine learning or other artificial intelligence techniques—and to respond to attacks at computer speeds.

While this is a laudable goal, there's a fundamental problem with doing this in the short term. You can only automate what you're certain about, and there is still an enormous amount of uncertainty in cybersecurity. Automation has its place in incident response, but the focus needs to be on making the people effective, not on replacing them—security orchestration, not automation.

This isn't just a choice of words—it's a difference in philosophy. The US military went through this in the 1990s. What was called the Revolution in Military Affairs (RMA) was supposed to change how warfare was fought. Satellites, drones and battlefield sensors were supposed to give commanders unprecedented information about what was going on, while networked soldiers and weaponry would enable troops to coordinate to a degree never before possible. In short, the traditional fog of war would be replaced by perfect information, providing certainty instead of uncertainty. They, too, believed certainty would fuel automation and, in many circumstances, allow technology to replace people.

Of course, it didn't work out that way. The US learned in Afghanistan and Iraq that there are a lot of holes in both its collection and coordination systems. Drones have their place, but they can't replace ground troops. The advances from the RMA brought with them some enormous advantages, especially against militaries that didn't have access to the same technologies, but never resulted in certainty. Uncertainty still rules the battlefield, and soldiers on the ground are still the only effective way to control a region of territory.

But along the way, we learned a lot about how the feeling of certainty affects military thinking. Last month, I attended a lecture on the topic by H.R. McMaster. This was before he became President Trump's national security advisor-designate. Then, he was the director of the Army Capabilities Integration Center. His lecture touched on many topics, but at one point he talked about the failure of the RMA. He confirmed that military strategists mistakenly believed that data would give them certainty. But he took this change in thinking further, outlining the ways this belief in certainty had repercussions in how military strategists thought about modern conflict.

McMaster's observations are directly relevant to Internet security incident response. We too have been led to believe that data will give us certainty, and we are making the same mistakes that the military did in the 1990s. In a world of uncertainty, there's a premium on understanding, because commanders need to figure out what's going on. In a world of certainty, knowing what's going on becomes a simple matter of data collection.

I see this same fallacy in Internet security. Many companies exhibiting at the RSA Conference promised to collect and display more data and that the data will reveal everything. This simply isn't true. Data does not equal information, and information does not equal understanding. We need data, but we also must prioritize understanding the data we have over collecting ever more data. Much like the problems with bulk surveillance, the "collect it all" approach provides minimal value over collecting the specific data that's useful.

In a world of uncertainty, the focus is on execution. In a world of certainty, the focus is on planning. I see this manifesting in Internet security as well. My own Resilient Systems—now part of IBM Security—allows incident response teams to manage security incidents and intrusions. While the tool is useful for planning and testing, its real focus is always on execution.

Uncertainty demands initiative, while certainty demands synchronization. Here, again, we are heading too far down the wrong path. The purpose of all incident response tools should be to make the human responders more effective. They need both the ability and the capability to exercise it effectively.

When things are uncertain, you want your systems to be decentralized. When things are certain, centralization is more important. Good incident response teams know that decentralization goes hand in hand with initiative. And finally, a world of uncertainty prioritizes command, while a world of certainty prioritizes control. Again, effective incident response teams know this, and effective managers aren't scared to release and delegate control.

Like the US military, we in the incident response field have shifted too much into the world of certainty. We have prioritized data collection, preplanning, synchronization, centralization and control. You can see it in the way people talk about the future of Internet security, and you can see it in the products and services offered on the show floor of the RSA Conference.

Automation, too, is fixed. Incident response needs to be dynamic and agile, because you are never certain and there is an adaptive, malicious adversary on the other end. You need a response system that has human controls and can modify itself on the fly. Automation just doesn't allow a system to do that to the extent that's needed in today's environment. Just as the military shifted from trying to replace the soldier to making the best soldier possible, we need to do the same.

For some time, I have been talking about incident response in terms of OODA loops. This is a way of thinking about real-time adversarial relationships, originally developed for airplane dogfights, but much more broadly applicable. OODA stands for observe-orient-decide-act, and it's what people responding to a cybersecurity incident do constantly, over and over again. We need tools that augment each of those four steps. These tools need to operate in a world of uncertainty, where there is never enough data to know everything that is going on. We need to prioritize understanding, execution, initiative, decentralization and command.

At the same time, we're going to have to make all of this scale. If anything, the most seductive promise of a world of certainty and automation is that it allows defense to scale. The problem is that we're not there yet. We can automate and scale parts of IT security, such as antivirus, automatic patching and firewall management, but we can't yet scale incident response. We still need people. And we need to understand what can be automated and what can't be.

The word I prefer is orchestration. Security orchestration represents the union of people, process and technology. It's computer automation where it works, and human coordination where that's necessary. It's networked systems giving people understanding and capabilities for execution. It's making those on the front lines of incident response the most effective they can be, instead of trying to replace them. It's the best approach we have for cyberdefense.

Automation has its place. If you think about the product categories where it has worked, they're all areas where we have pretty strong certainty. Automation works in antivirus, firewalls, patch management and authentication systems. None of them is perfect, but all those systems are right almost all the time, and we've developed ancillary systems to deal with it when they're wrong.

Automation fails in incident response because there's too much uncertainty. Actions can be automated once the people understand what's going on, but people are still required. For example, IBM's Watson for Cyber Security provides insights for incident response teams based on its ability to ingest and find patterns in an enormous amount of freeform data. It does not attempt a level of understanding necessary to take people out of the equation.

From within an orchestration model, automation can be incredibly powerful. But it's the human-centric orchestration model—the dashboards, the reports, the collaboration—that makes automation work. Otherwise, you're blindly trusting the machine. And when an uncertain process is automated, the results can be dangerous.

Technology continues to advance, and this is all a changing target. Eventually, computers will become intelligent enough to replace people at real-time incident response. My guess, though, is that computers are not going to get there by collecting enough data to be certain. More likely, they'll develop the ability to exhibit understanding and operate in a world of uncertainty. That's a much harder goal.

Yes, today, this is all science fiction. But it's not stupid science fiction, and it might become reality during the lifetimes of our children. Until then, we need people in the loop. Orchestration is a way to achieve that.

9

Leaking, Hacking, Doxing, and Whistleblowing

Government Secrets and the Need for Whistleblowers

Originally published in the Atlantic, *June 6, 2013*

Yesterday, we learned that the NSA received all calling records from Verizon customers for a three-month period starting in April. That's everything except the voice content: who called who, where they were, how long the call lasted—for millions of people, both Americans and foreigners. This "metadata" allows the government to track the movements of everyone during that period, and build a detailed picture of who talks to whom. It's exactly the same data the Justice Department collected about AP journalists.

The *Guardian* delivered this revelation after receiving a copy of a secret memo about this—presumably from a whistleblower. We don't know if the other phone companies handed data to the NSA too. We don't know if this was a one-off demand or a continuously renewed demand; the order started a few days after the Boston bombers were captured by police.

We don't know a lot about how the government spies on us, but we know some things. We know the FBI has issued tens of thousands of ultra-secret National Security Letters to collect all sorts of data on people—we believe on millions of people—and has been abusing them to spy on cloud-computer users. We know it can collect a wide array of personal data from the Internet without a warrant. We also know that the FBI has been intercepting cell-phone data, all but voice content, for the past 20 years without a warrant, and can use the microphone on some powered-off cell phones as a room bug—presumably only with a warrant.

We know that the NSA has many domestic-surveillance and data-mining programs with codenames like Trailblazer, Stellar Wind, and Ragtime—deliberately using different codenames for similar programs to stymie oversight and conceal what's really going on. We know that the NSA is building an enormous computer facility in Utah to store all this data, as well as faster computer networks to process it all. We know the US Cyber Command employs 4,000 people.

We know that the DHS is also collecting a massive amount of data on people, and that local police departments are running "fusion centers" to collect and analyze this data, and covering up its failures. This is all part of the militarization of the police.

Remember in 2003, when Congress defunded the decidedly creepy Total Information Awareness program? It didn't die; it just changed names and split into many smaller programs. We know that corporations are doing an enormous amount of spying on behalf of the government: all parts.

We know all of this not because the government is honest and forthcoming, but mostly through three backchannels—inadvertent hints or outright admissions by government officials in hearings and court cases, information gleaned from government documents received under FOIA, and government whistleblowers.

There's much more we don't know, and often what we know is obsolete. We know quite a bit about the NSA's ECHELON program from a 2000 European investigation, and about the DHS's plans for Total Information Awareness from 2002, but much less about how these programs have evolved. We can make inferences about the NSA's Utah facility based on the theoretical amount of data from various sources, the cost of computation, and the power requirements from the facility, but those are rough guesses at best. For a lot of this, we're completely in the dark.

And that's wrong.

The US government is on a secrecy binge. It overclassifies more information than ever. And we learn, again and again, that our government regularly classifies things not because they need to be secret, but because their release would be embarrassing.

Knowing how the government spies on us is important. Not only because so much of it is illegal—or, to be as charitable as possible, based on novel interpretations of the law—but because we have a right to know. Democracy requires an informed citizenry in order to function properly, and transparency and accountability are essential parts of that. That means knowing what our government is doing to us, in our name. That means knowing that the government is operating within the constraints of the law. Otherwise, we're living in a police state.

We need whistleblowers.

Leaking information without getting caught is difficult. It's almost impossible to maintain privacy in the Internet Age. The WikiLeaks platform seems to have been secure—Bradley Manning was caught not because of a technological flaw, but because someone he trusted betrayed him—but the US government seems to have successfully destroyed it as a platform. None of the spin-offs have risen to become viable yet. The *New Yorker* recently unveiled its Strongbox platform for leaking material, which is still new but looks good. This link contains the best advice on how to leak information to the press via phone, email, or the post office. The National Whistleblowers Center has a page on national-security whistleblowers and their rights.

Leaking information is also very dangerous. The Obama Administration has embarked on a war on whistleblowers, pursuing them—both legally and through intimidation—further than any previous administration has done. Mark Klein, Thomas Drake, and William Binney have all been persecuted for exposing technical details of our surveillance state. Bradley Manning has been treated cruelly and inhumanly—and possibly tortured—for his more-indiscriminate leaking of State Department secrets.

The Obama Administration's actions against the Associated Press, its persecution of Julian Assange, and its unprecedented prosecution of Manning on charges of "aiding the enemy" demonstrate how far it's willing to go to intimidate whistleblowers—as well as the journalists who talk to them.

But whistleblowing is vital, even more broadly than in government spying. It's necessary for good government, and to protect us from abuse of power.

We need details on the full extent of the FBI's spying capabilities. We don't know what information it routinely collects on American citizens, what extra information it collects on those on various watch lists, and what legal justifications it invokes for its actions. We don't know its plans for future data collection. We don't know what scandals and illegal actions—either past or present—are currently being covered up.

We also need information about what data the NSA gathers, either domestically or internationally. We don't know how much it collects surreptitiously, and how much it relies on arrangements with various companies. We don't know how much it uses password cracking to get at encrypted data, and how much it exploits existing system vulnerabilities. We don't know whether it deliberately inserts backdoors into systems it wants to monitor, either with or without the permission of the communications-system vendors.

And we need details about the sorts of analysis the organizations perform. We don't know what they quickly cull at the point of collection, and what they store for later analysis—and how long they store it. We don't know what sort of database profiling they do, how extensive their CCTV and surveillance-drone analysis is, how much they perform behavioral analysis, or how extensively they trace friends of people on their watch lists.

We don't know how big the US surveillance apparatus is today, either in terms of money and people or in terms of how many people are monitored or how much data is collected. Modern technology makes it possible to monitor vastly more people—yesterday's NSA revelations demonstrate that they could easily surveil *everyone*—than could ever be done manually.

Whistleblowing is the moral response to immoral activity by those in power. What's important here are government programs and methods, not data about individuals. I understand I am asking for people to engage in illegal and dangerous behavior. Do it carefully and do it safely, but—and I am talking directly to you, person working on one of these secret and probably illegal programs—do it.

If you see something, say something. There are many people in the US that will appreciate and admire you.

For the rest of us, we can help by protesting this war on whistleblowers. We need to force our politicians not to punish them—to investigate the abuses and not the messengers—and to ensure that those unjustly persecuted can obtain redress.

Our government is putting its own self-interest ahead of the interests of the country. That needs to change.

Protecting Against Leakers

Originally published in Bloomberg.com, *August 21, 2013*

Ever since Edward Snowden walked out of a National Security Agency facility in May with electronic copies of thousands of classified documents, the finger-pointing has concentrated on government's security failures. Yet the debacle illustrates the challenge with trusting people in any organization.

The problem is easy to describe. Organizations require trusted people, but they don't necessarily know whether those people are trustworthy. These individuals are essential, and can also betray organizations.

So how does an organization protect itself?

Securing trusted people requires three basic mechanisms (as I describe in my book *Beyond Fear*). The first is compartmentalization. Trust doesn't have to be all or nothing; it makes sense to give relevant workers only the access, capabilities and information they need to accomplish their assigned tasks. In the military, even if they have the requisite clearance, people are only told what they "need to know." The same policy occurs naturally in companies.

This isn't simply a matter of always granting more senior employees a higher degree of trust. For example, only authorized armored-car delivery people can unlock automated teller machines and put money inside; even the bank president can't do so. Think of an employee as operating within a sphere of trust—a set of assets and functions he or she has access to. Organizations act in their best interest by making that sphere as small as possible.

The idea is that if someone turns out to be untrustworthy, he or she can only do so much damage. This is where the NSA failed with Snowden. As a system administrator, he needed access to many of the agency's computer systems—and he needed access to everything on those machines. This allowed him to make copies of documents he didn't need to see.

The second mechanism for securing trust is defense in depth: Make sure a single person can't compromise an entire system. NSA Director General Keith Alexander has said he is doing this inside the agency by instituting what is called two-person control: There will always be two people performing system-administration tasks on highly classified computers.

Defense in depth reduces the ability of a single person to betray the organization. If this system had been in place and Snowden's superior had been notified every time he downloaded a file, Snowden would have been caught well before his flight to Hong Kong.

The final mechanism is to try to ensure that trusted people are, in fact, trustworthy. The NSA does this through its clearance process, which at high levels includes lie-detector tests (even though they don't work) and background investigations. Many organizations perform reference and credit checks and drug tests when they hire new employees. Companies may refuse to hire people with criminal records or noncitizens; they might hire only those with a particular certification or membership in certain professional organizations. Some of these measures aren't very effective—it's pretty clear that personality profiling doesn't tell you anything useful, for example—but the general idea is to verify, certify and test individuals to increase the chance they can be trusted.

These measures are expensive. It costs the US government about $4,000 to qualify someone for top-secret clearance. Even in a corporation, background checks and screenings are expensive and add considerable time to the hiring process. Giving employees access to only the information they need can hamper them in an agile organization in which needs constantly change. Security audits are expensive, and two-person control is even more expensive: it can double personnel costs. We're always making trade-offs between security and efficiency.

The best defense is to limit the number of trusted people needed within an organization. Alexander is doing this at the NSA—albeit too late—by trying to reduce the number of system administrators by 90 percent. This is just a tiny part of the problem; in the US government, as many as 4 million people, including contractors, hold top-secret or higher security clearances. That's far too many.

More surprising than Snowden's ability to get away with taking the information he downloaded is that there haven't been dozens more like him. His uniqueness—along with the few who have gone before him and how rare whistleblowers are in general—is a testament to how well we normally do at building security around trusted people.

Here's one last piece of advice, specifically about whistleblowers. It's much harder to keep secrets in a networked world, and whistle-blowing has become the civil disobedience of the information age. A public or private organization's best defense against whistleblowers is to refrain from doing things it doesn't want to read about on the front page of the newspaper. This may come as a shock in a market-based system, in which morally dubious behavior is often rewarded as long as it's legal and illegal activity is rewarded as long as you can get away with it.

No organization, whether it's a bank entrusted with the privacy of its customer data, an organized-crime syndicate intent on ruling the world, or a government agency spying on its citizens, wants to have its secrets disclosed. In the information age, though, it may be impossible to avoid.

Why the Government Should Help Leakers

Originally published in CNN.com, *November 4, 2013*

In the Information Age, it's easier than ever to steal and publish data. Corporations and governments have to adjust to their secrets being exposed, regularly.

When massive amounts of government documents are leaked, journalists sift through them to determine which pieces of information are newsworthy, and confer with government agencies over what needs to be redacted.

Managing this reality is going to require that governments actively engage with members of the press who receive leaked secrets, helping them secure those secrets—even while being unable to prevent them from publishing. It might seem abhorrent to help those who are seeking to bring your secrets to light, but it's the best way to ensure that the things that truly need to be secret remain secret, even as everything else becomes public.

The WikiLeaks cables serve as an excellent example of how a government should not deal with massive leaks of classified information.

WikiLeaks has said it asked US authorities for help in determining what should be redacted before publication of documents, although some government officials have challenged that statement. WikiLeaks' media partners did redact many documents, but eventually all 250,000 unredacted cables were released to the world as a result of a mistake.

The damage was nowhere near as serious as government officials initially claimed, but it had been avoidable.

Fast-forward to today, and we have an even bigger trove of classified documents. What Edward Snowden took—"exfiltrated" is the National Security Agency term—dwarfs the State Department cables, and contains considerably more important secrets. But again, the US government is doing nothing to prevent a massive data dump.

The government engages with the press on individual stories. The *Guardian*, the *Washington Post*, and the *New York Times* are all redacting the original Snowden documents based on discussions with the government. This isn't new. The US press regularly consults with the government before publishing something that might be damaging. In 2006, the *New York Times* consulted with both the NSA and the Bush administration before publishing Mark Klein's whistle-blowing about the NSA's eavesdropping on AT&T trunk circuits. In all these cases, the goal is to minimize actual harm to US security while ensuring the press can still report stories in the public interest, even if the government doesn't want it to.

In today's world of reduced secrecy, whistleblowing as civil disobedience, and massive document exfiltrations, negotiations over individual stories aren't enough. The government needs to develop a protocol to actively help news organizations expose their secrets safely and responsibly.

Here's what should have happened as soon as Snowden's whistle-blowing became public. The government should have told the reporters and publications with the classified documents something like this: "OK, you have them. We know that we can't undo the leak. But please let us help. Let us help you secure the documents as you write your stories, and securely dispose of the documents when you're done."

The people who have access to the Snowden documents say they don't want them to be made public in their raw form or to get in the hands of rival governments. But accidents happen, and reporters are not trained in military secrecy practices.

Copies of some of the Snowden documents are being circulated to journalists and others. With each copy, each person, each day, there's a greater chance that, once again, someone will make a mistake and some—or all—of the raw documents will appear on the Internet. A formal system of working with whistleblowers could prevent that.

I'm sure the suggestion sounds odious to a government that is actively engaging in a war on whistleblowers, and that views Snowden as a criminal and the reporters writing these stories as "helping the terrorists." But it makes sense. Harvard law professor Jonathan Zittrain compares this to plea bargaining.

The police regularly negotiate lenient sentences or probation for confessed criminals in order to convict more important criminals. They make deals with all sorts of unsavory people, giving them benefits they don't deserve, because the result is a greater good.

In the Snowden case, an agreement would safeguard the most important of NSA's secrets from other nations' intelligence agencies. It would help ensure that the truly secret information not be exposed. It would protect US interests.

Why would reporters agree to this? Two reasons. One, they actually do want these documents secured while they look for stories to publish. And two, it would be a public demonstration of that desire.

Why wouldn't the government just collect all the documents under the pretense of securing them and then delete them? For the same reason they don't renege on plea bargains: No one would trust them next time. And, of course, because smart reporters will probably keep encrypted backups under their own control.

We're nowhere near the point where this system could be put into practice, but it's worth thinking about how it could work. The government would need to establish a semi-independent group, called, say, a Leak Management unit, which could act as an intermediary. Since it would be isolated from the agencies that were the source of the leak, its officials would be less vested and—this is important—less angry over the leak. Over time, it would build a reputation, develop protocols that reporters could rely on. Leaks will be more common in the future, but they'll still be rare. Expecting each agency to develop expertise in this process is unrealistic.

If there were sufficient trust between the press and the government, this could work. And everyone would benefit.

Lessons from the Sony Hack

Originally published in the Wall Street Journal CIO Journal, *December 19, 2014*

Earlier this month, a mysterious group that calls itself Guardians of Peace hacked into Sony Pictures Entertainment's computer systems and began revealing many of the Hollywood studio's best-kept secrets, from details about unreleased movies to embarrassing emails (notably some racist notes from Sony bigwigs about President Barack Obama's presumed movie-watching preferences) to the personnel data of employees, including salaries and performance reviews. The Federal Bureau of Investigation now says it has evidence that North Korea was behind the attack, and Sony Pictures pulled its planned release of "The Interview," a satire targeting that country's dictator, after the hackers made some ridiculous threats about terrorist violence.

Your reaction to the massive hacking of such a prominent company will depend on whether you're fluent in information-technology security. If you're not, you're probably wondering how in the world this could happen. If you are, you're aware that this could happen to any company (though it is still amazing that Sony made it so easy).

To understand any given episode of hacking, you need to understand who your adversary is. I've spent decades dealing with Internet hackers (as I do now at my current firm), and I've learned to separate opportunistic attacks from targeted ones.

You can characterize attackers along two axes: skill and focus. Most attacks are low-skill and low-focus—people using common hacking tools against thousands of networks world-wide. These low-end attacks include sending spam out to millions of email addresses, hoping that someone will fall for it and click on a poisoned link. I think of them as the background radiation of the Internet.

High-skill, low-focus attacks are more serious. These include the more sophisticated attacks using newly discovered "zero-day" vulnerabilities in software, systems and networks. This is the sort of attack that affected Target, J.P. Morgan Chase and most of the other commercial networks that you've heard about in the past year or so.

But even scarier are the high-skill, high-focus attacks—the type that hit Sony. This includes sophisticated attacks seemingly run by national intelligence agencies, using such spying tools as Regin and Flame, which many in the IT world suspect were created by the US; Turla, a piece of malware that many blame on the Russian government; and a huge snooping effort called GhostNet, which spied on the Dalai Lama and Asian governments, leading many of my colleagues to blame China. (We're mostly guessing about the origins of these attacks; governments refuse to comment on such issues.) China has also been accused of trying to hack into the *New York Times* in 2010, and in May, Attorney General Eric Holder announced the indictment of five Chinese military officials for cyberattacks against US corporations.

This category also includes private actors, including the hacker group known as Anonymous, which mounted a Sony-style attack against the Internet-security firm HBGary Federal, and the unknown hackers who stole racy celebrity photos from Apple's iCloud and posted them. If you've heard the IT-security buzz phrase "advanced persistent threat," this is it.

There is a key difference among these kinds of hacking. In the first two categories, the attacker is an opportunist. The hackers who penetrated Home Depot's networks didn't seem to care much about Home Depot; they just wanted a large database of credit-card numbers. Any large retailer would do.

But a skilled, determined attacker wants to attack a specific victim. The reasons may be political: to hurt a government or leader enmeshed in a geopolitical battle. Or ethical: to punish an industry that the hacker abhors, like big oil or big pharma. Or maybe the victim is just a company that hackers love to hate. (Sony falls into this category: It has been infuriating hackers since 2005, when the company put malicious software on its CDs in a failed attempt to prevent copying.)

Low-focus attacks are easier to defend against: If Home Depot's systems had been better protected, the hackers would have just moved on to an easier target. With attackers who are highly skilled and highly focused, however, what matters is whether a targeted company's security is superior to the attacker's skills, not just to the security measures of other companies. Often, it isn't. We're much better at such relative security than we are at absolute security.

That is why security experts aren't surprised by the Sony story. We know people who do penetration testing for a living—real, no-holds-barred attacks that mimic a full-on assault by a dogged, expert attacker—and we know that the expert always gets in. Against a sufficiently skilled, funded and motivated attacker, all networks are vulnerable. But good security makes many kinds of attack harder, costlier and riskier. Against attackers who aren't sufficiently skilled, good security may protect you completely.

It is hard to put a dollar value on security that is strong enough to assure you that your embarrassing emails and personnel information won't end up posted online somewhere, but Sony clearly failed here. Its security turned out to be subpar. They didn't have to leave so much information exposed. And they didn't have to be so slow detecting the breach, giving the attackers free rein to wander about and take so much stuff.

For those worried that what happened to Sony could happen to you, I have two pieces of advice. The first is for organizations: take this stuff seriously. Security is a combination of protection, detection and response. You need prevention to defend against low-focus attacks and to make targeted attacks harder. You need detection to spot the attackers who inevitably get through. And you need response to minimize the damage, restore security and manage the fallout.

The time to start is before the attack hits: Sony would have fared much better if its executives simply hadn't made racist jokes about Mr. Obama or insulted its stars—or if their response systems had been agile enough to kick the hackers out before they grabbed everything.

My second piece of advice is for individuals. The worst invasion of privacy from the Sony hack didn't happen to the executives or the stars; it happened to the blameless random employees who were just using their company's email system. Because of that, they've had their most personal conversations—gossip, medical conditions, love lives—exposed. The press may not have divulged this information, but their friends and relatives peeked at it. Hundreds of personal tragedies must be unfolding right now.

This could be any of us. We have no choice but to entrust companies with our intimate conversations: on email, on Facebook, by text and so on. We have no choice but to entrust the retailers that we use with our financial details. And we have little choice but to use cloud services such as iCloud and Google Docs.

So be smart: Understand the risks. Know that your data are vulnerable. Opt out when you can. And agitate for government intervention to ensure that organizations protect your data as well as you would. Like many areas of our hyper-technical world, this isn't something markets can fix.

Reacting to the Sony Hack

Originally published in Vice Motherboard, *December 19, 2014*

First we thought North Korea was behind the Sony cyberattacks. Then we thought it was a couple of hacker guys with an axe to grind. Now we think North Korea is behind it again, but the connection is still tenuous. There have been accusations of cyberterrorism, and even cyberwar. I've heard calls for us to strike back, with actual missiles and bombs. We're collectively pegging the hype meter, and the best thing we can do is calm down and take a deep breath.

First, this is not an act of terrorism. There has been no senseless violence. No innocents are coming home in body bags. Yes, a company is seriously embarrassed—and financially hurt—by all of its information leaking to the public. But posting unreleased movies online is not terrorism. It's not even close.

Nor is this an act of war. Stealing and publishing a company's proprietary information is not an act of war. We wouldn't be talking about going to war if someone snuck in and photocopied everything, and it makes equally little sense to talk about it when someone does it over the Internet. The threshold of war is much, much higher, and we're not going to respond to this militarily. Over the years, North Korea has performed far more aggressive acts against US and South Korean soldiers. We didn't go to war then, and we're not going to war now.

Finally, we don't know these attacks were sanctioned by the North Korean government. The US government has made statements linking the attacks to North Korea, but hasn't officially blamed the government, nor have officials provided any evidence of the linkage. We've known about North Korea's cyberattack capabilities long before this attack, but it might not be the government at all. This wouldn't be the first time a nationalistic cyberattack was launched without government sanction. We have lots of examples of these sorts of attacks being conducted by regular hackers with nationalistic pride. Kids playing politics, I call them. This may be that, and it could also be a random hacker who just has it out for Sony.

Remember, the hackers didn't start talking about *The Interview* until the press did. Maybe the NSA has some secret information pinning this attack on the North Korean government, but unless the agency comes forward with the evidence, we should remain skeptical. We don't know who did this, and we may never find out. I personally think it is a disgruntled ex-employee, but I don't have any more evidence than anyone else does.

What we have is a very extreme case of hacking. By "extreme" I mean the quantity of the information stolen from Sony's networks, not the quality of the attack. The attackers seem to have been good, but no more than that. Sony made its situation worse by having substandard security.

Sony's reaction has all the markings of a company without any sort of coherent plan. Near as I can tell, every Sony executive is in full panic mode. They're certainly facing dozens of lawsuits: from shareholders, from companies who invested in those movies, from employees who had their medical and financial data exposed, from everyone who was affected. They're probably facing government fines, for leaking financial and medical information, and possibly for colluding with other studios to attack Google.

If previous major hacks are any guide, there will be multiple senior executives fired over this; everyone at Sony is probably scared for their jobs. In this sort of situation, the interests of the corporation are not the same as the interests of the people running the corporation. This might go a long way to explain some of the reactions we've seen.

Pulling *The Interview* was exactly the wrong thing to do, as there was no credible threat and it just emboldens the hackers. But it's the kind of response you get when you don't have a plan.

Politically motivated hacking isn't new, and the Sony hack is not unprecedented. In 2011 the hacker group Anonymous did something similar to the Internet-security company HBGary Federal, exposing corporate secrets and internal emails. This sort of thing has been possible for decades, although it's gotten increasingly damaging as more corporate information goes online. It will happen again; there's no doubt about that.

But it hasn't happened very often, and that's not likely to change. Most hackers are garden-variety criminals, less interested in internal emails and corporate secrets and more interested in personal information and credit card numbers that they can monetize. Their attacks are opportunistic, and very different from the targeted attack Sony fell victim to.

When a hacker releases personal data on an individual, it's called doxing. We don't have a name for it when it happens to a company, but it's what happened to Sony. Companies need to wake up to the possibility that a whistleblower, a civic-minded hacker, or just someone who is out to embarrass them will hack their networks and publish their proprietary data. They need to recognize that their chatty private emails and their internal memos might be front-page news.

In a world where *everything* happens online, including what we think of as ephemeral conversation, everything is potentially subject to public scrutiny. Companies need to make sure their computer and network security is up to snuff, and their incident response and crisis management plans can handle this sort of thing. But they should also remember how rare this sort of attack is, and not panic.

Attack Attribution in Cyberspace

Originally published in Time, *January 5, 2015*

When you're attacked by a missile, you can follow its trajectory back to where it was launched from. When you're attacked in cyberspace, figuring out who did it is much harder. The reality of international aggression in cyberspace will change how we approach defense.

Many of us in the computer-security field are skeptical of the US government's claim that it has positively identified North Korea as the perpetrator of the massive Sony hack in November 2014. The FBI's evidence is circumstantial and not very convincing. The attackers never mentioned the movie that became the centerpiece of the hack until the press did. More likely, the culprits are random hackers who have loved to hate Sony for over a decade, or possibly a disgruntled insider.

On the other hand, most people believe that the FBI would not sound so sure unless it was convinced. And President Obama would not have imposed sanctions against North Korea if he weren't convinced. This implies that there's classified evidence as well. A couple of weeks ago, I wrote for the *Atlantic*, "The NSA has been trying to eavesdrop on North Korea's government communications since the Korean War, and it's reasonable to assume that its analysts are in pretty deep. The agency might have intelligence on the planning process for the hack. It might, say, have phone calls discussing the project, weekly PowerPoint status reports, or even Kim Jong Un's sign-off on the plan. On the other hand, maybe not. I could have written the same thing about Iraq's weapons-of-mass-destruction program in the run-up to the 2003 invasion of that country, and we all know how wrong the government was about that."

The NSA is extremely reluctant to reveal its intelligence capabilities—or what it refers to as "sources and methods"—against

North Korea simply to convince all of us of its conclusion, because by revealing them, it tips North Korea off to its insecurities. At the same time, we rightly have reason to be skeptical of the government's unequivocal attribution of the attack without seeing the evidence. Iraq's mythical weapons of mass destruction is only the most recent example of a major intelligence failure. American history is littered with examples of claimed secret intelligence pointing us toward aggression against other countries, only for us to learn later that the evidence was wrong.

Cyberspace exacerbates this in two ways. First, it is very difficult to attribute attacks in cyberspace. Packets don't come with return addresses, and you can never be sure that what you think is the originating computer hasn't itself been hacked. Even worse, it's hard to tell the difference between attacks carried out by a couple of lone hackers and ones where a nation-state military is responsible. When we do know who did it, it's usually because a lone hacker admitted it or because there was a months-long forensic investigation.

Second, in cyberspace, it is much easier to attack than to defend. The primary defense we have against military attacks in cyberspace is counterattack and the threat of counterattack that leads to deterrence.

What this all means is that it's in the US's best interest to claim omniscient powers of attribution. More than anything else, those in charge want to signal to other countries that they cannot get away with attacking the US: If they try something, we will know. And we will retaliate, swiftly and effectively. This is also why the US has been cagey about whether it caused North Korea's Internet outage in late December.

It can be an effective bluff, but only if you get away with it. Otherwise, you lose credibility. The FBI is already starting to equivocate, saying others might have been involved in the attack, possibly hired by North Korea. If the real attackers surface and can demonstrate that they acted independently, it will be obvious that the FBI and NSA were overconfident in their attribution. Already, the FBI has lost significant credibility.

The only way out of this, with respect to the Sony hack and any other incident of cyber-aggression in which we're expected to support retaliatory action, is for the government to be much more forthcoming about its evidence. The secrecy of the NSA's sources and methods is going to have to take a backseat to the public's right to know. And in cyberspace, we're going to have to accept the uncomfortable fact that there's a lot we don't know.

Organizational Doxing

Originally published in CNN.com, *July 7, 2015*

Recently, WikiLeaks began publishing over half a million previously secret cables and other documents from the Foreign Ministry of Saudi Arabia. It's a huge trove, and already reporters are writing stories about the highly secretive government.

What Saudi Arabia is experiencing isn't common but part of a growing trend.

Just last week, unknown hackers broke into the network of the cyber-weapons arms manufacturer Hacking Team and published 400 gigabytes of internal data, describing, among other things, its sale of Internet surveillance software to totalitarian regimes around the world.

Last year, hundreds of gigabytes of Sony's sensitive data was published on the Internet, including executive salaries, corporate emails and contract negotiations. The attacker in this case was the government of North Korea, which was punishing Sony for producing a movie that made fun of its leader. In 2010, the US cyberweapons arms manufacturer HBGary Federal was a victim, and its attackers were members of a loose hacker collective called LulzSec.

Edward Snowden stole a still-unknown number of documents from the National Security Agency in 2013 and gave them to reporters to publish. Chelsea Manning stole three-quarters of a million documents from the US State Department and gave them to WikiLeaks to publish. The person who stole the Saudi Arabian documents might also be a whistleblower and insider but is more likely a hacker who wanted to punish the kingdom.

Organizations are increasingly getting hacked, and not by criminals wanting to steal credit card numbers or account information in order to commit fraud, but by people intent on stealing as much data as they can and publishing it. Law professor and privacy expert Peter Swire refers to "the declining half-life of secrets." Secrets are simply harder to keep in the information age. This is bad news for all of us who value our privacy, but there's a hidden benefit when it comes to organizations.

The decline of secrecy means the rise of transparency. Organizational transparency is vital to any open and free society.

Open government laws and freedom of information laws let citizens know what the government is doing, and enable them to carry out their democratic duty to oversee its activities. Corporate disclosure laws perform similar functions in the private sphere. Of course, both corporations and governments have some need for secrecy, but the more they can be open, the more we can knowledgeably decide whether to trust them.

This makes the debate more complicated than simple personal privacy. Publishing someone's private writings and communications is bad, because in a free and diverse society people should have private space to think and act in ways that would embarrass them if public.

But organizations are not people and, while there are legitimate trade secrets, their information should otherwise be transparent. Holding government and corporate private behavior to public scrutiny is good.

Most organizational secrets are only valuable for a short term: negotiations, new product designs, earnings numbers before they're released, patents before filing, and so on.

Forever secrets, like the formula for Coca-Cola, are few and far between. The one exception is embarrassments. If an organization had to assume that anything it did would become public in a few years, people within that organization would behave differently.

The NSA would have had to weigh its collection programs against the possibility of public scrutiny. Sony would have had to think about how it would look to the world if it paid its female executives significantly less than its male executives. HBGary would have thought twice before launching an intimidation campaign against a journalist it didn't like, and Hacking Team wouldn't have lied to the UN about selling surveillance software to Sudan. Even the government of Saudi Arabia would have behaved differently. Such embarrassment might be the first significant downside of hiring a psychopath as CEO.

I don't want to imply that this forced transparency is a good thing, though. The threat of disclosure chills all speech, not just illegal, embarrassing, or objectionable speech. There will be less honest and candid discourse. People in organizations need the freedom to write and say things that they wouldn't want to be made public.

State Department officials need to be able to describe foreign leaders, even if their descriptions are unflattering. Movie executives need to be able to say unkind things about their movie stars. If they can't, their organizations will suffer.

With few exceptions, our secrets are stored on computers and networks vulnerable to hacking. It's much easier to break into networks than it is to secure them, and large organizational networks are very complicated and full of security holes. Bottom line: If someone sufficiently skilled, funded and motivated wants to steal an organization's secrets, they will succeed. This includes hacktivists (HBGary Federal, Hacking Team), foreign governments (Sony), and trusted insiders (State Department and NSA).

It's not likely that your organization's secrets will be posted on the Internet for everyone to see, but it's always a possibility.

Dumping an organization's secret information is going to become increasingly common as individuals realize its effectiveness for whistleblowing and revenge. While some hackers will use journalists to separate the news stories from mere personal information, not all will.

Both governments and corporations need to assume that their secrets are more likely to be exposed, and exposed sooner, than ever. They should do all they can to protect their data and networks, but have to realize that their best defense might be to refrain from doing things that don't look good on the front pages of the world's newspapers.

The Security Risks of Third-Party Data

Originally published in the Atlantic, *September 8, 2015*

Most of us get to be thoroughly relieved that our emails weren't in the Ashley Madison database. But don't get too comfortable. Whatever secrets you have, even the ones you don't think of as secret, are more likely than you think to get dumped on the Internet. It's not your fault, and there's largely nothing you can do about it.

Welcome to the age of organizational doxing.

Organizational doxing—stealing data from an organization's network and indiscriminately dumping it all on the Internet—is an increasingly popular attack against organizations. Because our data is connected to the Internet, and stored in corporate networks, we are all in the potential blast-radius of these attacks. While the risk that any particular bit of data gets published is low, we have to start thinking about what could happen if a larger-scale breach affects us or the people we care about. It's going to get a lot uglier before security improves.

We don't know why anonymous hackers broke into the networks of Avid Life Media, then stole and published 37 million—so far—personal records of AshleyMadison.com users. The hackers say it was because of the company's deceptive practices. They expressed indifference to the "cheating dirtbags" who had signed up for the site. The primary target, the hackers said, was the company itself. That philanderers were exposed, marriages were ruined, and people were driven to suicide was apparently a side effect.

Last November, the North Korean government stole and published gigabytes of corporate email from Sony Pictures. This was part of a much larger doxing—a hack aimed at punishing the company for making a movie parodying the North Korean leader Kim Jong-un. The press focused on Sony's corporate executives, who had sniped at celebrities and made racist jokes about President Obama. But also buried in those emails were loves, losses, confidences, and private conversations of thousands of innocent employees. The press didn't bother with those emails—and we know nothing of any personal tragedies that resulted from their friends' searches. They, too, were caught in the blast radius of the larger attack.

The Internet is more than a way for us to get information or connect with our friends. It has become a place for us to store our personal information. Our email is in the cloud. So are our address books and calendars, whether we use Google, Apple, Microsoft, or someone else. We store to-do lists on Remember the Milk and keep our jottings on Evernote. Fitbit and Jawbone store our fitness data. Flickr, Facebook, and iCloud are the repositories for our personal photos. Facebook and Twitter store many of our intimate conversations.

It often feels like everyone is collecting our personal information. Smartphone apps collect our location data. Google can draw a surprisingly intimate portrait of what we're thinking about from our Internet searches. Dating sites (even those less titillating than Ashley Madison), medical-information sites, and travel sites all have detailed portraits of who we are and where we go. Retailers save records of our purchases, and those databases are stored on the Internet. Data brokers have detailed dossiers that can include all of this and more.

Many people don't think about the security implications of this information existing in the first place. They might be aware that it's mined for advertising and other marketing purposes. They might even know that the government can get its hands on such data, with different levels of ease depending on the country. But it doesn't generally occur to people that their personal information might be available to anyone who wants to look.

In reality, all these networks are vulnerable to organizational doxing. Most aren't any more secure than Ashley Madison or Sony were. We could wake up one morning and find detailed information about our Uber rides, our Amazon purchases, our subscriptions to pornographic websites—anything we do on the Internet—published and available. It's not likely, but it's certainly possible.

Right now, you can search the Ashley Madison database for any email address, and read that person's details. You can search the Sony data dump and read the personal chatter of people who work for the company. Tempting though it may be, there are many reasons not to search for people you know on Ashley Madison. The one I most want to focus on is context. An email address might be in that database for many reasons, not all of them lascivious. But if you find your spouse or your friend in there, you don't necessarily know the context. It's the same with the Sony employee emails, and the data from whatever company is doxed next. You'll be able to read the data, but without the full story, it can be hard to judge the meaning of what you're reading.

Even so, of course people are going to look. Reporters will search for public figures. Individuals will search for people they know. Secrets will be read and passed around. Anguish and embarrassment will result. In some cases, lives will be destroyed.

Privacy isn't about hiding something. It's about being able to control how we present ourselves to the world. It's about maintaining a public face while at the same time being permitted private thoughts and actions. It's about personal dignity.

Organizational doxing is a powerful attack against organizations, and one that will continue because it's so effective. And while the network owners and the hackers might be battling it out for their own reasons, sometimes it's our data that's the prize. Having information we thought private turn out to be public and searchable is what happens when the hackers win. It's a result of the information age that hasn't been fully appreciated, and one that we're still not prepared to face.

The Rise of Political Doxing

Originally published in Vice Motherboard, *October 28, 2015*

Last week, CIA director John O. Brennan became the latest victim of what's become a popular way to embarrass and harass people on the Internet. A hacker allegedly broke into his AOL account and published emails and documents found inside, many of them personal and sensitive.

It's called doxing—sometimes doxxing—from the word "documents." It emerged in the 1990s as a hacker revenge tactic, and has since been as a tool to harass and intimidate people, primarily women, on the Internet. Someone would threaten a woman with physical harm, or try to incite others to harm her, and publish her personal information as a way of saying "I know a lot about you—like where you live and work." Victims of doxing talk about the fear that this tactic instills. It's very effective, by which I mean that it's horrible.

Brennan's doxing was slightly different. Here, the attacker had a more political motive. He wasn't out to intimidate Brennan; he simply wanted to embarrass him. His personal papers were dumped indiscriminately, fodder for an eager press. This doxing was a political act, and we're seeing this kind of thing more and more.

Last year, the government of North Korea did this to Sony. Hackers the FBI believes were working for North Korea broke into the company's networks, stole a huge amount of corporate data, and published it. This included unreleased movies, financial information, company plans, and personal emails. The reputational damage to the company was enormous; the company estimated the cost at $41 million.

In July, hackers stole and published sensitive documents from the cyberweapons arms manufacturer Hacking Team. That same month, different hackers did the same thing to the infidelity website Ashley Madison. In 2014, hackers broke into the iCloud accounts of over 100 celebrities and published personal photographs, most containing some nudity. In 2013, Edward Snowden doxed the NSA.

These aren't the first instances of politically motivated doxing, but there's a clear trend. As people realize what an effective attack this can be, and how an individual can use the tactic to do considerable damage to powerful people and institutions, we're going to see a lot more of it.

On the Internet, attack is easier than defense. We're living in a world where a sufficiently skilled and motivated attacker will circumvent network security. Even worse, most Internet security assumes it needs to defend against an opportunistic attacker who will attack the weakest network in order to get—for example—a pile of credit card numbers. The notion of a targeted attacker, who wants Sony or Ashley Madison or John Brennan because of what they stand for, is still new. And it's even harder to defend against.

What this means is that we're going to see more political doxing in the future, against both people and institutions. It's going to be a factor in elections. It's going to be a factor in anti-corporate activism. More people will find their personal information exposed to the world: politicians, corporate executives, celebrities, divisive and outspoken individuals.

Of course they won't all be doxed, but some of them will. Some of them will be doxed directly, like Brennan. Some of them will be inadvertent victims of a doxing attack aimed at a company where their information is stored, like those celebrities with iPhone accounts and every customer of Ashley Madison. Regardless of the method, lots of people will have to face the publication of personal correspondence, documents, and information they would rather be private.

In the end, doxing is a tactic that the powerless can effectively use against the powerful. It can be used for whistleblowing. It can be used as a vehicle for social change. And it can be used to embarrass, harass, and intimidate. Its popularity will rise and fall on this effectiveness, especially in a world where prosecuting the doxers is so difficult.

There's no good solution for this right now. We all have the right to privacy, and we should be free from doxing. But we're not, and those of us who are in the public eye have no choice but to rethink our online data shadows.

Data Is a Toxic Asset

Originally published in CNN.com, *March 1, 2016*

Thefts of personal information aren't unusual. Every week, thieves break into networks and steal data about people, often tens of millions at a time. Most of the time it's information that's needed to commit fraud, as happened in 2015 to Experian and the IRS.

Sometimes it's stolen for purposes of embarrassment or coercion, as in the 2015 cases of Ashley Madison and the US Office of Personnel Management. The latter exposed highly sensitive personal data that affects security of millions of government employees, probably to the Chinese. Always it's personal information about us, information that we shared with the expectation that the recipients would keep it secret. And in every case, they did not.

The telecommunications company TalkTalk admitted that its data breach last year resulted in criminals using customer information to commit fraud. This was more bad news for a company that's been hacked three times in the past 12 months, and has already seen some disastrous effects from losing customer data, including £60 million (about $83 million) in damages and over 100,000 customers. Its stock price took a pummeling as well.

People have been writing about 2015 as the year of data theft. I'm not sure if more personal records were stolen last year than in other recent years, but it certainly was a year for big stories about data thefts. I also think it was the year that industry started to realize that data is a toxic asset.

The phrase "big data" refers to the idea that large databases of seemingly random data about people are valuable. Retailers save our purchasing habits. Cell phone companies and app providers save our location information.

Telecommunications providers, social networks, and many other types of companies save information about who we talk to and share things with. Data brokers save everything about us they can get their hands on. This data is saved and analyzed, bought and sold, and used for marketing and other persuasive purposes.

And because the cost of saving all this data is so cheap, there's no reason not to save as much as possible, and save it all forever. Figuring out what isn't worth saving is hard. And because someday the companies might figure out how to turn the data into money, until recently there was absolutely no downside to saving everything. That changed this past year.

What all these data breaches are teaching us is that data is a toxic asset and saving it is dangerous.

Saving it is dangerous because it's highly personal. Location data reveals where we live, where we work, and how we spend our time. If we all have a location tracker like a smartphone, correlating data reveals who we spend our time with—including who we spend the night with.

Our Internet search data reveals what's important to us, including our hopes, fears, desires and secrets. Communications data reveals who our intimates are, and what we talk about with them. I could go on. Our reading habits, or purchasing data, or data from sensors as diverse as cameras and fitness trackers: All of it can be intimate.

Saving it is dangerous because many people want it. Of course companies want it; that's why they collect it in the first place. But governments want it, too. In the United States, the National Security Agency and FBI use secret deals, coercion, threats and legal compulsion to get at the data. Foreign governments just come in and steal it. When a company with personal data goes bankrupt, it's one of the assets that gets sold.

Saving it is dangerous because it's hard for companies to secure. For a lot of reasons, computer and network security is very difficult. Attackers have an inherent advantage over defenders, and a sufficiently skilled, funded and motivated attacker will always get in.

And saving it is dangerous because failing to secure it is damaging. It will reduce a company's profits, reduce its market share, hurt its stock price, cause it public embarrassment, and—in some cases—result in expensive lawsuits and occasionally, criminal charges.

All this makes data a toxic asset, and it continues to be toxic as long as it sits in a company's computers and networks. The data is vulnerable, and the company is vulnerable. It's vulnerable to hackers and governments. It's vulnerable to employee error. And when there's a toxic data spill, millions of people can be affected. The 2015 Anthem Health data breach affected 80 million people. The 2013 Target Corp. breach affected 110 million.

This toxic data can sit in organizational databases for a long time. Some of the stolen Office of Personnel Management data was decades old. Do you have any idea which companies still have your earliest emails, or your earliest posts on that now-defunct social network?

If data is toxic, why do organizations save it?

There are three reasons. The first is that we're in the middle of the hype cycle of big data. Companies and governments are still punch-drunk on data, and have believed the wildest of promises on how valuable that data is. The research showing that more data isn't necessarily better, and that there are serious diminishing returns when adding additional data to processes like personalized advertising, is just starting to come out.

The second is that many organizations are still downplaying the risks. Some simply don't realize just how damaging a data breach would be. Some believe they can completely protect themselves against a data breach, or at least that their legal and public relations teams can minimize the damage if they fail. And while there's certainly a lot that companies can do technically to better secure the data they hold about all of us, there's no better security than deleting the data.

The last reason is that some organizations understand both the first two reasons and are saving the data anyway. The culture of venture-capital-funded start-up companies is one of extreme risk taking. These are companies that are always running out of money, that always know their impending death date.

They are so far from profitability that their only hope for surviving is to get even more money, which means they need to demonstrate rapid growth or increasing value. This motivates those companies to take risks that larger, more established, companies would never take. They might take extreme chances with our data, even flout regulations, because they literally have nothing to lose. And often, the most profitable business models are the most risky and dangerous ones.

We can be smarter than this. We need to regulate what corporations can do with our data at every stage: collection, storage, use, resale and disposal. We can make corporate executives personally liable so they know there's a downside to taking chances. We can make the business models that involve massively surveilling people the less compelling ones, simply by making certain business practices illegal.

The Ashley Madison data breach was such a disaster for the company because it saved its customers' real names and credit card numbers. It didn't have to do it this way. It could have processed the credit card information, given the user access, and then deleted all identifying information.

To be sure, it would have been a different company. It would have had less revenue, because it couldn't charge users a monthly recurring fee. Users who lost their password would have had more trouble re-accessing their account. But it would have been safer for its customers.

Similarly, the Office of Personnel Management didn't have to store everyone's information online and accessible. It could have taken older records offline, or at least onto a separate network with more secure access controls. Yes, it wouldn't be immediately available to government employees doing research, but it would have been much more secure.

Data is a toxic asset. We need to start thinking about it as such, and treat it as we would any other source of toxicity. To do anything else is to risk our security and privacy.

Credential Stealing as an Attack Vector

Originally published in Xconomy, *April 20, 2016*

Traditional computer security concerns itself with vulnerabilities. We employ antivirus software to detect malware that exploits vulnerabilities. We have automatic patching systems to fix vulnerabilities. We debate whether the FBI should be permitted to introduce vulnerabilities in our software so it can get access to systems with a warrant. This is all important, but what's missing is a recognition that software vulnerabilities aren't the most common attack vector: credential stealing is.

The most common way hackers of all stripes, from criminals to hacktivists to foreign governments, break into networks is by stealing and using a valid credential. Basically, they steal passwords, set up man-in-the-middle attacks to piggy-back on legitimate logins, or engage in cleverer attacks to masquerade as authorized users. It's a more effective avenue of attack in many ways: it doesn't involve finding a zero-day or unpatched vulnerability, there's less chance of discovery, and it gives the attacker more flexibility in technique.

Rob Joyce, the head of the NSA's Tailored Access Operations (TAO) group—basically the country's chief hacker—gave a rare public talk at a conference in January. In essence, he said that zero-day vulnerabilities are overrated, and credential stealing is how he gets into networks: "A lot of people think that nation states are running their operations on zero days, but it's not that common. For big corporate networks, persistence and focus will get you in without a zero day; there are so many more vectors that are easier, less risky, and more productive."

This is true for us, and it's also true for those attacking us. It's how the Chinese hackers breached the Office of Personnel Management in 2015. The 2014 criminal attack against Target Corporation started when hackers stole the login credentials of the company's HVAC vendor. Iranian hackers stole US login credentials. And the hacktivist that broke into the cyber-arms manufacturer Hacking Team and published pretty much every proprietary document from that company used stolen credentials.

As Joyce said, stealing a valid credential and using it to access a network is easier, less risky, and ultimately more productive than using an existing vulnerability, even a zero-day.

Our notions of defense need to adapt to this change. First, organizations need to beef up their authentication systems. There are lots of tricks that help here: two-factor authentication, one-time passwords, physical tokens, smartphone-based authentication, and so on. None of these is foolproof, but they all make credential stealing harder.

Second, organizations need to invest in breach detection and—most importantly—incident response. Credential-stealing attacks tend to bypass traditional IT security software. But attacks are complex and multi-step. Being able to detect them in process, and to respond quickly and effectively enough to kick attackers out and restore security, is essential to resilient network security today.

Vulnerabilities are still critical. Fixing vulnerabilities is still vital for security, and introducing new vulnerabilities into existing systems is still a disaster. But strong authentication and robust incident response are also critical. And an organization that skimps on these will find itself unable to keep its networks secure.

Someone Is Learning How to Take Down the Internet

Originally published in Lawfare.com, *September 13, 2016*

Over the past year or two, someone has been probing the defenses of the companies that run critical pieces of the Internet. These probes take the form of precisely calibrated attacks designed to determine exactly how well these companies can defend themselves, and what would be required to take them down. We don't know who is doing this, but it feels like a large nation state. China or Russia would be my first guesses.

First, a little background. If you want to take a network off the Internet, the easiest way to do it is with a distributed denial-of-service attack (DDoS). Like the name says, this is an attack designed to prevent legitimate users from getting to the site. There are subtleties, but basically it means blasting so much data at the site that it's overwhelmed. These attacks are not new: hackers do this to sites they don't like, and criminals have done it as a method of extortion. There is an entire industry, with an arsenal of technologies, devoted to DDoS defense. But largely it's a matter of bandwidth. If the attacker has a bigger fire hose of data than the defender has, the attacker wins.

Recently, some of the major companies that provide the basic infrastructure that makes the Internet work have seen an increase in DDoS attacks against them. Moreover, they have seen a certain profile of attacks. These attacks are significantly larger than the ones they're used to seeing. They last longer. They're more sophisticated. And they look like probing. One week, the attack would start at a particular level of attack and slowly ramp up before stopping. The next week, it would start at that higher point and continue. And so on, along those lines, as if the attacker were looking for the exact point of failure.

The attacks are also configured in such a way as to see what the company's total defenses are. There are many different ways to launch a DDoS attack. The more attack vectors you employ simultaneously, the more different defenses the defender has to counter with. These companies are seeing more attacks using three or four different vectors. This means that the companies have to use everything they've got to defend themselves. They can't hold anything back. They're forced to demonstrate their defense capabilities for the attacker.

I am unable to give details, because these companies spoke with me under condition of anonymity. But this all is consistent with what Verisign is reporting. Verisign is the registrar for many popular top-level Internet domains, like .com and .net. If it goes down, there's a global blackout of all websites and email addresses in the most common top-level domains. Every quarter, Verisign publishes a DDoS trends report. While its publication doesn't have the level of detail I heard from the companies I spoke with, the trends are the same: "in Q2 2016, attacks continued to become more frequent, persistent, and complex."

There's more. One company told me about a variety of probing attacks in addition to the DDoS attacks: testing the ability to manipulate Internet addresses and routes, seeing how long it takes the defenders to respond, and so on. Someone is extensively testing the core defensive capabilities of the companies that provide critical Internet services.

Who would do this? It doesn't seem like something an activist, criminal, or researcher would do. Profiling core infrastructure is common practice in espionage and intelligence gathering. It's not normal for companies to do that. Furthermore, the size and scale of these probes—and especially their persistence—points to state actors. It feels like a nation's military cybercommand trying to calibrate its weaponry in the case of cyberwar. It reminds me of the US's Cold War program of flying high-altitude planes over the Soviet Union to force their air-defense systems to turn on, to map their capabilities.

What can we do about this? Nothing, really. We don't know where the attacks come from. The data I see suggests China, an assessment shared by the people I spoke with. On the other hand, it's possible to disguise the country of origin for these sorts of attacks. The NSA, which has more surveillance in the Internet backbone than everyone else combined, probably has a better idea, but unless the US decides to make an international incident over this, we won't see any attribution.

But this is happening. And people should know.

Who Is Publishing NSA and CIA Secrets, and Why?

Originally published in Lawfare.com, *April 27, 2017*

There's something going on inside the intelligence communities in at least two countries, and we have no idea what it is.

Consider these three data points. One: someone, probably a country's intelligence organization, is dumping massive amounts of cyberattack tools belonging to the NSA onto the Internet. Two: someone else, or maybe the same someone, is doing the same thing to the CIA.

Three: in March, NSA Deputy Director Richard Ledgett described how the NSA penetrated the computer networks of a Russian intelligence agency and was able to monitor them as they attacked the US

State Department in 2014. Even more explicitly, a US ally—my guess is the UK—was not only hacking the Russian intelligence agency's computers, but also the surveillance cameras inside their building. "They [the US ally] monitored the [Russian] hackers as they maneuvered inside the US systems and as they walked in and out of the workspace, and were able to see faces, the officials said."

Countries don't often reveal intelligence capabilities: "sources and methods." Because it gives their adversaries important information about what to fix, it's a deliberate decision done with good reason. And it's not just the target country who learns from a reveal. When the US announces that it can see through the cameras inside the buildings of Russia's cyber warriors, other countries immediately check the security of their own cameras.

With all this in mind, let's talk about the recent leaks at NSA and the CIA.

Last year, a previously unknown group called the Shadow Brokers started releasing NSA hacking tools and documents from about three years ago. They continued to do so this year—five sets of files in all—and have implied that more classified documents are to come. We don't know how they got the files. When the Shadow Brokers first emerged, the general consensus was that someone had found and hacked an external NSA staging server. These are third-party computers that the NSA's TAO hackers use to launch attacks from. Those servers are necessarily stocked with TAO attack tools. This matched the leaks, which included a "script" directory and working attack notes. We're not sure if someone inside the NSA made a mistake that left these files exposed, or if the hackers that found the cache got lucky.

That explanation stopped making sense after the latest Shadow Brokers release, which included attack tools against Windows, PowerPoint presentations, and operational notes—documents that are definitely not going to be on an external NSA staging server. A credible theory, which I first heard from Nicholas Weaver, is that the Shadow Brokers are publishing NSA data from multiple sources. The first leaks were from an external staging server, but the more recent leaks are from inside the NSA itself.

So what happened? Did someone inside the NSA accidentally mount the wrong server on some external network? That's possible, but seems very unlikely. Did someone hack the NSA itself? Could there be a mole inside the NSA, as Kevin Poulsen speculated?

If it is a mole, my guess is that he's already been arrested. There are enough individualities in the files to pinpoint exactly where and when they came from. Surely the NSA knows who could have taken the files. No country would burn a mole working for it by publishing what he delivered. Intelligence agencies know that if they betray a source this severely, they'll never get another one.

That points to two options. The first is that the files came from Hal Martin. He's the NSA contractor who was arrested in August for hoarding agency secrets in his house for two years. He can't be the publisher, because the Shadow Brokers are in business even though he is in prison. But maybe the leaker got the documents from his stash: either because Martin gave the documents to them or because he himself was hacked. The dates line up, so it's theoretically possible, but the contents of the documents speak to someone with a different sort of access. There's also nothing in the public indictment against Martin that speaks to his selling secrets to a foreign power, and I think it's exactly the sort of thing that the NSA would leak. But maybe I'm wrong about all of this; Occam's Razor suggests that it's him.

The other option is a mysterious second NSA leak of cyberattack tools. The only thing I have ever heard about this is from a Washington Post story about Martin: "But there was a second, previously undisclosed breach of cybertools, discovered in the summer of 2015, which was also carried out by a TAO employee, one official said. That individual also has been arrested, but his case has not been made public. The individual is not thought to have shared the material with another country, the official said." But "not thought to have" is not the same as not having done so.

On the other hand, it's possible that someone penetrated the internal NSA network. We've already seen NSA tools that can do that kind of thing to other networks. That would be huge, and explain why there were calls to fire NSA Director Mike Rogers last year.

The CIA leak is both similar and different. It consists of a series of attack tools from about a year ago. The most educated guess amongst people who know stuff is that the data is from an almost-certainly air-gapped internal development wiki—a Confluence server—and either someone on the inside was somehow coerced into giving up a copy of it, or someone on the outside hacked into the CIA and got themselves a copy. They turned the documents over to WikiLeaks, which continues to publish it.

This is also a really big deal, and hugely damaging for the CIA. Those tools were new, and they're impressive. I have been told that the CIA is desperately trying to hire coders to replace what was lost.

For both of these leaks, one big question is attribution: who did this? A whistleblower wouldn't sit on attack tools for years before publishing. A whistleblower would act more like Snowden or Manning, publishing immediately—and publishing documents that discuss what the US is doing to whom, not simply a bunch of attack tools. It just doesn't make sense. Neither does random hackers. Or cybercriminals. I think it's being done by a country or countries.

My guess was, and is still, Russia in both cases. Here's my reasoning. Whoever got this information years before and is leaking it now has to 1) be capable of hacking the NSA and/or the CIA, and 2) willing to publish it all. Countries like Israel and France are certainly capable, but wouldn't ever publish. Countries like North Korea or Iran probably aren't capable. The list of countries who fit both criteria is small: Russia, China, and...and...and I'm out of ideas. And China is currently trying to make nice with the US.

Last August, Edward Snowden guessed Russia, too.

So Russia—or someone else—steals these secrets, and presumably uses them to both defend its own networks and hack other countries while deflecting blame for a couple of years. For it to publish now means that the intelligence value of the information is now lower than the embarrassment value to the NSA and CIA. This could be because the US figured out that its tools were hacked, and maybe even by whom; which would make the tools less valuable against US government targets, although still valuable against third parties.

The message that comes with publishing seems clear to me: "We are so deep into your business that we don't care if we burn these few-years-old capabilities, as well as the fact that we have them. There's just nothing you can do about it." It's bragging.

Which is exactly the same thing Ledgett is doing to the Russians. Maybe the capabilities he talked about are long gone, so there's nothing lost in exposing sources and methods. Or maybe he too is bragging: saying to the Russians that he doesn't care if they know. He's certainly bragging to every other country that is paying attention to his remarks. (He may be bluffing, of course, hoping to convince others that the US has intelligence capabilities it doesn't.)

What happens when intelligence agencies go to war with each other and don't tell the rest of us? I think there's something going on between the US and Russia that the public is just seeing pieces of. We have no idea why, or where it will go next, and can only speculate.

Who Are the Shadow Brokers?

Originally published in the Atlantic, *May 23, 2017*

In 2013, a mysterious group of hackers that calls itself the Shadow Brokers stole a few disks full of NSA secrets. Since last summer, they've been dumping these secrets on the Internet. They have publicly embarrassed the NSA and damaged its intelligence-gathering capabilities, while at the same time have put sophisticated cyberweapons in the hands of anyone who wants them. They have exposed major vulnerabilities in Cisco routers, Microsoft Windows, and Linux mail servers, forcing those companies and their customers to scramble. And they gave the authors of the WannaCry ransomware the exploit they needed to infect hundreds of thousands of computer worldwide this month.

After the WannaCry outbreak, the Shadow Brokers threatened to release more NSA secrets every month, giving cybercriminals and other governments worldwide even more exploits and hacking tools.

Who are these guys? And how did they steal this information? The short answer is: we don't know. But we can make some educated guesses based on the material they've published.

The Shadow Brokers suddenly appeared last August, when they published a series of hacking tools and computer exploits—vulnerabilities in common software—from the NSA. The material was from autumn 2013, and seems to have been collected from an external NSA staging server, a machine that is owned, leased, or otherwise controlled by the US, but with no connection to the agency. NSA hackers find obscure corners of the Internet to hide the tools they need as they go about their work, and it seems the Shadow Brokers successfully hacked one of those caches.

In total, the group has published four sets of NSA material: a set of exploits and hacking tools against routers, the devices that direct data throughout computer networks; a similar collection against mail servers; another collection against Microsoft Windows; and a working directory of an NSA analyst breaking into the SWIFT banking network. Looking at the time stamps on the files and other material, they all come from around 2013. The Windows attack tools, published last month, might be a year or so older, based on which versions of Windows the tools support.

The releases are so different that they're almost certainly from multiple sources at the NSA. The SWIFT files seem to come from an internal NSA computer, albeit one connected to the Internet. The Microsoft files seem different, too; they don't have the same identifying information that the router and mail server files do. The Shadow Brokers have released all the material unredacted, without the care journalists took with the Snowden documents or even the care WikiLeaks has taken with the CIA secrets it's publishing. They also posted anonymous messages in bad English but with American cultural references.

Given all of this, I don't think the agent responsible is a whistleblower. While possible, it seems like a whistleblower wouldn't sit on attack tools for three years before publishing. They would act more like Edward Snowden or Chelsea Manning, collecting for a time and then publishing immediately—and publishing documents that discuss what the US is doing to whom. That's not what we're seeing here; it's simply a bunch of exploit code, which doesn't have the political or ethical implications that a whistleblower would want to highlight. The SWIFT documents are records of an NSA operation, and the other posted files demonstrate that the NSA is hoarding vulnerabilities for attack rather than helping fix them and improve all of our security.

I also don't think that it's random hackers who stumbled on these tools and are just trying to harm the NSA or the US. Again, the three-year wait makes no sense. These documents and tools are cyber-Kryptonite; anyone who is secretly hoarding them is in danger from half the intelligence agencies in the world. Additionally, the publication schedule doesn't make sense for the leakers to be cybercriminals. Criminals would use the hacking tools for themselves, incorporating the exploits into worms and viruses, and generally profiting from the theft.

That leaves a nation state. Whoever got this information years before and is leaking it now has to be both capable of hacking the

NSA and willing to publish it all. Countries like Israel and France are capable, but would never publish, because they wouldn't want to incur the wrath of the US. Countries like North Korea or Iran probably aren't capable. (Additionally, North Korea is suspected of being behind WannaCry, which was written after the Shadow Brokers released that vulnerability to the public.) As I've written previously, the obvious list of countries who fit my two criteria is small: Russia, China, and—I'm out of ideas. And China is currently trying to make nice with the US.

It was generally believed last August, when the first documents were released and before it became politically controversial to say so, that the Russians were behind the leak, and that it was a warning message to President Barack Obama not to retaliate for the Democratic National Committee hacks. Edward Snowden guessed Russia, too. But the problem with the Russia theory is, why? These leaked tools are much more valuable if kept secret. Russia could use the knowledge to detect NSA hacking in its own country and to attack other countries. By publishing the tools, the Shadow Brokers are signaling that they don't care if the US knows the tools were stolen.

Sure, there's a chance the attackers knew that the US knew that the attackers knew—and round and round we go. But the "we don't give a damn" nature of the releases points to an attacker who isn't thinking strategically: a lone hacker or hacking group, which clashes with the nation-state theory.

This is all speculation on my part, based on discussion with others who don't have access to the classified forensic and intelligence analysis. Inside the NSA, they have a lot more information. Many of the files published include operational notes and identifying information. NSA researchers know exactly which servers were compromised, and through that know what other information the attackers would have access to. As with the Snowden documents, though, they only know what the attackers could have taken and not what they did take. But they did alert Microsoft about the Windows vulnerability the Shadow Brokers released months in advance. Did they have eavesdropping capability inside whoever stole the files, as they claimed to when the Russians attacked the State Department? We have no idea.

So, how did the Shadow Brokers do it? Did someone inside the NSA accidentally mount the wrong server on some external network?

That's possible, but seems very unlikely for the organization to make that kind of rookie mistake. Did someone hack the NSA itself? Could there be a mole inside the NSA?

If it is a mole, my guess is that the person was arrested before the Shadow Brokers released anything. No country would burn a mole working for it by publishing what that person delivered while he or she was still in danger. Intelligence agencies know that if they betray a source this severely, they'll never get another one.

That points to two possibilities. The first is that the files came from Hal Martin. He's the NSA contractor who was arrested in August for hoarding agency secrets in his house for two years. He can't be the publisher, because the Shadow Brokers are in business even though he is in prison. But maybe the leaker got the documents from his stash, either because Martin gave the documents to them or because he himself was hacked. The dates line up, so it's theoretically possible. There's nothing in the public indictment against Martin that speaks to his selling secrets to a foreign power, but that's just the sort of thing that would be left out. It's not needed for a conviction.

If the source of the documents *is* Hal Martin, then we can speculate that a random hacker did in fact stumble on it—no need for nation-state cyberattack skills.

The other option is a mysterious second NSA leaker of cyberattack tools. Could this be the person who stole the NSA documents and passed them on to someone else? The only time I have ever heard about this was from a *Washington Post* story about Martin:

> There was a second, previously undisclosed breach of cyber-tools, discovered in the summer of 2015, which was also carried out by a TAO employee [a worker in the Office of Tailored Access Operations], one official said. That individual also has been arrested, but his case has not been made public. The individual is not thought to have shared the material with another country, the official said.

Of course, "not thought to have" is not the same as not having done so.

It is interesting that there have been no public arrests of anyone in connection with these hacks. If the NSA knows where the files came from, it knows who had access to them—and it's long since questioned everyone involved and should know if someone deliberately or accidentally lost control of them. I know that many people, both inside the government and out, think there is some sort of domestic involvement; things may be more complicated than I realize.

It's also not over. Last week, the Shadow Brokers were back, with a rambling and taunting message announcing a "Data Dump of the Month" service. They're offering to sell unreleased NSA attack tools— something they also tried last August—with the threat to publish them if no one pays. The group has made good on their previous boasts: In the coming months, we might see new exploits against web browsers, networking equipment, smartphones, and operating systems— Windows in particular. Even scarier, they're threatening to release raw NSA intercepts: data from the SWIFT network and banks, and "compromised data from Russian, Chinese, Iranian, or North Korean nukes and missile programs."

Whoever the Shadow Brokers are, however they stole these disks full of NSA secrets, and for whatever reason they're releasing them, it's going to be a long summer inside of Fort Meade—as it will be for the rest of us.

On the Equifax Data Breach

Originally published in CNN.com *September 11, 2017*

Last Thursday, Equifax reported a data breach that affects 143 million US customers, about 44% of the population. It's an extremely serious breach; hackers got access to full names, Social Security numbers, birth dates, addresses, driver's license numbers—exactly the sort of information criminals can use to impersonate victims to banks, credit card companies, insurance companies, and other businesses vulnerable to fraud.

Many sites posted guides to protecting yourself now that it's happened. But if you want to prevent this kind of thing from happening again, your only solution is government regulation (as unlikely as that may be at the moment).

The market can't fix this. Markets work because buyers choose between sellers, and sellers compete for buyers. In case you didn't notice, you're not Equifax's customer. You're its product.

This happened because your personal information is valuable, and Equifax is in the business of selling it. The company is much more than a credit reporting agency. It's a data broker. It collects information about all of us, analyzes it all, and then sells those insights.

Its customers are people and organizations who want to buy information: banks looking to lend you money, landlords deciding whether to rent you an apartment, employers deciding whether to hire you, companies trying to figure out whether you'd be a profitable customer—everyone who wants to sell you something, even governments.

It's not just Equifax. It might be one of the biggest, but there are 2,500 to 4,000 other data brokers that are collecting, storing, and selling information about you—almost all of them companies you've never heard of and have no business relationship with.

Surveillance capitalism fuels the Internet, and sometimes it seems that everyone is spying on you. You're secretly tracked on pretty much every commercial website you visit. Facebook is the largest surveillance organization mankind has created; collecting data on you is its business model. I don't have a Facebook account, but Facebook still keeps a surprisingly complete dossier on me and my associations— just in case I ever decide to join.

I also don't have a Gmail account, because I don't want Google storing my email. But my guess is that it has about half of my email anyway, because so many people I correspond with have accounts. I can't even avoid it by choosing not to write to gmail.com addresses, because I have no way of knowing if newperson@company.com is hosted at Gmail.

And again, many companies that track us do so in secret, without our knowledge and consent. And most of the time we can't opt out. Sometimes it's a company like Equifax that doesn't answer to us in any way. Sometimes it's a company like Facebook, which is effectively a monopoly because of its sheer size. And sometimes it's our cell phone provider. All of them have decided to track us and not compete by offering consumers privacy. Sure, you can tell people not to have an email account or cell phone, but that's not a realistic option for most people living in 21st-century America.

The companies that collect and sell our data don't need to keep it secure in order to maintain their market share. They don't have to answer to us, their products. They know it's more profitable to save money on security and weather the occasional bout of bad press after a data loss. Yes, we are the ones who suffer when criminals get our data, or when our private information is exposed to the public, but ultimately why should Equifax care?

Yes, it's a huge black eye for the company—this week. Soon, another company will have suffered a massive data breach and few will remember Equifax's problem. Does anyone remember last year when Yahoo admitted that it exposed personal information of a billion users in 2013 and another half billion in 2014?

This market failure isn't unique to data security. There is little improvement in safety and security in any industry until government steps in. Think of food, pharmaceuticals, cars, airplanes, restaurants, workplace conditions, and flame-retardant pajamas.

Market failures like this can only be solved through government intervention. By regulating the security practices of companies that store our data, and fining companies that fail to comply, governments can raise the cost of insecurity high enough that security becomes a cheaper alternative. They can do the same thing by giving individuals affected by these breaches the ability to sue successfully, citing the exposure of personal data itself as a harm.

By all means, take the recommended steps to protect yourself from identity theft in the wake of Equifax's data breach, but recognize that these steps are only effective on the margins, and that most data security is out of your hands. Perhaps the Federal Trade Commission will get involved, but without evidence of "unfair and deceptive trade practices," there's nothing it can do. Perhaps there will be a class-action lawsuit, but because it's hard to draw a line between any of the many data breaches you're subjected to and a specific harm, courts are not likely to side with you.

If you don't like how careless Equifax was with your data, don't waste your breath complaining to Equifax. Complain to your government.

10 Security, Policy, Liberty, and Law

Our Newfound Fear of Risk

Originally published in Forbes.com, *August 23, 2013*

We're afraid of risk. It's a normal part of life, but we're increasingly unwilling to accept it at any level. So we turn to technology to protect us. The problem is that technological security measures aren't free. They cost money, of course, but they cost other things as well. They often don't provide the security they advertise, and—paradoxically—they often increase risk somewhere else. This problem is particularly stark when the risk involves another person: crime, terrorism, and so on. While technology has made us much safer against natural risks like accidents and disease, it works less well against man-made risks.

Three examples:

1. We have allowed the police to turn themselves into a paramilitary organization. They deploy SWAT teams multiple times a day, almost always in nondangerous situations. They tase people at minimal provocation, often when it's not warranted. Unprovoked shootings are on the rise. One result of these measures is that honest mistakes—a wrong address on a warrant, a misunderstanding—result in the terrorizing of innocent people, and more death in what were once nonviolent confrontations with police.

2. We accept zero-tolerance policies in schools. This results in ridiculous situations, where young children are suspended for pointing gun-shaped fingers at other students or drawing pictures of guns with crayons, and high-school students are disciplined for giving each other over-the-counter pain relievers. The cost of

these policies is enormous, both in dollars to implement and its long-lasting effects on students.

3. We have spent over one trillion dollars and thousands of lives fighting terrorism in the past decade—including the wars in Iraq and Afghanistan—money that could have been better used in all sorts of ways. We now know that the NSA has turned into a massive domestic surveillance organization, and that its data is also used by other government organizations, which then lie about it. Our foreign policy has changed for the worse: we spy on everyone, we trample human rights abroad, our drones kill indiscriminately, and our diplomatic outposts have either closed down or become fortresses. In the months after 9/11, so many people chose to drive instead of fly that the resulting deaths dwarfed the deaths from the terrorist attack itself, because cars are much more dangerous than airplanes.

There are lots more examples, but the general point is that we tend to fixate on a particular risk and then do everything we can to mitigate it, including giving up our freedoms and liberties.

There's a subtle psychological explanation. Risk tolerance is both cultural and dependent on the environment around us. As we have advanced technologically as a society, we have reduced many of the risks that have been with us for millennia. Fatal childhood diseases are things of the past, many adult diseases are curable, accidents are rarer and more survivable, buildings collapse less often, death by violence has declined considerably, and so on. All over the world—among the wealthier of us who live in peaceful Western countries—our lives have become safer.

Our notions of risk are not absolute; they're based more on how far they are from whatever we think of as "normal." So as our perception of what is normal gets safer, the remaining risks stand out more. When your population is dying of the plague, protecting yourself from the occasional thief or murderer is a luxury. When everyone is healthy, it becomes a necessity.

Some of this fear results from imperfect risk perception. We're bad at accurately assessing risk; we tend to exaggerate spectacular, strange, and rare events, and downplay ordinary, familiar, and common ones. This leads us to believe that violence against police, school shootings, and terrorist attacks are more common and more deadly than they actually are—and that the costs, dangers, and risks of a militarized police, a school system without flexibility, and a surveillance state without privacy are less than they really are.

Some of this fear stems from the fact that we put people in charge of just one aspect of the risk equation. No one wants to be the senior officer who didn't approve the SWAT team for the one subpoena delivery that resulted in an officer being shot. No one wants to be the school principal who didn't discipline—no matter how benign the infraction—the one student who became a shooter. No one wants to be the president who rolled back counterterrorism measures, just in time to have a plot succeed. Those in charge will be naturally risk averse, since they personally shoulder so much of the burden.

We also expect that science and technology should be able to mitigate these risks, as they mitigate so many others. There's a fundamental problem at the intersection of these security measures with science and technology; it has to do with the types of risk they're arrayed against. Most of the risks we face in life are against nature: disease, accident, weather, random chance. As our science has improved—medicine is the big one, but other sciences as well—we become better at mitigating and recovering from those sorts of risks.

Security measures combat a very different sort of risk: a risk stemming from another person. People are intelligent, and they can adapt to new security measures in ways nature cannot. An earthquake isn't able to figure out how to topple structures constructed under some new and safer building code, and an automobile won't invent a new form of accident that undermines medical advances that have made existing accidents more survivable. But a terrorist will change his tactics and targets in response to new security measures. An otherwise innocent person will change his behavior in response to a police force that compels compliance at the threat of a Taser. We will all change, living in a surveillance state.

When you implement measures to mitigate the effects of the random risks of the world, you're safer as a result. When you implement measures to reduce the risks from your fellow human beings, the human beings adapt and you get less risk reduction than you'd expect—and you also get more side effects, because we *all* adapt.

We need to relearn how to recognize the trade-offs that come from risk management, especially risk from our fellow human beings. We need to relearn how to accept risk, and even embrace it, as essential to human progress and our free society. The more we expect technology to protect us from people in the same way it protects us from nature, the more we will sacrifice the very values of our society in futile attempts to achieve this security.

Take Back the Internet

Originally published in the Guardian, *September 5, 2013*

Government and industry have betrayed the Internet, and us.

By subverting the Internet at every level to make it a vast, multi-layered and robust surveillance platform, the NSA has undermined a fundamental social contract. The companies that build and manage our Internet infrastructure, the companies that create and sell us our hardware and software, or the companies that host our data: we can no longer trust them to be ethical Internet stewards.

This is not the Internet the world needs, or the Internet its creators envisioned. We need to take it back.

And by we, I mean the engineering community.

Yes, this is primarily a political problem, a policy matter that requires political intervention.

But this is also an engineering problem, and there are several things engineers can—and should—do.

One, we should expose. If you do not have a security clearance, and if you have not received a National Security Letter, you are not bound by a federal confidentially requirements or a gag order. If you have been contacted by the NSA to subvert a product or protocol, you need to come forward with your story. Your employer obligations don't cover illegal or unethical activity. If you work with classified data and are truly brave, expose what you know. We need whistleblowers.

We need to know how exactly how the NSA and other agencies are subverting routers, switches, the Internet backbone, encryption technologies and cloud systems. I already have five stories from people like you, and I've just started collecting. I want 50. There's safety in numbers, and this form of civil disobedience is the moral thing to do.

Two, we can design. We need to figure out how to re-engineer the Internet to prevent this kind of wholesale spying. We need new techniques to prevent communications intermediaries from leaking private information.

We can make surveillance expensive again. In particular, we need open protocols, open implementations, open systems—these will be harder for the NSA to subvert.

The Internet Engineering Task Force, the group that defines the standards that make the Internet run, has a meeting planned for early November in Vancouver. This group needs to dedicate its next meeting to this task. This is an emergency, and demands an emergency response.

Three, we can influence governance. I have resisted saying this up to now, and I am saddened to say it, but the US has proved to be an unethical steward of the Internet. The UK is no better. The NSA's actions are legitimizing the Internet abuses by China, Russia, Iran and others. We need to figure out new means of Internet governance, ones that makes it harder for powerful tech countries to monitor everything. For example, we need to demand transparency, oversight, and accountability from our governments and corporations.

Unfortunately, this is going play directly into the hands of totalitarian governments that want to control their country's Internet for even more extreme forms of surveillance. We need to figure out how to prevent that, too. We need to avoid the mistakes of the International Telecommunications Union, which has become a forum to legitimize bad government behavior, and create truly international governance that can't be dominated or abused by any one country.

Generations from now, when people look back on these early decades of the Internet, I hope they will not be disappointed in us. We can ensure that they don't only if each of us makes this a priority, and engages in the debate. We have a moral duty to do this, and we have no time to lose.

Dismantling the surveillance state won't be easy. Has any country that engaged in mass surveillance of its own citizens voluntarily given up that capability? Has any mass surveillance country avoided becoming totalitarian? Whatever happens, we're going to be breaking new ground.

Again, the politics of this is a bigger task than the engineering, but the engineering is critical. We need to demand that real technologists be involved in any key government decision making on these issues. We've had enough of lawyers and politicians not fully understanding technology; we need technologists at the table when we build tech policy.

To the engineers, I say this: we built the Internet, and some of us have helped to subvert it. Now, those of us who love liberty have to fix it.

The Battle for Power on the Internet

Originally published in the Atlantic, *October 24, 2013*

We're in the middle of an epic battle for power in cyberspace. On one side are the traditional, organized, institutional powers such as governments and large multinational corporations. On the other are the distributed and nimble: grassroots movements, dissident groups, hackers, and criminals. Initially, the Internet empowered the second side. It gave them a place to coordinate and communicate efficiently, and made them seem unbeatable. But now, the more traditional institutional powers are winning, and winning big. How these two sides fare in the long term, and the fate of the rest of us who don't fall into either group, is an open question—and one vitally important to the future of the Internet.

In the Internet's early days, there was a lot of talk about its "natural laws"—how it would upend traditional power blocks, empower the masses, and spread freedom throughout the world. The international nature of the Internet circumvented national laws. Anonymity was easy. Censorship was impossible. Police were clueless about cybercrime. And bigger changes seemed inevitable. Digital cash would undermine national sovereignty. Citizen journalism would topple traditional media, corporate PR, and political parties. Easy digital copying would destroy the traditional movie and music industries. Web marketing would allow even the smallest companies to compete against corporate giants. It really would be a new world order.

This was a utopian vision, but some of it did come to pass. Internet marketing has transformed commerce. The entertainment industries have been transformed by things like MySpace and YouTube, and are now more open to outsiders. Mass media has changed dramatically, and some of the most influential people in the media have come from the blogging world. There are new ways to organize politically and run elections. Crowdfunding has made tens of thousands of projects possible to finance, and crowdsourcing made more types of projects possible. Facebook and Twitter really did help topple governments.

But that is just one side of the Internet's disruptive character. The Internet has emboldened traditional power as well.

On the corporate side, power is consolidating, a result of two current trends in computing. First, the rise of cloud computing means that we no longer have control of our data. Our email, photos, calendars, address books, messages, and documents are on servers belonging to Google, Apple, Microsoft, Facebook, and so on. And second, we are increasingly accessing our data using devices that we have much less control over: iPhones, iPads, Android phones, Kindles, Chrome-Books, and so on. Unlike traditional operating systems, those devices are controlled much more tightly by the vendors, who limit what software can run, what they can do, how they're updated, and so on. Even Windows 8 and Apple's Mountain Lion operating system are heading in the direction of more vendor control.

I have previously characterized this model of computing as "feudal." Users pledge their allegiance to more powerful companies that, in turn, promise to protect them from both sysadmin duties and security threats. It's a metaphor that's rich in history and in fiction, and a model that's increasingly permeating computing today.

Medieval feudalism was a hierarchical political system, with obligations in both directions. Lords offered protection, and vassals offered service. The lord-peasant relationship was similar, with a much greater power differential. It was a response to a dangerous world.

Feudal security consolidates power in the hands of the few. Internet companies, like lords before them, act in their own self-interest. They use their relationship with us to increase their profits, sometimes at our expense. They act arbitrarily. They make mistakes. They're deliberately—and incidentally—changing social norms. Medieval feudalism gave the lords vast powers over the landless peasants; we're seeing the same thing on the Internet.

It's not all bad, of course. We, especially those of us who are not technical, like the convenience, redundancy, portability, automation, and shareability of vendor-managed devices. We like cloud backup. We like automatic updates. We like not having to deal with security ourselves. We like that Facebook just works—from any device, anywhere.

Government power is also increasing on the Internet. There is more government surveillance than ever before. There is more government censorship than ever before. There is more government propaganda, and an increasing number of governments are controlling what their users can and cannot do on the Internet. Totalitarian governments are embracing a growing "cyber sovereignty" movement to further consolidate their power. And the cyberwar arms race is on, pumping an enormous amount of money into cyber-weapons and consolidated cyber-defenses, further increasing government power.

In many cases, the interests of corporate and government powers are aligning. Both corporations and governments benefit from ubiquitous surveillance, and the NSA is using Google, Facebook, Verizon, and others to get access to data it couldn't otherwise. The entertainment industry is looking to governments to enforce its antiquated business models. Commercial security equipment from companies like BlueCoat and Sophos is being used by oppressive governments to surveil and censor their citizens. The same facial recognition technology that Disney uses in its theme parks can also identify protesters in China and Occupy Wall Street activists in New York. Think of it as a public/private surveillance partnership.

What happened? How, in those early Internet years, did we get the future so wrong?

The truth is that technology magnifies power in general, but rates of adoption are different. The unorganized, the distributed, the marginal, the dissidents, the powerless, the criminal: they can make use of new technologies very quickly. And when those groups discovered the Internet, suddenly they had power. But later, when the already-powerful big institutions finally figured out how to harness the Internet, they had more power to magnify. That's the difference: the distributed were more nimble and were faster to make use of their new power, while the institutional were slower but were able to use their power more effectively.

So while the Syrian dissidents used Facebook to organize, the Syrian government used Facebook to identify dissidents to arrest.

All isn't lost for distributed power, though. For institutional power, the Internet is a change in degree, but for distributed power, it's a qualitative one. The Internet gives decentralized groups—for the first time—the ability to coordinate. This can have incredible ramifications, as we saw in the SOPA/PIPA debate, Gezi, Brazil, and the rising use of crowdfunding. It can invert power dynamics, even in the presence of surveillance, censorship, and use control. But aside from political coordination, the Internet allows for social coordination as well—to unite, for example, ethnic diasporas, gender minorities, sufferers of rare diseases, and people with obscure interests.

This isn't static: Technological advances continue to provide advantage to the nimble. I discussed this trend in my book *Liars and Outliers*. If you think of security as an arms race between attackers and defenders, any technological advance gives one side or the other a temporary advantage. But most of the time, a new technology benefits the nimble first. They are not hindered by bureaucracy—and sometimes not by laws or ethics, either. They can evolve faster.

We saw it with the Internet. As soon as the Internet started being used for commerce, a new breed of cybercriminal emerged, immediately able to take advantage of the new technology. It took police a decade to catch up. And we saw it on social media, as political dissidents made use of its organizational powers before totalitarian regimes did.

This delay is what I call a "security gap." It's greater when there's more technology, and in times of rapid technological change. Basically, if there are more innovations to exploit, there will be more damage resulting from society's inability to keep up with exploiters of all of them. And since our world is one in which there's more technology than ever before, and a faster rate of technological change than ever before, we should expect to see a greater security gap than ever before. In other words, there will be an increasing time period during which nimble distributed powers can make use of new technologies before slow institutional powers can make better use of those technologies.

This is the battle: quick vs. strong. To return to medieval metaphors, you can think of a nimble distributed power—whether marginal, dissident, or criminal—as Robin Hood; and ponderous institutional powers—both government and corporate—as the feudal lords.

So who wins? Which type of power dominates in the coming decades?

Right now, it looks like traditional power. Ubiquitous surveillance means that it's easier for the government to identify dissidents than it is for the dissidents to remain anonymous. Data monitoring means easier for the Great Firewall of China to block data than it is for people to circumvent it. The way we all use the Internet makes it much easier for the NSA to spy on everyone than it is for anyone to maintain privacy. And even though it is easy to circumvent digital copy protection, most users still can't do it.

The problem is that leveraging Internet power requires technical expertise. Those with sufficient ability will be able to stay ahead of institutional powers. Whether it's setting up your own email server, effectively using encryption and anonymity tools, or breaking copy protection, there will always be technologies that can evade institutional powers. This is why cybercrime is still pervasive, even as police savvy increases; why technically capable whistleblowers can do so much damage; and why organizations like Anonymous are still a viable social and political force. Assuming technology continues to advance—and there's no reason to believe it won't—there will always be a security gap in which technically advanced Robin Hoods can operate.

Most people, though, are stuck in the middle. These are people who don't have the technical ability to evade large governments and corporations, avoid the criminal and hacker groups who prey on us, or join any resistance or dissident movements. These are the people who accept default configuration options, arbitrary terms of service, NSA-installed back doors, and the occasional complete loss of their data. These are the people who get increasingly isolated as government and corporate power align. In the feudal world, these are the hapless peasants. And it's even worse when the feudal lords—or any powers—fight each other. As anyone watching *Game of Thrones* knows, peasants get trampled when powers fight: when Facebook, Google, Apple, and Amazon fight it out in the market; when the US, EU, China, and Russia fight it out in geopolitics; or when it's the US vs. "the terrorists" or China vs. its dissidents.

The abuse will only get worse as technology continues to advance. In the battle between institutional power and distributed power, more technology means more damage. We've already seen this: Cybercriminals can rob more people more quickly than criminals who have to physically visit everyone they rob. Digital pirates can make more copies of more things much more quickly than their analog forebears. And we'll see it in the future: 3D printers mean that the computer restriction debate will soon involves guns, not movies. Big data will mean that more companies will be able to identify and track you more easily. It's the same problem as the "weapons of mass destruction" fear: terrorists with nuclear or biological weapons can do a lot more damage than terrorists with conventional explosives. And by the same token, terrorists with large-scale cyberweapons can potentially do more damage than terrorists with those same bombs.

It's a numbers game. Very broadly, because of the way humans behave as a species and as a society, every society is going to have a certain amount of crime. And there's a particular crime rate society is willing to tolerate. With historically inefficient criminals, we were willing to live with some percentage of criminals in our society. As technology makes each individual criminal more powerful, the percentage we can tolerate decreases. Again, remember the "weapons of mass destruction" debate: As the amount of damage each individual terrorist can do increases, we need to do increasingly more to prevent even a single terrorist from succeeding.

The more destabilizing the technologies, the greater the rhetoric of fear, and the stronger institutional powers will get. This means increasingly repressive security measures, even if the security gap means that such measures become increasingly ineffective. And it will squeeze the peasants in the middle even more.

Without the protection of his own feudal lord, the peasant was subject to abuse both by criminals and other feudal lords. But both corporations and the government—and often the two in cahoots—are using their power to their own advantage, trampling on our rights in the process. And without the technical savvy to become Robin Hoods ourselves, we have no recourse but to submit to whatever the ruling institutional power wants.

So what happens as technology increases? Is a police state the only effective way to control distributed power and keep our society safe? Or do the fringe elements inevitably destroy society as technology increases their power? Probably neither doomsday scenario will come to pass, but figuring out a stable middle ground is hard. These questions are complicated, and dependent on future technological advances that we cannot predict. But they are primarily political questions, and any solutions will be political.

In the short term, we need more transparency and oversight. The more we know of what institutional powers are doing, the more we can trust that they are not abusing their authority. We have long known this to be true in government, but we have increasingly ignored it in our fear of terrorism and other modern threats. This is also true for corporate power. Unfortunately, market dynamics will not necessarily force corporations to be transparent; we need laws to do that. The same is true for decentralized power; transparency is how we'll differentiate political dissidents from criminal organizations.

Oversight is also critically important, and is another long-understood mechanism for checking power. This can be a combination of things: courts that act as third-party advocates for the rule of law rather than rubber-stamp organizations, legislatures that understand the technologies and how they affect power balances, and vibrant public-sector press and watchdog groups that analyze and debate the actions of those wielding power.

Transparency and oversight give us the confidence to trust institutional powers to fight the bad side of distributed power, while still allowing the good side to flourish. For if we're going to entrust our security to institutional powers, we need to know they will act in our interests and not abuse that power. Otherwise, democracy fails.

In the longer term, we need to work to reduce power differences. The key to all of this is access to data. On the Internet, data is power. To the extent the powerless have access to it, they gain in power. To the extent that the already powerful have access to it, they further consolidate their power. As we look to reducing power imbalances, we have to look at data: data privacy for individuals, mandatory disclosure laws for corporations, and open government laws.

Medieval feudalism evolved into a more balanced relationship in which lords had responsibilities as well as rights. Today's Internet feudalism is both ad-hoc and one-sided. Those in power have a lot of rights, but increasingly few responsibilities or limits. We need to rebalance this relationship. In medieval Europe, the rise of the centralized state and the rule of law provided the stability that feudalism lacked. The Magna Carta first forced responsibilities on governments and put humans on the long road toward government by the people and for the people. In addition to re-reigning in government power, we need similar restrictions on corporate power: a new Magna Carta focused on the institutions that abuse power in the 21st century.

Today's Internet is a fortuitous accident: a combination of an initial lack of commercial interests, government benign neglect, military requirements for survivability and resilience, and computer engineers building open systems that worked simply and easily.

We're at the beginning of some critical debates about the future of the Internet: the proper role of law enforcement, the character of ubiquitous surveillance, the collection and retention of our entire life's history, how automatic algorithms should judge us, government control over the Internet, cyberwar rules of engagement, national sovereignty on the Internet, limitations on the power of corporations over our data, the ramifications of information consumerism, and so on.

Data is the pollution problem of the information age. All computer processes produce it. It stays around. How we deal with it—how we reuse and recycle it, who has access to it, how we dispose of it, and what laws regulate it—is central to how the information age functions. And I believe that just as we look back at the early decades of the industrial age and wonder how society could ignore pollution in their rush to build an industrial world, our grandchildren will look back at us during these early decades of the information age and judge us on how we dealt with the rebalancing of power resulting from all this new data.

This won't be an easy period for us as we try to work these issues out. Historically, no shift in power has ever been easy. Corporations have turned our personal data into an enormous revenue generator, and they're not going to back down. Neither will governments, who have harnessed that same data for their own purposes. But we have a duty to tackle this problem.

I can't tell you what the result will be. These are all complicated issues, and require meaningful debate, international cooperation, and innovative solutions. We need to decide on the proper balance between institutional and decentralized power, and how to build tools that amplify what is good in each while suppressing the bad.

How the NSA Threatens National Security

Originally published in the Atlantic, *January 6, 2014*

Secret NSA eavesdropping is still in the news. Details about once secret programs continue to leak. The Director of National Intelligence has recently declassified additional information, and the President's Review Group has just released its report and recommendations.

With all this going on, it's easy to become inured to the breadth and depth of the NSA's activities. But through the disclosures, we've learned an enormous amount about the agency's capabilities, how it is failing to protect us, and what we need to do to regain security in the Information Age.

First and foremost, the surveillance state is robust. It is robust politically, legally, and technically. I can name three different NSA programs to collect Gmail user data. These programs are based on three different technical eavesdropping capabilities. They rely on three different legal authorities. They involve collaborations with three different companies. And this is just Gmail. The same is true for cell phone call records, Internet chats, cell phone location data.

Second, the NSA continues to lie about its capabilities. It hides behind tortured interpretations of words like "collect," "incidentally," "target," and "directed." It cloaks programs in multiple code names to obscure their full extent and capabilities. Officials testify that a particular surveillance activity is not done under one particular program or authority, conveniently omitting that it is done under some other program or authority.

Third, U.S. government surveillance is not just about the NSA. The Snowden documents have given us extraordinary details about the NSA's activities, but we now know that the CIA, NRO, FBI, DEA, and local police all engage in ubiquitous surveillance using the same sorts of eavesdropping tools, and that they regularly share information with each other.

The NSA's collect-everything mentality is largely a hold-over from the Cold War, when a voyeuristic interest in the Soviet Union was the norm. Still, it is unclear how effective targeted surveillance against "enemy" countries really is. Even when we learn actual secrets, as we did regarding Syria's use of chemical weapons earlier this year, we often can't do anything with the information.

Ubiquitous surveillance should have died with the fall of Communism, but it got a new—and even more dangerous—life with the intelligence community's post-9/11 "never again" terrorism mission. This quixotic goal of preventing something from happening forces us to try to know everything that does happen. This pushes the NSA to eavesdrop on online gaming worlds and on every cell phone in the world. But it's a fool's errand; there are simply too many ways to communicate.

We have no evidence that any of this surveillance makes us safer. NSA Director General Keith Alexander responded to these stories in

June by claiming that he disrupted 54 terrorist plots. In October, he revised that number downward to 13, and then to "one or two." At this point, the only "plot" prevented was that of a San Diego man sending $8,500 to support a Somali militant group. We have been repeatedly told that these surveillance programs would have been able to stop 9/11, yet the NSA didn't detect the Boston bombings—even though one of the two terrorists was on the watch list and the other had a sloppy social media trail. Bulk collection of data and metadata is an ineffective counterterrorism tool.

Not only is ubiquitous surveillance ineffective, it is extraordinarily costly. I don't mean just the budgets, which will continue to skyrocket. Or the diplomatic costs, as country after country learns of our surveillance programs against their citizens. I'm also talking about the cost to our society. It breaks so much of what our society has built. It breaks our political systems, as Congress is unable to provide any meaningful oversight and citizens are kept in the dark about what government does. It breaks our legal systems, as laws are ignored or reinterpreted, and people are unable to challenge government actions in court. It breaks our commercial systems, as U.S. computer products and services are no longer trusted worldwide. It breaks our technical systems, as the very protocols of the Internet become untrusted. And it breaks our social systems; the loss of privacy, freedom, and liberty is much more damaging to our society than the occasional act of random violence.

And finally, these systems are susceptible to abuse. This is not just a hypothetical problem. Recent history illustrates many episodes where this information was, or would have been, abused: Hoover and his FBI spying, McCarthy, Martin Luther King Jr. and the civil rights movement, antiwar Vietnam protesters, and—more recently—the Occupy movement. Outside the U.S., there are even more extreme examples. Building the surveillance state makes it too easy for people and organizations to slip over the line into abuse.

It's not just domestic abuse we have to worry about; it's the rest of the world, too. The more we choose to eavesdrop on the Internet and other communications technologies, the less we are secure from eavesdropping by others. Our choice isn't between a digital world where the NSA can eavesdrop and one where the NSA is prevented from eavesdropping; it's between a digital world that is vulnerable to all attackers, and one that is secure for all users.

Fixing this problem is going to be hard. We are long past the point where simple legal interventions can help. The bill in Congress to limit NSA surveillance won't actually do much to limit NSA surveillance. Maybe the NSA will figure out an interpretation of the law that will allow it to do what it wants anyway. Maybe it'll do it another way, using another justification. Maybe the FBI will do it and give it a copy. And when asked, it'll lie about it.

NSA-level surveillance is like the Maginot Line was in the years before World War II: ineffective and wasteful. We need to openly disclose what surveillance we have been doing, and the known insecurities that make it possible. We need to work toward security, even if other countries like China continue to use the Internet as a giant surveillance platform. We need to build a coalition of free-world nations dedicated to a secure global Internet, and we need to continually push back against bad actors—both state and non-state—that work against that goal.

Securing the Internet requires both laws and technology. It requires Internet technology that secures data wherever it is and however it travels. It requires broad laws that put security ahead of both domestic and international surveillance. It requires additional technology to enforce those laws, and a worldwide enforcement regime to deal with bad actors. It's not easy, and has all the problems that other international issues have: nuclear, chemical, and biological weapon nonproliferation; small arms trafficking; human trafficking; money laundering; intellectual property. Global information security and anti-surveillance needs to join those difficult global problems, so we can start making progress.

The President's Review Group recommendations are largely positive, but they don't go nearly far enough. We need to recognize that security is more important than surveillance, and work towards that goal.

Who Should Store NSA Surveillance Data?

Originally published in Slate.com, *February 14, 2014*

One of the recommendations by the president's Review Group on Intelligence and Communications Technologies on reforming the National Security Agency—No. 5, if you're counting—is that the government should not collect and store telephone metadata. Instead, a private company—either the phone companies themselves or some other third party—should store the metadata and provide it to the government only upon a court order.

This isn't a new idea. Over the past decade, several countries have enacted mandatory data retention laws, in which companies are required to save Internet or telephony data about customers for a specified period of time, in case the government needs it for an investigation. But does it make sense? In December, Harvard Law professor Jack Goldsmith asked: "I understand the Report's concerns about the storage of bulk meta-data by the government. But I do not understand the Report's implicit assumption that the storage of bulk meta-data by private entities is an improvement from the perspective of privacy, or data security, or potential abuse."

It's a good question, and in the almost two months since the report was released, it hasn't received enough attention. I think the proposal makes things worse in several respects.

First, the NSA is going to do a better job at database security than corporations are. I say this not because the NSA has any magic computer security powers, but because it has more experience at it and is better funded. (And, yes, that's true even though Edward Snowden was able to copy so many of their documents.) The difference is of degree, not of kind. Both options leave the data vulnerable to insider attacks—more so in the case of a third-party data repository because there will be more insiders. And although neither will be perfect, I would trust the NSA to protect my data *against unauthorized access* more than I would trust a private corporation to do the same.

Second, there's the greater risk of authorized access. This is the risk that the Review Group is most concerned about. The thought is that if the data were in private hands, and the only legal way at the data was a court order, then it would be less likely for the NSA to exceed its authority by making bulk queries on the data or accessing more of it than it is allowed to. I don't believe that this is true. Any system that has the data outside of the NSA's control is going to include provisions for emergency access, because ... well, because the word *terrorism* will scare any lawmaker enough to give the NSA that capability. Already the NSA goes through whatever legal processes it and the secret FISA court have agreed to. Adding another party into this process doesn't slow things down, provide more oversight, or in any way make it better. I don't trust a corporate employee not to turn data over for NSA analysis any more than I trust an NSA employee.

On the corporate side, the corresponding risk is that the data will be used for all sorts of things that wouldn't be possible otherwise. If corporations are forced by governments to hold on to customer data, they're going to start thinking things like: "We're already storing this personal data on all of our customers for the government. Why don't we mine it for interesting tidbits, use it for marketing purposes, sell it to data brokers, and on and on and on?" At least the NSA isn't going to use our personal data for large-scale individual psychological manipulation designed to separate us from as much money as possible—which is the business model of companies like Google and Facebook.

The final claimed benefit—and this one is from the president's Review Group—is that putting the data in private hands will make us all feel better. They write: "Knowing that the government has ready access to one's phone call records can seriously chill 'associational and expressive freedoms,' and knowing that the government is one flick of a switch away from such information can profoundly 'alter the relationship between citizen and government in a way that is inimical to society.'" Those quotes within the quote are from Justice Sonia Sotomayor's opinion in the *U.S. v. Jones* GPS monitoring case.

The Review Group believes that moving the data to some other organization, either the companies that generate it in the first place or some third-party data repository, fixes that problem. But is that something we really want fixed? The fact that a government has us all under constant and ubiquitous surveillance *should* be chilling. It *should* limit freedom of expression. It is inimical to society, and to the extent we hide what we're doing from the people or do things that only pretend to fix the problem, we do ourselves a disservice.

Where does this leave us? If the corporations are storing the data already—for some business purpose—then the answer is easy: Only they should store it. If the corporations are not already storing the data, then—on balance—it's safer for the NSA to store the data. And in many cases, the right answer is for no one to store the data. It should be deleted because keeping it makes us all less secure.

This question is much bigger than the NSA. There are going to be data—medical data, movement data, transactional data—that are both valuable to us all in aggregate and private to us individually. And in every one of those instances, we're going to be faced with the same question: How do we extract that societal value, while at the same protecting its personal nature? This is one of the key challenges of the Information Age, and figuring out where to store the data is a major part of that challenge. There certainly isn't going to be one solution for all instances of this problem, but learning how to weigh the costs and benefits of different solutions will be a key component to harnessing the power of big data without suffering the societal harms.

Ephemeral Apps

Originally published in CNN.com, *March 26, 2014*

Ephemeral messaging apps such as Snapchat, Wickr and Frankly, all of which advertise that your photo, message or update will only be accessible for a short period, are on the rise. Snapchat and Frankly, for example, claim they permanently delete messages, photos and videos after 10 seconds. After that, there's no record.

This notion is especially popular with young people, and these apps are an antidote to sites such as Facebook where everything you post lasts forever unless you take it down—and taking it down is no guarantee that it isn't still available.

These ephemeral apps are the first concerted push against the permanence of Internet conversation. We started losing ephemeral conversation when computers began to mediate our communications. Computers naturally produce conversation records, and that data was often saved and archived.

The powerful and famous—from Oliver North back in 1987 to Anthony Weiner in 2011—have been brought down by emails, texts, tweets and posts they thought private. Lots of us have been embroiled in more personal embarrassments resulting from things we've said either being saved for too long or shared too widely.

People have reacted to this permanent nature of Internet communications in ad hoc ways. We've deleted our stuff where possible and asked others not to forward our writings without permission. "Wall scrubbing" is the term used to describe the deletion of Facebook posts.

Sociologist danah boyd has written about teens who systematically delete every post they make on Facebook soon after they make it. Apps such as Wickr just automate the process. And it turns out there's a huge market in that.

Ephemeral conversation is easy to promise but hard to get right. In 2013, researchers discovered that Snapchat doesn't delete images as advertised; it merely changes their names so they're not easy to see. Whether this is a problem for users depends on how technically savvy their adversaries are, but it illustrates the difficulty of making instant deletion actually work.

The problem is that these new "ephemeral" conversations aren't really ephemeral the way a face-to-face unrecorded conversation would be. They're not ephemeral like a conversation during a walk in a deserted woods used to be before the invention of cell phones and GPS receivers.

At best, the data is recorded, used, saved and then deliberately deleted. At worst, the ephemeral nature is faked. While the apps make the posts, texts or messages unavailable to users quickly, they probably don't erase them off their systems immediately. They certainly don't erase them from their backup tapes, if they end up there.

The companies offering these apps might very well analyze their content and make that information available to advertisers. We don't know how much metadata is saved. In SnapChat, users can see the metadata even though they can't see the content and what it's used for. And if the government demanded copies of those conversations—either through a secret NSA demand or a more normal legal process involving an employer or school—the companies would have no choice but to hand them over.

Even worse, if the FBI or NSA demanded that American companies secretly store those conversations and *not tell their users*, breaking their promise of deletion, the companies would have no choice but to comply.

That last bit isn't just paranoia.

We know the US government has done this to companies large and small. Lavabit was a small secure email service, with an encryption system designed so that even the company had no access to users' email. Last year, the NSA presented it with a secret court order demanding that it turn over its master key, thereby compromising the security of every user. Lavabit shut down its service rather than comply, but that option isn't feasible for larger companies. In 2011, Microsoft made some still-unknown changes to Skype to make NSA eavesdropping easier, but the security promises they advertised didn't change.

This is one of the reasons President Barack Obama's announcement that he will end one particular NSA collection program under one particular legal authority barely begins to solve the problem: the surveillance state is so robust that anything other than a major overhaul won't make a difference.

Of course, the typical Snapchat user doesn't care whether the US government is monitoring his conversations. He's more concerned about his high school friends and his parents. But if these platforms are insecure, it's not just the NSA that one should worry about.

Dissidents in the Ukraine and elsewhere need security, and if they rely on ephemeral apps, they need to know that their own governments aren't saving copies of their chats. And even US high school students need to know that their photos won't be surreptitiously saved and used against them years later.

The need for ephemeral conversation isn't some weird privacy fetish or the exclusive purview of criminals with something to hide. It represents a basic need for human privacy, and something every one of us had as a matter of course before the invention of microphones and recording devices.

We need ephemeral apps, but we need credible assurances from the companies that they are actually secure and credible assurances from the government that they won't be subverted.

Disclosing vs. Hoarding Vulnerabilities

Originally published in TheAtlantic.com, *May 19, 2014*

There's a debate going on about whether the US government—specifically, the NSA and United States Cyber Command—should stockpile Internet vulnerabilities or disclose and fix them. It's a complicated problem, and one that starkly illustrates the difficulty of separating attack and defense in cyberspace.

A software vulnerability is a programming mistake that allows an adversary access into that system. Heartbleed is a recent example, but hundreds are discovered every year.

Unpublished vulnerabilities are called "zero-day" vulnerabilities, and they're very valuable because no one is protected. Someone with one of those can attack systems world-wide with impunity.

When someone discovers one, he can either use it for defense or for offense. Defense means alerting the vendor and getting it patched. Lots of vulnerabilities are discovered by the vendors themselves and patched without any fanfare. Others are discovered by researchers and hackers. A patch doesn't make the vulnerability go away, but most users protect themselves by patching their systems regularly.

Offense means using the vulnerability to attack others. This is the quintessential zero-day, because the vendor doesn't even know the vulnerability exists until it starts being used by criminals or hackers. Eventually the affected software's vendor finds out—the timing depends on how extensively the vulnerability is used—and issues a patch to close the vulnerability.

If an offensive military cyber unit discovers the vulnerability—or a cyber-weapons arms manufacturer—it keeps that vulnerability secret for use to deliver a cyber-weapon. If it is used stealthily, it might remain secret for a long time. If unused, it'll remain secret until someone else discovers it.

Discoverers can sell vulnerabilities. There's a rich market in zero-days for attack purposes—both military/commercial and black markets. Some vendors offer bounties for vulnerabilities to incent defense, but the amounts are much lower.

The NSA can play either defense or offense. It can either alert the vendor and get a still-secret vulnerability fixed, or it can hold on to it and use it to eavesdrop on foreign computer systems. Both are important US policy goals, but the NSA has to choose which one to pursue. By fixing the vulnerability, it strengthens the security of the Internet against all attackers: other countries, criminals, hackers. By leaving the vulnerability open, it is better able to attack others on the Internet. But each use runs the risk of the target government learning of, and using for itself, the vulnerability—or of the vulnerability becoming public and criminals starting to use it.

There is no way to simultaneously defend US networks while leaving foreign networks open to attack. Everyone uses the same software, so fixing us means fixing them, and leaving them vulnerable means leaving us vulnerable. As Harvard Law Professor Jack Goldsmith wrote, "every offensive weapon is a (potential) chink in our defense—and vice versa."

To make matters even more difficult, there is an arms race going on in cyberspace. The Chinese, the Russians, and many other countries are finding vulnerabilities as well. If we leave a vulnerability unpatched, we run the risk of another country independently discovering it and using it in a cyber-weapon that we will be vulnerable to. But if we patch all the vulnerabilities we find, we won't have any cyber-weapons to use against other countries.

Many people have weighed in on this debate. The president's Review Group on Intelligence and Communications Technologies, convened post-Snowden, concluded (recommendation 30), that vulnerabilities should only be hoarded in rare instances and for short times. Cory Doctorow calls it a public health problem. I have said similar things. Dan Geer recommends that the US government corner the vulnerabilities market and fix them all. Both the FBI and the intelligence agencies claim that this amounts to unilateral disarmament.

It seems like an impossible puzzle, but the answer hinges on how vulnerabilities are distributed in software.

If vulnerabilities are sparse, then it's obvious that every vulnerability we find and fix improves security. We render a vulnerability unusable, even if the Chinese government already knows about it. We make it impossible for criminals to find and use it. We improve the general security of our software, because we can find and fix most of the vulnerabilities.

If vulnerabilities are plentiful—and this seems to be true—the ones the US finds and the ones the Chinese find will largely be different. This means that patching the vulnerabilities we find won't make it appreciably harder for criminals to find the next one. We don't really improve general software security by disclosing and patching unknown vulnerabilities, because the percentage we find and fix is small compared to the total number that are out there.

But while vulnerabilities are plentiful, they're not uniformly distributed. There are easier-to-find ones, and harder-to-find ones. Tools that automatically find and fix entire classes of vulnerabilities, and coding practices that eliminate many easy-to-find ones, greatly improve software security. And when a person finds a vulnerability, it is likely that another person soon will, or recently has, found the same vulnerability. Heartbleed, for example, remained undiscovered for two years, and then two independent researchers discovered it within two days of each other. This is why it is important for the government to err on the side of disclosing and fixing.

The NSA, and by extension US Cyber Command, tries its best to play both ends of this game. Former NSA Director Michael Hayden talks about NOBUS, "nobody but us." The NSA has a classified process to determine what it should do about vulnerabilities, disclosing and closing most of the ones it finds, but holding back some—we don't know how many—vulnerabilities that "nobody but us" could find for attack purposes.

This approach seems to be the appropriate general framework, but the devil is in the details. Many of us in the security field don't know how to make NOBUS decisions, and the recent White House clarification posed more questions than it answered.

Who makes these decisions, and how? How often are they reviewed? Does this review process happen inside Department of Defense, or is it broader? Surely there needs to be a technical review of each vulnerability, but there should also be policy reviews regarding the sorts of vulnerabilities we are hoarding. Do we hold these vulnerabilities until someone else finds them, or only for a short period of time? How many do we stockpile? The US/Israeli cyberweapon Stuxnet used four zero-day vulnerabilities. Burning four on a single military operation implies that we are not hoarding a small number, but more like 100 or more.

There's one more interesting wrinkle. Cyber-weapons are a combination of a payload—the damage the weapon does—and a delivery mechanism: the vulnerability used to get the payload into the enemy network. Imagine that China knows about a vulnerability and is using it in a still-unfired cyber-weapon, and that the NSA learns about it through espionage. Should the NSA disclose and patch the vulnerability, or should it use it itself for attack? If it discloses, then China could find a replacement vulnerability that the NSA won't know about it. But if it doesn't, it's deliberately leaving the US vulnerable to cyber-attack. Maybe someday we can get to the point where we can patch vulnerabilities faster than the enemy can use them in an attack, but we're nowhere near that point today.

The implications of US policy can be felt on a variety of levels. The NSA's actions have resulted in a widespread mistrust of the security of US Internet products and services, greatly affecting American business. If we show that we're putting security ahead of surveillance, we can begin to restore that trust. And by making the decision process much more public than it is today, we can demonstrate both our trust-worthiness and the value of open government.

An unpatched vulnerability puts everyone at risk, but not to the same degree. The US and other Western countries are highly vulnerable, because of our critical electronic infrastructure, intellectual property, and personal wealth. Countries like China and Russia are less vulnerable—North Korea much less—so they have considerably less incentive to see vulnerabilities fixed. Fixing vulnerabilities isn't disarmament; it's making our own countries much safer. We also regain the moral authority to negotiate any broad international reductions in cyber-weapons; and we can decide not to use them even if others do.

Regardless of our policy towards hoarding vulnerabilities, the most important thing we can do is patch vulnerabilities quickly once they are disclosed. And that's what companies are doing, even without any government involvement, because so many vulnerabilities are discovered by criminals.

We also need more research in automatically finding and fixing vulnerabilities, and in building secure and resilient software in the first place. Research over the last decade or so has resulted in software vendors being able to find and close entire classes of vulnerabilities. Although there are many cases of these security analysis tools not being used, all of our security is improved when they are. That alone is a good reason to continue disclosing vulnerability details, and something the NSA can do to vastly improve the security of the Internet worldwide. Here again, though, they would have to make the tools they have to automatically find vulnerabilities available for defense and not attack.

In today's cyberwar arms race, unpatched vulnerabilities and stockpiled cyber-weapons are inherently destabilizing, especially because they are only effective for a limited time. The world's militaries are investing more money in finding vulnerabilities than the commercial world is investing in fixing them. The vulnerabilities they discover affect the security of us all. No matter what cybercriminals do, no matter what other countries do, we in the US need to err on the side of security and fix almost all the vulnerabilities we find. But not all, yet.

The Limits of Police Subterfuge

Originally published in the Atlantic, *December 17, 2014*

"The next time you call for assistance because the Internet service in your home is not working, the 'technician' who comes to your door may actually be an undercover government agent. He will have secretly disconnected the service, knowing that you will naturally call for help and—when he shows up at your door, impersonating a technician— let him in. He will walk through each room of your house, claiming to diagnose the problem. Actually, he will be videotaping everything (and everyone) inside. He will have no reason to suspect you have broken the law, much less probable cause to obtain a search warrant. But that makes no difference, because by letting him in, you will have 'consented' to an intrusive search of your home."

This chilling scenario is the first paragraph of a motion to suppress evidence gathered by the police in exactly this manner, from a hotel room. Unbelievably, this isn't a story from some totalitarian government on the other side of an ocean. This happened in the United States, and by the FBI. Eventually—I'm sure there will be appeals—higher US courts will decide whether this sort of practice is legal. If it is, the country will slide even further into a society where the police have even more unchecked power than they already possess.

The facts are these. In June, Two wealthy Macau residents stayed at Caesar's Palace in Las Vegas. The hotel suspected that they were running an illegal gambling operation out of their room. They enlisted the police and the FBI, but could not provide enough evidence for them to get a warrant. So instead they repeatedly cut the guests' Internet connection. When the guests complained to the hotel, FBI agents wearing hidden cameras and recorders pretended to be Internet repair technicians and convinced the guests to let them in. They filmed and recorded everything under the pretense of fixing the Internet, and then used the information collected from that to get an actual search warrant. To make matters even worse, they lied to the judge about how they got their evidence.

The FBI claims that their actions are no different from any conventional sting operation. For example, an undercover policeman can legitimately look around and report on what he sees when he invited into a suspect's home under the pretext of trying to buy drugs. But there are two very important differences: one of consent, and the other of trust. The former is easier to see in this specific instance, but the latter is much more important for society.

You can't give consent to something you don't know and understand. The FBI agents did not enter the hotel room under the pretext of making an illegal bet. They entered under a false pretext, and relied on that for consent of their true mission. That makes things different. The occupants of the hotel room didn't realize who they were giving access to, and they didn't know their intentions. The FBI knew this would be a problem. According to the *New York Times*, "a federal prosecutor had initially warned the agents not to use trickery because of the 'consent issue.' In fact, a previous ruse by agents had failed when a person in one of the rooms refused to let them in." Claiming that a person granting an Internet technician access is consenting to a police search makes no sense, and is no different than one of those "click through" Internet license agreements that you didn't read saying one thing and while meaning another. It's not consent in any meaningful sense of the term.

Far more important is the matter of trust. Trust is central to how a society functions. No one, not even the most hardened survivalists who live in backwoods log cabins, can do everything by themselves. Humans need help from each other, and most of us need a lot of help from each other. And that requires trust. Many Americans' homes, for example, are filled with systems that require outside technical expertise when they break: phone, cable, Internet, power, heat, water. Citizens need to trust each other enough to give them access to their hotel rooms, their homes, their cars, their person. Americans simply can't live any other way.

It cannot be that every time someone allows one of those technicians into our homes they are consenting to a police search. Again from the motion to suppress: "Our lives cannot be private—and our personal relationships intimate—if each physical connection that links our homes to the outside world doubles as a ready-made excuse for the government to conduct a secret, suspicionless, warrantless search." The resultant breakdown in trust would be catastrophic. People would not be able to get the assistance they need. Legitimate servicemen would find it much harder to do their job. Everyone would suffer.

It all comes back to the warrant. Through warrants, Americans legitimately grant the police an incredible level of access into our personal lives. This is a reasonable choice because the police need this access in order to solve crimes. But to protect ordinary citizens, the law requires the police to go before a neutral third party and convince them that they have a legitimate reason to demand that access. That neutral third party, a judge, then issues the warrant when he or she is convinced. This check on the police's power is for Americans' security, and is an important part of the Constitution.

In recent years, the FBI has been pushing the boundaries of its warrantless investigative powers in disturbing and dangerous ways. It collects phone-call records of millions of innocent people. It uses hacking tools against unknown individuals without warrants. It impersonates legitimate news sites. If the lower court sanctions this particular FBI subterfuge, the matter needs to be taken up—and reversed—by the Supreme Court.

When Thinking Machines Break the Law

Originally published in Edge.org *as one of the answers to the 2015 Edge Question:* "What do you think about machines that think?", *January 28, 2015*

Last year, two Swiss artists programmed a Random Botnot Shopper, which every week would spend $100 in bitcoin to buy a random item from an anonymous Internet black market...all for an art project on display in Switzerland. It was a clever concept, except there was a problem. Most of the stuff the bot purchased was benign—fake Diesel jeans, a baseball cap with a hidden camera, a stash can, a pair of Nike trainers—but it also purchased ten ecstasy tablets and a fake Hungarian passport.

What do we do when a machine breaks the law? Traditionally, we hold the person controlling the machine responsible. People commit the crimes; the guns, lockpicks, or computer viruses are merely their tools. But as machines become more autonomous, the link between machine and controller becomes more tenuous.

Who is responsible if an autonomous military drone accidentally kills a crowd of civilians? Is it the military officer who keyed in the mission, the programmers of the enemy detection software that misidentified the people, or the programmers of the software that made the actual kill decision? What if those programmers had no idea that their software was being used for military purposes? And what if the drone can improve its algorithms by modifying its own software based on what the entire fleet of drones learns on earlier missions?

Maybe our courts can decide where the culpability lies, but that's only because while current drones may be autonomous, they're not very smart. As drones get smarter, their links to the humans who originally built them become more tenuous.

What if there are no programmers, and the drones program themselves? What if they are both smart and autonomous, and make strategic as well as tactical decisions on targets? What if one of the drones decides, based on whatever means it has at its disposal, that it no longer maintains allegiance to the country that built it and goes rogue?

Our society has many approaches, using both informal social rules and more formal laws, for dealing with people who won't follow the rules of society. We have informal mechanisms for small infractions, and a complex legal system for larger ones. If you are obnoxious at a party I throw, I won't invite you back. Do it regularly, and you'll be shamed and ostracized from the group. If you steal some of my stuff, I might report you to the police. Steal from a bank, and you'll almost certainly go to jail for a long time. A lot of this might seem more ad hoc than situation-specific, but we humans have spent millennia working this all out. Security is both political and social, but it's also psychological. Door locks, for example, only work because our social and legal prohibitions on theft keep the overwhelming majority of us honest. That's how we live peacefully together at a scale unimaginable for any other species on the planet.

How does any of this work when the perpetrator is a machine with whatever passes for free will? Machines probably won't have any concept of shame or praise. They won't refrain from doing something because of what other machines might think. They won't follow laws simply because it's the right thing to do, nor will they have a natural deference to authority. When they're caught stealing, how can they be punished? What does it mean to fine a machine? Does it make any sense at all to incarcerate it? And unless they are deliberately programmed with a self-preservation function, threatening them with execution will have no meaningful effect.

We are already talking about programming morality into thinking machines, and we can imagine programming other human tendencies into our machines, but we're certainly going to get it wrong. No matter how much we try to avoid it, we're going to have machines that break the law.

This, in turn, will break our legal system. Fundamentally, our legal system doesn't prevent crime. Its effectiveness is based on arresting and convicting criminals after the fact, and their punishment providing a deterrent to others. This completely fails if there's no punishment that makes sense.

We already experienced a small example of this after 9/11, which was when most of us first started thinking about suicide terrorists and how post-facto security was irrelevant to them. That was just one change in motivation, and look at how those actions affected the way we think about security. Our laws will have the same problem with thinking machines, along with related problems we can't even imagine yet. The social and legal systems that have dealt so effectively with human rulebreakers of all sorts will fail in unexpected ways in the face of thinking machines.

A machine that thinks won't always think in the ways we want it to. And we're not ready for the ramifications of that.

The Democratization of Cyberattack

Originally published in Vice Motherboard, *February 25, 2015*

The thing about infrastructure is that everyone uses it. If it's secure, it's secure for everyone. And if it's insecure, it's insecure for everyone. This forces some hard policy choices.

When I was working with the *Guardian* on the Snowden documents, the one top-secret program the NSA desperately did not want us to expose was QUANTUM. This is the NSA's program for what is called packet injection—basically, a technology that allows the agency to hack into computers.

Turns out, though, that the NSA was not alone in its use of this technology. The Chinese government uses packet injection to attack computers. The cyberweapons manufacturer Hacking Team sells packet injection technology to any government willing to pay for it. Criminals use it. And there are hacker tools that give the capability to individuals as well.

All of these existed before I wrote about QUANTUM. By using its knowledge to attack others rather than to build up the Internet's defenses, the NSA has worked to ensure that anyone can use packet injection to hack into computers.

This isn't the only example of once-top-secret US government attack capabilities being used against US government interests. StingRay is a particular brand of IMSI catcher, and is used to intercept cell phone calls and metadata. This technology was once the FBI's secret, but not anymore. There are dozens of these devices scattered around Washington, DC, as well as the rest of the country, run by who-knows-what government or organization. By accepting the vulnerabilities in these devices so the FBI can use them to solve crimes, we necessarily allow foreign governments and criminals to use them against us.

Similarly, vulnerabilities in phone switches—SS7 switches, for those who like jargon—have been long used by the NSA to locate cell phones. This same technology is sold by the US company Verint and the UK company Cobham to third-world governments, and hackers have demonstrated the same capabilities at conferences. An eavesdropping capability that was built into phone switches to enable lawful intercepts was used by still-unidentified unlawful intercepters in Greece between 2004 and 2005.

These are the stories you need to keep in mind when thinking about proposals to ensure that all communications systems can be eavesdropped on by government. Both the FBI's James Comey and UK Prime Minister David Cameron recently proposed limiting secure cryptography in favor of cryptography they can have access to.

But here's the problem: technological capabilities cannot distinguish based on morality, nationality, or legality; if the US government is able to use a backdoor in a communications system to spy on its enemies, the Chinese government can use the same backdoor to spy on its dissidents.

Even worse, modern computer technology is inherently democratizing. Today's NSA secrets become tomorrow's PhD theses and the next day's hacker tools. As long as we're all using the same computers, phones, social networking platforms, and computer networks, a vulnerability that allows us to spy also allows us to be spied upon.

We can't choose a world where the US gets to spy but China doesn't, or even a world where governments get to spy and criminals don't. We need to choose, as a matter of policy, communications systems that are secure for all users, or ones that are vulnerable to all attackers. It's security or surveillance.

As long as criminals are breaking into corporate networks and stealing our data, as long as totalitarian governments are spying on their citizens, as long as cyberterrorism and cyberwar remain a threat, and as long as the beneficial uses of computer technology outweighs the harmful uses, we have to choose security. Anything else is just too dangerous.

This essay previously appeared on Vice Motherboard.

Using Law against Technology

Originally published in CNN.com, *December 21, 2015*

On Thursday, a Brazilian judge ordered the text messaging service WhatsApp shut down for 48 hours. It was a monumental action.

WhatsApp is the most popular app in Brazil, used by about 100 million people. The Brazilian telecoms hate the service because it entices people away from more expensive text messaging services, and they have been lobbying for months to convince the government that it's unregulated and illegal. A judge finally agreed.

In Brazil's case, WhatsApp was blocked for allegedly failing to respond to a court order. Another judge reversed the ban 12 hours later, but there is a pattern forming here. In Egypt, Vodafone has complained about the legality of WhatsApp's free voice-calls, while India's telecoms firms have been lobbying hard to curb messaging apps such as WhatsApp and Viber. Earlier this year, the United Arab Emirates blocked WhatsApp's free voice call feature.

All this is part of a massive power struggle going on right now between traditional companies and new Internet companies, and we're all in the blast radius.

It's one aspect of a tech policy problem that has been plaguing us for at least 25 years: technologists and policymakers don't understand each other, and they inflict damage on society because of that. But it's worse today. The speed of technological progress makes it worse. And the types of technology—especially the current Internet of mobile devices everywhere, cloud computing, always-on connections and the Internet of Things—make it worse.

The Internet has been disrupting and destroying long-standing business models since its popularization in the mid-1990s. And traditional industries have long fought back with every tool at their disposal. The movie and music industries have tried for decades to hamstring computers in an effort to prevent illegal copying of their products. Publishers have battled with Google over whether their books could be indexed for online searching.

More recently, municipal taxi companies and large hotel chains are fighting with ride-sharing companies such as Uber and apartment-sharing companies such as Airbnb. Both the old companies and the new upstarts have tried to bend laws to their will in an effort to out-maneuver each other.

Sometimes the actions of these companies harm the users of these systems and services. And the results can seem crazy. Why would the Brazilian telecoms want to provoke the ire of almost everyone in the country? They're trying to protect their monopoly. If they win in not just shutting down WhatsApp, but Telegram and all the other text-message services, their customers will have no choice. This is how high-stakes these battles can be.

This isn't just companies competing in the marketplace. These are battles between competing visions of how technology should apply to business, and traditional businesses and "disruptive" new businesses. The fundamental problem is that technology and law are in conflict, and what's worked in the past is increasingly failing today.

First, the speeds of technology and law have reversed. Traditionally, new technologies were adopted slowly over decades. There was time for people to figure them out, and for their social repercussions to percolate through society. Legislatures and courts had time to figure out rules for these technologies and how they should integrate into the existing legal structures.

They don't always get it right—the sad history of copyright law in the United States is an example of how they can get it badly wrong again and again—but at least they had a chance before the technologies become widely adopted.

That's just not true anymore. A new technology can go from zero to a hundred million users in a year or less. That's just too fast for the political or legal process. By the time they're asked to make rules, these technologies are well-entrenched in society.

Second, the technologies have become more complicated and specialized. This means that the normal system of legislators passing laws, regulators making rules based on those laws and courts providing a second check on those rules fails. None of these people has the expertise necessary to understand these technologies, let alone the subtle and potentially pernicious ramifications of any rules they make.

We see the same thing between governments and law-enforcement and militaries. In the United States, we're expecting policymakers to understand the debate between the FBI's desire to read the encrypted emails and computers of crime suspects and the security researchers who maintain that giving them that capability will render everyone insecure. We're expecting legislators to provide meaningful oversight over the National Security Agency, when they can only read highly technical documents about the agency's activities in special rooms and without any aides who might be conversant in the issues.

The result is that we end up in situations such as the one Brazil finds itself in. WhatsApp went from zero to 100 million users in five years. The telecoms are advancing all sorts of weird legal arguments to get the service banned, and judges are ill-equipped to separate fact from fiction.

This isn't a simple matter of needing government to get out of the way and let companies battle in the marketplace. These companies are for-profit entities, and their business models are so complicated that they regularly don't do what's best for their users. (For example, remember that you're not really Facebook's customer. You're their product.)

The fact that people's resumes are effectively the first 10 hits on a Google search of their name is a problem—something that the European "right to be forgotten" tried ham-fistedly to address. There's a lot of smart writing that says that Uber's disruption of traditional taxis will be worse for the people who regularly use the services. And many people worry about Amazon's increasing dominance of the publishing industry.

We need a better way of regulating new technologies.

That's going to require bridging the gap between technologists and policymakers. Each needs to understand the other—not enough to be experts in each other's fields, but enough to engage in meaningful conversations and debates. That's also going to require laws that are agile and written to be as technologically invariant as possible.

It's a tall order, I know, and one that has been on the wish list of every tech policymaker for decades. But today, the stakes are higher and the issues come faster. Not doing so will become increasingly harmful for all of us.

Decrypting an iPhone for the FBI ====

Originally published in the Washington Post,
February 18, 2016

Earlier this week, a federal magistrate ordered Apple to assist the FBI in hacking into the iPhone used by one of the San Bernardino shooters. Apple will fight this order in court.

The policy implications are complicated. The FBI wants to set a precedent that tech companies will assist law enforcement in breaking their users' security, and the technology community is afraid that the precedent will limit what sorts of security features it can offer customers. The FBI sees this as a privacy vs. security debate, while the tech community sees it as a security vs. surveillance debate.

The technology considerations are more straightforward, and shine a light on the policy questions.

The iPhone 5c in question is encrypted. This means that someone without the key cannot get at the data. This is a good security feature. Your phone is a very intimate device. It is likely that you use it for private text conversations, and that it's connected to your bank accounts. Location data reveals where you've been, and correlating multiple phones reveals who you associate with. Encryption protects your phone if it's stolen by criminals. Encryption protects the phones of dissidents around the world if they're taken by local police. It protects all the data on your phone, and the apps that increasingly control the world around you.

This encryption depends on the user choosing a secure password, of course. If you had an older iPhone, you probably just used the default four-digit password. That's only 10,000 possible passwords, making it pretty easy to guess. If the user enabled the more-secure alphanumeric password, that means a harder-to-guess password.

Apple added two more security features on the iPhone. First, a phone could be configured to erase the data after too many incorrect password guesses. And it enforced a delay between password guesses. This delay isn't really noticeable by the user if you type the wrong password and then have to retype the correct password, but it's a large barrier for anyone trying to guess password after password in a brute-force attempt to break into the phone.

But that iPhone has a security flaw. While the data is encrypted, the software controlling the phone is not. This means that someone can create a hacked version of the software and install it on the phone without the consent of the phone's owner and without knowing the encryption key. This is what the FBI—and now the court—is demanding Apple do: It wants Apple to rewrite the phone's software to make it possible to guess possible passwords quickly and automatically.

The FBI's demands are specific to one phone, which might make its request seem reasonable if you don't consider the technological implications: Authorities have the phone in their lawful possession, and they only need help seeing what's on it in case it can tell them something about how the San Bernardino shooters operated. But the hacked software the court and the FBI wants Apple to provide would be general. It would work on any phone of the same model. It has to.

Make no mistake; this is what a backdoor looks like. This is an existing vulnerability in iPhone security that could be exploited by anyone.

There's nothing preventing the FBI from writing that hacked software itself, aside from budget and manpower issues. There's every reason to believe, in fact, that such hacked software has been written by intelligence organizations around the world. Have the Chinese, for instance, written a hacked Apple operating system that records conversations and automatically forwards them to police? They would need to have stolen Apple's code-signing key so that the phone would recognize the hacked as valid, but governments have done that in the past with other keys and other companies. We simply have no idea who already has this capability.

And while this sort of attack might be limited to state actors today, remember that attacks always get easier. Technology broadly spreads capabilities, and what was hard yesterday becomes easy tomorrow. Today's top-secret NSA programs become tomorrow's PhD theses and the next day's hacker tools. Soon this flaw will be exploitable by cyber-criminals to steal your financial data. Everyone with an iPhone is at risk, regardless of what the FBI demands Apple do

What the FBI wants to do would make us less secure, even though it's in the name of keeping us safe from harm. Powerful governments, democratic and totalitarian alike, want access to user data for both law enforcement and social control. We cannot build a backdoor that only works for a particular type of government, or only in the presence of a particular court order.

Either everyone gets security or no one does. Either everyone gets access or no one does. The current case is about a single iPhone 5c, but the precedent it sets will apply to all smartphones, computers, cars and everything the Internet of Things promises. The danger is that the court's demands will pave the way to the FBI forcing Apple and others to reduce the security levels of their smart phones and computers, as well as the security of cars, medical devices, homes, and everything else that will soon be computerized. The FBI may be targeting the iPhone of the San Bernardino shooter, but its actions imperil us all.

The original essay contained a major error.

I wrote: "This is why Apple fixed this security flaw in 2014. Apple's iOS 8.0 and its phones with an A7 or later processor protect the phone's software as well as the data. If you have a newer iPhone, you are not vulnerable to this attack. You are more secure - from the government of whatever country you're living in, from cybercriminals and from hackers." Also: "We are all more secure now that Apple has closed that vulnerability."

That was based on a misunderstanding of the security changes Apple made in what is known as the "Secure Enclave." It turns out that all iPhones have this security vulnerability: all can have their software updated without knowing the password. The updated code has to be signed with Apple's key, of course, which adds a major difficulty to the attack.

Lawful Hacking and Continuing Vulnerabilities

Originally published in the Washington Post, *March 29, 2016*

The FBI's legal battle with Apple is over, but the way it ended may not be good news for anyone.

Federal agents had been seeking to compel Apple to break the security of an iPhone 5c that had been used by one of the San Bernardino, Calif., terrorists. Apple had been fighting a court order to cooperate with the FBI, arguing that the authorities' request was illegal and that creating a tool to break into the phone was itself harmful to the security of every iPhone user worldwide.

Last week, the FBI told the court it had learned of a possible way to break into the phone using a third party's solution, without Apple's help. On Monday, the agency dropped the case because the method worked. We don't know who that third party is. We don't know what the method is, or which iPhone models it applies to. Now it seems like we never will.

The FBI plans to classify this access method and to use it to break into other phones in other criminal investigations.

Compare this iPhone vulnerability with another, one that was made public on the same day the FBI said it might have found its own way into the San Bernardino phone. Researchers at Johns Hopkins University sity announced last week that they had found a significant vulnerability in the iMessage protocol. They disclosed the vulnerability to Apple in the fall, and last Monday, Apple released an updated version of its operating system that fixed the vulnerability. (That's iOS 9.3—you should download and install it right now.) The Hopkins team didn't publish its findings until Apple's patch was available, so devices could be updated to protect them from attacks using the researchers' discovery.

This is how vulnerability research is supposed to work.

Vulnerabilities are found, fixed, then published. The entire security community is able to learn from the research, and—more important—everyone is more secure as a result of the work.

The FBI is doing the exact opposite. It has been given whatever vulnerability it used to get into the San Bernardino phone in secret, and it is keeping it secret. All of our iPhones remain vulnerable to this exploit. This includes the iPhones used by elected officials and federal workers and the phones used by people who protect our nation's critical infrastructure and carry out other law enforcement duties, including lots of FBI agents.

This is the trade-off we have to consider: do we prioritize security over surveillance, or do we sacrifice security for surveillance?

The problem with computer vulnerabilities is that they're general. There's no such thing as a vulnerability that affects only one device. If it affects one copy of an application, operating system or piece of hardware, then it affects all identical copies. A vulnerability in Windows 10, for example, affects all of us who use Windows 10. And it can be used by anyone who knows it, be they the FBI, a gang of cyber criminals, the intelligence agency of another country—anyone.

And once a vulnerability is found, it can be used for attack—like the FBI is doing—or for defense, as in the Johns Hopkins example.

Over years of battling attackers and intruders, we've learned a lot about computer vulnerabilities. They're plentiful: vulnerabilities are found and fixed in major systems all the time. They're regularly discovered independently, by outsiders rather than by the original manufacturers or programmers. And once they're discovered, word gets out. Today's top-secret National Security Agency attack techniques become tomorrow's PhD theses and the next day's hacker tools.

The attack/defense trade-off is not new to the US government. They even have a process for deciding what to do when a vulnerability is discovered: whether they should be disclosed to improve all of our security, or kept secret to be used for offense. The White House claims that it prioritizes defense, and that general vulnerabilities in widely used computer systems are patched.

Whatever method the FBI used to get into the San Bernardino shooter's iPhone is one such vulnerability. The FBI did the right thing by using an existing vulnerability rather than forcing Apple to create a new one, but it should be disclosed to Apple and patched immediately.

This case has always been more about the PR battle and potential legal precedent than about the particular phone. And while the legal dispute is over, there are other cases involving other encrypted devices in other courts across the country. But while there will always be a few computers—corporate servers, individual laptops or personal smartphones—that the FBI would like to break into, there are far more such devices that we need to be secure.

One of the most surprising things about this debate is the number of former national security officials who came out on Apple's side. They understand that we are singularly vulnerable to cyberattack, and that our cyberdefense needs to be as strong as possible.

The FBI's myopic focus on this one investigation is understandable, but in the long run, it's damaging to our national security.

The NSA Is Hoarding Vulnerabilities

Originally published in Vox.com, *August 24, 2016*

The National Security Agency is lying to us. We know that because data stolen from an NSA server was dumped on the Internet. The agency is hoarding information about security vulnerabilities in the products you use, because it wants to use it to hack others' computers.

Those vulnerabilities aren't being reported, and aren't getting fixed, making your computers and networks unsafe.

On August 13, a group calling itself the Shadow Brokers released 300 megabytes of NSA cyberweapon code on the Internet. Near as we experts can tell, the NSA network itself wasn't hacked; what probably happened was that a "staging server" for NSA cyberweapons—that is, a server the NSA was making use of to mask its surveillance activities—was hacked in 2013.

The NSA inadvertently resecured itself in what was coincidentally the early weeks of the Snowden document release. The people behind the link used casual hacker lingo, and made a weird, implausible proposal involving holding a bitcoin auction for the rest of the data: "!!! Attention government sponsors of cyber warfare and those who profit from it !!!! How much you pay for enemies cyber weapons?"

Still, most people believe the hack was the work of the Russian government and the data release some sort of political message. Perhaps it was a warning that if the US government exposes the Russians as being behind the hack of the Democratic National Committee—or other high-profile data breaches—the Russians will expose NSA exploits in turn.

But what I want to talk about is the data. The sophisticated cyberweapons in the data dump include vulnerabilities and "exploit code" that can be deployed against common Internet security systems. Products targeted include those made by Cisco, Fortinet, TOPSEC, Watchguard, and Juniper—systems that are used by both private and government organizations around the world. Some of these vulnerabilities have been independently discovered and fixed since 2013, and some had remained unknown until now.

All of them are examples of the NSA—despite what it and other representatives of the US government say—prioritizing its ability to conduct surveillance over our security. Here's one example. Security researcher Mustafa al-Bassam found an attack tool codenamed BENIGHCERTAIN that tricks certain Cisco firewalls into exposing some of their memory, including their authentication passwords. Those passwords can then be used to decrypt virtual private network, or VPN, traffic, completely bypassing the firewalls' security. Cisco hasn't sold these firewalls since 2009, but they're still in use today.

Vulnerabilities like that one could have, and should have, been fixed years ago. And they would have been, if the NSA had made good on its word to alert American companies and organizations when it had identified security holes.

Over the past few years, different parts of the US government have repeatedly assured us that the NSA does not hoard "zero days"—the term used by security experts for vulnerabilities unknown to software vendors. After we learned from the Snowden documents that the NSA purchases zero-day vulnerabilities from cyberweapons arms manufacturers, the Obama administration announced, in early 2014, that the NSA must disclose flaws in common software so they can be patched (unless there is "a clear national security or law enforcement" use).

Later that year, National Security Council cybersecurity coordinator and special adviser to the president on cybersecurity issues Michael Daniel insisted that US doesn't stockpile zero-days (except for the same narrow exemption). An official statement from the White House in 2014 said the same thing.

The Shadow Brokers data shows this is not true. The NSA hoards vulnerabilities.

Hoarding zero-day vulnerabilities is a bad idea. It means that we're all less secure. When Edward Snowden exposed many of the NSA's surveillance programs, there was considerable discussion about what the agency does with vulnerabilities in common software products that it finds. Inside the US government, the system of figuring out what to do with individual vulnerabilities is called the Vulnerabilities Equities Process (VEP). It's an inter-agency process, and it's complicated.

There is a fundamental tension between attack and defense. The NSA can keep the vulnerability secret and use it to attack other networks. In such a case, we are all at risk of someone else finding and using the same vulnerability. Alternatively, the NSA can disclose the vulnerability to the product vendor and see it gets fixed. In this case, we are all secure against whoever might be using the vulnerability, but the NSA can't use it to attack other systems.

There are probably some overly pedantic word games going on. Last year, the NSA said that it discloses 91 percent of the vulnerabilities it finds. Leaving aside the question of whether that remaining 9 percent represents 1, 10, or 1,000 vulnerabilities, there's the bigger question of what qualifies in the NSA's eyes as a "vulnerability."

Not all vulnerabilities can be turned into exploit code. The NSA loses no attack capabilities by disclosing the vulnerabilities it can't use, and doing so gets its numbers up; it's good PR. The vulnerabilities we care about are the ones in the Shadow Brokers data dump. We care about them because those are the ones whose existence leaves us all vulnerable.

Because everyone uses the same software, hardware, and networking protocols, there is no way to simultaneously secure our systems while attacking their systems—whoever "they" are. Either everyone is more secure, or everyone is more vulnerable.

Pretty much uniformly, security experts believe we ought to disclose and fix vulnerabilities. And the NSA continues to say things that appear to reflect that view, too. Recently, the NSA told everyone that it doesn't rely on zero days—very much, anyway.

Earlier this year at a security conference, Rob Joyce, the head of the NSA's Tailored Access Operations (TAO) organization—basically the country's chief hacker—gave a rare public talk, in which he said that credential stealing is a more fruitful method of attack than are zero days: "A lot of people think that nation states are running their operations on zero days, but it's not that common. For big corporate networks, persistence and focus will get you in without a zero day; there are so many more vectors that are easier, less risky, and more productive."

The distinction he's referring to is the one between exploiting a technical hole in software and waiting for a human being to, say, get sloppy with a password.

A phrase you often hear in any discussion of the Vulnerabilities Equities Process is NOBUS, which stands for "nobody but us." Basically, when the NSA finds a vulnerability, it tries to figure out if it is unique in its ability to find it, or whether someone else could find it, too. If it believes no one else will find the problem, it may decline to make it public. It's an evaluation prone to both hubris and optimism, and many security experts have cast doubt on the very notion that there is some unique American ability to conduct vulnerability research.

The vulnerabilities in the Shadow Brokers data dump are definitely not NOBUS-level. They are run-of-the-mill vulnerabilities that anyone—another government, cybercriminals, amateur hackers—could discover, as evidenced by the fact that many of them *were* discovered between 2013, when the data was stolen, and this summer, when it was published. They are vulnerabilities in common systems used by people and companies all over the world.

So what are all these vulnerabilities doing in a secret stash of NSA code that was stolen in 2013? Assuming the Russians were the ones who did the stealing, how many US companies did they hack with these vulnerabilities? This is what the Vulnerabilities Equities Process is designed to prevent, and it has clearly failed.

If there are any vulnerabilities that—according to the standards established by the White House and the NSA—should have been disclosed and fixed, it's these. That they have not been during the three-plus years that the NSA knew about and exploited them—despite Joyce's insistence that they're not very important—demonstrates that the Vulnerable Equities Process is badly broken.

We need to fix this. This is exactly the sort of thing a congressional investigation is for. This whole process needs a lot more transparency, oversight, and accountability. It needs guiding principles that prioritize security over surveillance. A good place to start are the recommendations by Ari Schwartz and Rob Knake in their report: these include a clearly defined and more public process, more oversight by Congress and other independent bodies, and a strong bias toward fixing vulnerabilities instead of exploiting them.

And as long as I'm dreaming, we really need to separate our nation's intelligence-gathering mission from our computer security mission: we should break up the NSA. The agency's mission should be limited to nation state espionage. Individual investigation should be part of the FBI, cyberwar capabilities should be within US Cyber Command, and critical infrastructure defense should be part of DHS's mission.

I doubt we're going to see any congressional investigations this year, but we're going to have to figure this out eventually. In my 2014 book *Data and Goliath*, I write that "no matter what cybercriminals do, no matter what other countries do, we in the US need to err on the side of security by fixing almost all the vulnerabilities we find…" Our nation's cybersecurity is just too important to let the NSA sacrifice it in order to gain a fleeting advantage over a foreign adversary.

WannaCry and Vulnerabilities

Originally published in Foreign Affairs, *May 30, 2017*

There is plenty of blame to go around for the WannaCry ransomware that spread throughout the Internet earlier this month, disrupting work at hospitals, factories, businesses, and universities. First, there are the writers of the malicious software, which blocks victims' access to their computers until they pay a fee. Then there are the users who didn't install the Windows security patch that would have prevented an attack. A small portion of the blame falls on Microsoft, which wrote the insecure code in the first place. One could certainly condemn the Shadow Brokers, a group of hackers with links to Russia who stole and published the National Security Agency attack tools that included the exploit code used in the ransomware. But before all of this, there was the NSA, which found the vulnerability years ago and decided to exploit it rather than disclose it.

All software contains bugs or errors in the code. Some of these bugs have security implications, granting an attacker unauthorized access to or control of a computer. These vulnerabilities are rampant in the software we all use. A piece of software as large and complex as Microsoft Windows will contain hundreds of them, maybe more. These vulnerabilities have obvious criminal uses that can be neutralized if patched. Modern software is patched all the time—either on a fixed schedule, such as once a month with Microsoft, or whenever required, as with the Chrome browser.

When the US government discovers a vulnerability in a piece of software, however, it decides between two competing equities. It can keep it secret and use it offensively, to gather foreign intelligence, help execute search warrants, or deliver malware. Or it can alert the software vendor and see that the vulnerability is patched, protecting the country—and, for that matter, the world—from similar attacks by foreign governments and cybercriminals. It's an either-or choice. As former US Assistant Attorney General Jack Goldsmith has said, "Every offensive weapon is a (potential) chink in our defense—and vice versa."

This is all well-trod ground, and in 2010 the US government put in place an interagency Vulnerabilities Equities Process (VEP) to help balance the trade-off. The details are largely secret, but a 2014 blog post by then President Barack Obama's cybersecurity coordinator, Michael Daniel, laid out the criteria that the government uses to decide when to keep a software flaw undisclosed. The post's contents were unsurprising, listing questions such as "How much is the vulnerable system used in the core Internet infrastructure, in other critical infrastructure systems, in the US economy, and/or in national security systems?" and "Does the vulnerability, if left unpatched, impose significant risk?" They were balanced by questions like "How badly do we need the intelligence we think we can get from exploiting the vulnerability?" Elsewhere, Daniel has noted that the US government discloses to vendors the "overwhelming majority" of the vulnerabilities that it discovers—91 percent, according to NSA Director Michael S. Rogers.

The particular vulnerability in WannaCry is code-named Eternal-Blue, and it was discovered by the US government—most likely the NSA—sometime before 2014. The *Washington Post* reported both how useful the bug was for attack and how much the NSA worried about it being used by others. It was a reasonable concern: many of our national security and critical infrastructure systems contain the vulnerable software, which imposed significant risk if left unpatched. And yet it was left unpatched.

There's a lot we don't know about the VEP. The *Washington Post* says that the NSA used EternalBlue "for more than five years," which implies that it was discovered after the 2010 process was put in place. It's not clear if all vulnerabilities are given such consideration, or if bugs are periodically reviewed to determine if they should be disclosed. That said, any VEP that allows something as dangerous as Eternal-Blue—or the Cisco vulnerabilities that the Shadow Brokers leaked last August to remain unpatched for years isn't serving national security very well. As a former NSA employee said, the quality of intelligence that could be gathered was "unreal." But so was the potential damage. The NSA must avoid hoarding vulnerabilities.

Perhaps the NSA thought that no one else would discover EternalBlue. That's another one of Daniel's criteria: "How likely is it that someone else will discover the vulnerability?" This is often referred to as NOBUS, short for "nobody but us." Can the NSA discover vulnerabilities that no one else will? Or are vulnerabilities discovered by one intelligence agency likely to be discovered by another, or by cybercriminals?

In the past few months, the tech community has acquired some data about this question. In one study, two colleagues from Harvard and I examined over 4,300 disclosed vulnerabilities in common software and concluded that 15 to 20 percent of them are rediscovered within a year. Separately, researchers at the Rand Corporation looked at a different and much smaller data set and concluded that fewer than six percent of vulnerabilities are rediscovered within a year. The questions the two papers ask are slightly different and the results are not directly comparable (we'll both be discussing these results in more detail at the Black Hat Conference in July), but clearly, more research is needed.

People inside the NSA are quick to discount these studies, saying that the data don't reflect their reality. They claim that there are entire classes of vulnerabilities the NSA uses that are not known in the research world, making rediscovery less likely. This may be true, but the evidence we have from the Shadow Brokers is that the vulnerabilities that the NSA keeps secret aren't consistently different from those that researchers discover. And given the alarming ease with which both the NSA and CIA are having their attack tools stolen, rediscovery isn't limited to independent security research.

But even if it is difficult to make definitive statements about vulnerability rediscovery, it is clear that vulnerabilities are plentiful. Any vulnerabilities that are discovered and used for offense should only remain secret for as short a time as possible. I have proposed six months, with the right to appeal for another six months in exceptional circumstances. The United States should satisfy its offensive requirements through a steady stream of newly discovered vulnerabilities that, when fixed, also improve the country's defense.

The VEP needs to be reformed and strengthened as well. A report from last year by Ari Schwartz and Rob Knake, who both previously worked on cybersecurity policy at the White House National Security Council, makes some good suggestions on how to further formalize the process, increase its transparency and oversight, and ensure periodic review of the vulnerabilities that are kept secret and used for offense. This is the least we can do. A bill recently introduced in both the Senate and the House calls for this and more.

In the case of EternalBlue, the VEP did have some positive effects. When the NSA realized that the Shadow Brokers had stolen the tool, it alerted Microsoft, which released a patch in March. This prevented a true disaster when the Shadow Brokers exposed the vulnerability on the Internet. It was only unpatched systems that were susceptible to WannaCry a month later, including versions of Windows so old that Microsoft normally didn't support them. Although the NSA must take its share of the responsibility, no matter how good the VEP is, or how many vulnerabilities the NSA reports and the vendors fix, security won't improve unless users download and install patches, and organizations take responsibility for keeping their software and systems up to date. That is one of the important lessons to be learned from WannaCry.

NSA Document Outlining Russian Attempts to Hack Voter Rolls

Originally published in the Washington Post, *June 9, 2017*

This week brought new public evidence about Russian interference in the 2016 election. On Monday, the *Intercept* published a top-secret National Security Agency document describing Russian hacking attempts against the US election system. While the attacks seem more exploratory than operational—and there's no evidence that they had any actual effect—they further illustrate the real threats and vulnerabilities facing our elections, and they point to solutions.

The document describes how the GRU, Russia's military intelligence agency, attacked a company called VR Systems that, according to its website, provides software to manage voter rolls in eight states. The August 2016 attack was successful, and the attackers used the information they stole from the company's network to launch targeted attacks against 122 local election officials on October 27, 12 days before the election.

That is where the NSA's analysis ends. We don't know whether those 122 targeted attacks were successful, or what their effects were if so. We don't know whether other election software companies besides VR Systems were targeted, or what the GRU's overall plan was—if it had one. Certainly, there are ways to disrupt voting by interfering with the voter registration process or voter rolls. But there was no indication on Election Day that people found their names removed from the system, or their address changed, or anything else that would have had an effect—anywhere in the country, let alone in the eight states where VR Systems is deployed. (There were Election Day problems with the voting rolls in Durham, NC—one of the states that VR Systems supports—but they seem like conventional errors and not malicious action.)

And 12 days before the election (with early voting already well underway in many jurisdictions) seems far too late to start an operation like that. That is why these attacks feel exploratory to me, rather than part of an operational attack. The Russians were seeing how far they could get, and keeping those accesses in their pocket for potential future use.

Presumably, this document was intended for the Justice Department, including the FBI, which would be the proper agency to continue looking into these hacks. We don't know what happened next, if anything. VR Systems isn't commenting, and the names of the local election officials targeted did not appear in the NSA document.

So while this document isn't much of a smoking gun, it's yet more evidence of widespread Russian attempts to interfere last year.

The document was, allegedly, sent to the *Intercept* anonymously. An NSA contractor, Reality Leigh Winner, was arrested Saturday and charged with mishandling classified information. The speed with which the government identified her serves as a caution to anyone wanting to leak official US secrets.

The *Intercept* sent a scan of the document to another source during its reporting. That scan showed a crease in the original document, which implied that someone had printed the document and then carried it out of some secure location. The second source, according to the FBI's affidavit against Winner, passed it on to the NSA. From there, NSA investigators were able to look at their records and determine that only six people had printed out the document. (The government may also have been able to track the printout through secret dots that identified the printer.) Winner was the only one of those six who had been in email contact with the *Intercept*. It is unclear whether the email evidence was from Winner's NSA account or her personal account, but in either case, it's incredibly sloppy tradecraft.

With President Trump's election, the issue of Russian interference in last year's campaign has become highly politicized. Reports like the one from the Office of the Director of National Intelligence in January have been criticized by partisan supporters of the White House. It's interesting that this document was reported by the *Intercept*, which has been historically skeptical about claims of Russian interference. (I was quoted in their story, and they showed me a copy of the NSA document before it was published.) The leaker was even praised by WikiLeaks founder Julian Assange, who up until now has been traditionally critical of allegations of Russian election interference.

This demonstrates the power of source documents. It's easy to discount a Justice Department official or a summary report. A detailed NSA document is much more convincing. Right now, there's a federal suit to force the ODNI to release the entire January report, not just the unclassified summary. These efforts are vital.

This hack will certainly come up at the Senate hearing where former FBI director James B. Comey is scheduled to testify Thursday. Last year, there were several stories about voter databases being targeted by Russia. Last August, the FBI confirmed that the Russians successfully hacked voter databases in Illinois and Arizona. And a month later, an unnamed Department of Homeland Security official said that the Russians targeted voter databases in 20 states. Again, we don't know of anything that came of these hacks, but expect Comey to be asked about them. Unfortunately, any details he does know are almost certainly classified, and won't be revealed in open testimony.

But more important than any of this, we need to better secure our election systems going forward. We have significant vulnerabilities in our voting machines, our voter rolls and registration process, and the vote tabulation systems after the polls close. In January, DHS designated our voting systems as critical national infrastructure, but so far that has been entirely for show. In the United States, we don't have a single integrated election. We have 50-plus individual elections, each with its own rules and its own regulatory authorities. Federal standards that mandate voter-verified paper ballots and post-election auditing would go a long way to secure our voting system. These attacks demonstrate that we need to secure the voter rolls, as well.

Democratic elections serve two purposes. The first is to elect the winner. But the second is to convince the loser. After the votes are all counted, everyone needs to trust that the election was fair and the results accurate. Attacks against our election system, even if they are ultimately ineffective, undermine that trust and—by extension—our democracy. Yes, fixing this will be expensive. Yes, it will require federal action in what's historically been state-run systems. But as a country, we have no other option.

Warrant Protections against Police Searches of Our Data

Originally published in the Washington Post, *November 27, 2017*

The cell phones we carry with us constantly are the most perfect surveillance device ever invented, and our laws haven't caught up to that reality. That might change soon.

This week, the Supreme Court will hear a case with profound implications for your security and privacy in the coming years. The Fourth Amendment's prohibition of unlawful search and seizure is a vital right that protects us all from police overreach, and the way the courts interpret it is increasingly nonsensical in our computerized and networked world. The Supreme Court can either update current law to reflect the world, or it can further solidify an unnecessary and dangerous police power.

The case centers on cell phone location data and whether the police need a warrant to get it, or if they can use a simple subpoena, which is easier to obtain. Current Fourth Amendment doctrine holds that you lose all privacy protections over any data you willingly share with a third party. Your cellular provider, under this interpretation, is a third party with whom you've willingly shared your movements, 24 hours a day, going back months—even though you don't really have any choice about whether to share with them. So police can request records of where you've been from cell carriers without any judicial oversight. The case before the court, *Carpenter v. United States*, could change that.

Traditionally, information that was most precious to us was physically close to us. It was on our bodies, in our homes and offices, in our cars. Because of that, the courts gave that information extra protections. Information that we stored far away from us, or gave to other people, afforded fewer protections. Police searches have been governed by the "third-party doctrine," which explicitly says that information we share with others is not considered private.

The Internet has turned that thinking upside-down. Our cell phones know who we talk to and, if we're talking via text or email, what we say. They track our location constantly, so they know where we live and work. Because they're the first and last thing we check every day, they know when we go to sleep and when we wake up. Because everyone has one, they know whom we sleep with. And because of how those phones work, all that information is naturally shared with third parties.

More generally, all our data is literally stored on computers belonging to other people. It's our email, text messages, photos, Google docs, and more—all in the cloud. We store it there not because it's unimportant, but precisely because it is important. And as the Internet of Things computerizes the rest our lives, even more data will be collected by other people: data from our health trackers and medical devices, data from our home sensors and appliances, data from Internet-connected "listeners" like Alexa, Siri, and your voice-activated television.

All this data will be collected and saved by third parties, sometimes for years. The result is a detailed dossier of your activities more complete than any private investigator—or police officer—could possibly collect by following you around.

The issue here is not whether the police should be allowed to use that data to help solve crimes. Of course they should. The issue is whether that information should be protected by the warrant process that requires the police to have probable cause to investigate you and get approval by a court.

Warrants are a security mechanism. They prevent the police from abusing their authority to investigate someone they have no reason to suspect of a crime. They prevent the police from going on "fishing expeditions." They protect our rights and liberties, even as we willingly give up our privacy to the legitimate needs of law enforcement.

The third-party doctrine never made a lot of sense. Just because I share an intimate secret with my spouse, friend, or doctor doesn't mean that I no longer consider it private. It makes even less sense in today's hyper-connected world. It's long past time the Supreme Court recognized that a months-long history of my movements is private, and my emails and other personal data deserve the same protections, whether they're on my laptop or on Google's servers.

References

Chapter 1: Crime, Terrorism, Spying, and War

Cyberconflicts and National Security
https://www.un.org/wcm/content/site/chronicle/home/archive/issues2013/
        security/cyberconfzictsandnationalsecurity

Counterterrorism Mission Creep
http://www.theatlantic.com/politics/archive/2013/07/
        mission-creep-when-everything-is-terrorism/277844/

Syrian Electronic Army Cyberattacks
http://blogs.wsj.com/speakeasy/2013/08/29/syrian-electronic-army-a-brief-
        look-at-what-businesses-need-to-know/

The Limitations of Intelligence
http://www.cnn.com/2013/09/11/opinion/schneier-intelligence-limitation

Computer Network Exploitation vs. Computer Network Attack
http://www.theatlantic.com/technology/archive/2014/03/theres-no-real-
        difference-between-online-espionage-and-online-attack/284233/

iPhone Encryption and the Return of the Crypto Wars
https://www.schneier.com/essays/archives/2014/10/stop_the_hysteria_ov.html

Attack Attribution and Cyber Conflict
http://www.csmonitor.com/World/Passcode/Passcode-Voices/2015/0304/
        Hacker-or-spy-In-today-s-cyberattacks-finding-the-culprit-is-a-
        troubling-puzzle

Metal Detectors at Sports Stadiums
http://www.washingtonpost.com/posteverything/wp/2015/04/14/baseballs-new-
        metal-detectors-wont-keep-you-safe-theyll-just-make-you-miss-a-
        few-innings/

The Future of Ransomware

https://www.washingtonpost.com/posteverything/wp/2017/05/16/the-next-
    ransomware-hack-will-be-worse-than-the-current-one/?utm_
    term=.8bb09d30bb61

Chapter 2: Travel and Security ════════

Hacking Airplanes

http://edition.cnn.com/2015/04/16/opinions/schneier-hacking-airplanes/

Reassessing Airport Security

http://www.cnn.com/2015/06/05/opinions/schneier-tsa-security/index.html

Chapter 3: Internet of Things ════════

Hacking Consumer Devices

http://www.cnn.com/2013/08/14/opinion/schneier-hacking-baby-monitor/
    index.html

Security Risks of Embedded Systems

http://www.wired.com/opinion/2014/01/theres-no-good-way-to-patch-the-
    internet-of-things-and-thats-a-huge-problem/

Samsung Television Spies on Viewers

http://www.cnn.com/2015/02/11/opinion/schneier-samsung-tv-listening/
    index.html

Volkswagen and Cheating Software

http://www.cnn.com/2015/09/28/opinions/schneier-vw-cheating-software/
    index.html

DMCA and the Internet of Things

http://www.theatlantic.com/technology/archive/2015/12/
    internet-of-things-philips-hue-lightbulbs/421884/

Real-World Security and the Internet of Things

https://motherboard.vice.com/read/the-internet-of-things-will-cause-the-
    first-ever-large-scale-internet-disaster

Lessons From the Dyn DDoS Attack

https://securityintelligence.com/lessons-from-the-dyn-ddos-attack/

Regulation of the Internet of Things

https://www.washingtonpost.com/posteverything/wp/2016/11/03/your–wifi–
    connected–thermostat–can–take–down–the–whole–internet–we–need–
    new–regulations/

Security and the Internet of Things

http://nymag.com/selectall/2017/01/the–internet–of–things–dangerous–future–
    bruce–schneier.html

Botnets

https://www.technologyreview.com/s/603500/10–breakthrough–
    technologies–2017–botnets–of–things/

Chapter 4: Security and Technology

The NSA's Cryptographic Capabilities

http://www.wired.com/opinion/2013/09/black–budget–what–exactly–are–the–nsas–
    cryptanalytic–capabilities/

iPhone Fingerprint Authentication

http://www.wired.com/opinion/2013/09/what–if–apples–new–phone–has–
    fingerprint–authentication/

The Future of Incident Response Drone Self-Defense and the Law

http://www.cnn.com/2015/09/09/opinions/schneier–shoot–down–drones/index.html

Replacing Judgment with Algorithms

http://www.cnn.com/2016/01/06/opinions/schneier–china–social–scores/
    index.html

Class Breaks

https://www.edge.org/annual–question/2017/response/27229

Chapter 5: Elections and Voting

Candidates Won't Hesitate to Use Manipulative Advertising to Score Votes

http://www.theguardian.com/commentisfree/2016/feb/04/
    presidential–election–voter–data–manipulative–advertising–privacy

The Security of Our Election Systems

https://www.washingtonpost.com/posteverything/wp/2016/07/27/
    by–november–russian–hackers–could–target–voting–machines/

Election Security

http://www.nytimes.com/2016/11/09/opinion/american-elections-will-be-hacked.html

Hacking and the 2016 Presidential Election

https://www.washingtonpost.com/posteverything/wp/2016/11/23/u-s-elections-are-a-mess-whether-this-one-was-hacked-or-not/

Chapter 6: Privacy and Surveillance

Restoring Trust in Government and the Internet

http://www.cnn.com/2013/07/31/opinion/schneier-nsa-trust/index.html

The NSA is Commandeering the Internet

http://www.theatlantic.com/technology/archive/2013/08/the-nsa-is-commandeering-the-internet/278572/

Conspiracy Theories and the NSA

http://www.theatlantic.com/politics/archive/2013/09/the-only-way-to-restore-trust-in-the-nsa/279314/

How to Remain Secure Against the NSA

http://www.theguardian.com/world/2013/sep/05/nsa-how-to-remain-secure-surveillance

Air Gaps

http://www.wired.com/opinion/2013/10/149481/

Why the NSA's Defense of Mass Data Collection Makes No Sense

http://www.theatlantic.com/politics/archive/2013/10/why-the-nsas-defense-of-mass-data-collection-makes-no-sense/280715/

Defending Against Crypto Backdoors

http://www.wired.com/opinion/2013/10/how-to-design-and-defend-against-the-perfect-backdoor/

A Fraying of the Public/Private Surveillance Partnership

http://www.theatlantic.com/technology/archive/2013/11/a-fraying-of-the-public-private-surveillance-partnership/281289/

Surveillance as a Business Model

http://edition.cnn.com/2013/11/20/opinion/schneier-stalker-economy/index.html

Finding People's Locations Based on Their Activities in Cyberspace

http://www.theatlantic.com/technology/archive/2014/02/everything-we-know-about-how-the-nsa-tracks-peoples-physical-location/283745/

Surveillance by Algorithm

https://www.theguardian.com/commentisfree/2014/feb/27/
        nsa-robots-algorithm-surveillance-bruce-schneier

Everyone Wants You To Have Security, But Not from Them

http://www.forbes.com/sites/bruceschneier/2015/02/23/
        everyone-wants-you-to-have-security-but-not-from-them/

Why We Encrypt

https://www.privacyinternational.org/?q=node/599

Automatic Face Recognition and Surveillance

http://www.forbes.com/sites/bruceschneier/2015/09/29/
        the-era-of-automatic-facial-recognition-and-surveillance-is-here/

The Internet of Things that Talk About You Behind Your Back

https://motherboard.vice.com/en_ca/read/
        the-internet-of-things-that-talk-about-you-behind-your-back

Security vs. Surveillance

https://cyber.law.harvard.edu/pubrelease/dont-panic/

The Value of Encryption

http://www.riponsociety.org/article/the-value-
        of-encryption/

Congress Removes FCC Privacy Protections on your Internet Usage

https://www.theguardian.com/commentisfree/2017/mar/30/
        snoops-buy-your-browsing-history-us-congress

Infrastructure Vulnerabilities Make Surveillance Easy

http://www.aljazeera.com/indepth/opinion/2017/04/infrastructure-
        vulnerabilities-surveillance-easy-170409071533166.html

Chapter 7: Business and Economics of Security

More on Feudal Security

http://blogs.hbr.org/cs/2013/06/you_have_no_control_over_s.html

The Public/Private Surveillance Partnership

http://www.bloomberg.com/news/2013-07-31/the-public-private-surveillance-
        partnership.html

Should Companies Do Most of Their Computing in the Cloud?

http://debates.economist.com/debate/cloud-computing

Security Economics of the Internet of Things

https://motherboard.vice.com/read/we-need-to-save-the-internet-from-
the-internet-of-things

Chapter 8: Human Aspects of Security

Human-Machine Trust Failures

https://www.schneier.com/essay-445.html

Government Secrecy and the Generation Gap

http://www.ft.com/cms/s/0/420a9a64-163c-11e3-a57d-00144feabdc0.html

Choosing Secure Passwords

http://boingboing.net/2014/02/25/choosing-a-secure-password.html

The Human Side of Heartbleed

http://www.themarknews.com/2014/05/19/a-human-problem/

The Security of Data Deletion

http://arstechnica.com/security/2015/01/the-importance-of-deleting-old-
stuff-another-lesson-from-the-sony-attack/

Living in a Code Yellow World

http://fusion.net/story/200747/living-in-code-yellow/

Security Orchestration and Incident Response

https://securityintelligence.com/security-
orchestration-for-an-uncertain-world/

Chapter 9: Leaking, Hacking, Doxing, and Whistleblowing

Government Secrets and the Need for Whistleblowers

http://www.schneier.com/essay-429.html

Protecting Against Leakers

http://www.bloomberg.com/news/2013-08-21/how-companies-can-protect-against-
leakers.html

Why the Government Should Help Leakers
http://edition.cnn.com/2013/11/04/opinion/schneier-leakers-government/
index.html

Lessons from the Sony Hack
http://www.wsj.com/articles/sony-made-it-easy-but-any-of-us-could-get-
hacked-1419002701

Reacting to the Sony Hack
https://www.schneier.com/essays/archives/2014/12/the_best_thing_we_ca.html

Attack Attribution in Cyberspace
http://time.com/3653625/sony-hack-obama-sanctions-north-korea/

Organizational Doxing
https://www.schneier.com/essays/archives/2015/07/should_some_secrets_.html

The Security Risks of Third-Party Data
http://www.theatlantic.com/technology/archive/2015/09/
organizational-doxing-ashley-madison-hack/403900/

The Rise of Political Doxing
http://motherboard.vice.com/read/the-rise-
of-political-doxing

Data Is a Toxic Asset
http://www.cnn.com/2016/03/01/opinions/data-is-a-toxic-asset-opinion-
schneier/index.html

Credential Stealing as an Attack Vector
http://www.xconomy.com/boston/2016/04/20/
credential-stealing-as-attack-vector/

Someone Is Learning How to Take Down the Internet
https://www.lawfareblog.com/someone-learning-how-take-down-internet

Who is Publishing NSA and CIA Secrets, and Why?
https://www.lawfareblog.com/who-publishing-nsa-and-cia-secrets-and-why

Who Are the Shadow Brokers?
https://www.theatlantic.com/technology/archive/2017/05/shadow-brokers/527778/

On the Equifax Data Breach
http://www.cnn.com/2017/09/11/opinions/dont-complain-to-equifax-demand-
government-act-opinion-schneier/index.html

Chapter 10: Security, Policy, Liberty, and Law

Our Newfound Fear of Risk
https://www.schneier.com/essay-442.html

Take Back the Internet
http://www.theguardian.com/commentisfree/2013/sep/05/
government-betrayed-internet-nsa-spying

The Battle for Power on the Internet
http://www.theatlantic.com/technology/archive/2013/10/
the-battle-for-power-on-the-internet/280824/

How the NSA Threatens National Security
http://www.theatlantic.com/technology/archive/2014/01/
how-the-nsa-threatens-national-security/282822/

Who Should Store NSA Surveillance Data
http://www.slate.com/articles/technology/future_tense/2014/02/nsa_
surveillance_metadata_the_government_not_private_companies_should_
store.html

Ephemeral Apps
http://www.cnn.com/2014/03/26/opinion/schneier-snapchat-wickr/index.html

Disclosing vs. Hoarding Vulnerabilities
http://www.theatlantic.com/technology/archive/2014/05/
should-hackers-fix-cybersecurity-holes-or-exploit-them/371197/

The Limits of Police Subterfuge
http://www.theatlantic.com/national/archive/2014/12/
what-are-the-limits-of-police-subterfuge/383815/

When Thinking Machines Break the Law
http://edge.org/response-detail/26249

The Democratization of Cyberattack
http://motherboard.vice.com/read/cyberweapons-have-no-allegiance

Using Law against Technology
http://www.cnn.com/2015/12/21/opinions/schneier-whatsapp-blocked-brazil/
index.html

Decrypting an iPhone for the FBI
https://www.washingtonpost.com/posteverything/wp/2016/02/18/why-you-should-
side-with-apple-not-the-fbi-in-the-san-bernardino-iphone-case/

Lawful Hacking and Continuing Vulnerabilities

https://www.washingtonpost.com/posteverything/wp/2016/03/29/
your-iphone-just-got-a-lot-less-secure-and-the-fbi-is-to-blame/

The NSA Is Hoarding Vulnerabilities

http://www.vox.com/2016/8/24/12615258/nsa-security-
breach-hoard

WannaCry and Vulnerabilities

https://www.foreignaffairs.com/articles/2017-05-30/
why-nsa-makes-us-more-vulnerable-cyberattacks

NSA Document Outlining Russian Attempts to Hack Voter Rolls

https://www.washingtonpost.com/posteverything/wp/2017/06/06/russias-
attempt-to-hack-voting-systems-shows-that-our-elections-need-
better-security/

Warrant Protections against Police Searches of Our Data

https://www.washingtonpost.com/news/posteverything/wp/2017/11/27/how-the-
supreme-court-could-keep-police-from-using-your-cellphone-to-
spy-on-you/